Black Knights

Black Knights

ON THE BLOODY ROAD TO BAGHDAD

OLIVER POOLE

HarperCollins*Publishers*

HarperCollins*Publishers*
77–85 Fulham Palace Road,
Hammersmith, London w6 8jb

www.harpercollins.co.uk

Published by HarperCollins*Publishers* 2003

9 8 7 6 5 4 3 2 1

A catalogue record for this book is
available from the British Library

ISBN 0 00 717438 1

Maps by Hardlines

Set in PostScript Linotype Minion with Photina display by
Rowland Phototypesetting Ltd, Bury St Edmunds, Suffolk

Printed and bound in Great Britain by
Clays Ltd, St Ives plc

To the memory of John Donald

Contents

Illustrations

Myself interviewing Captain James Montgomery at the base camp in Kuwait.

The press pack receives its final anti-biochemical warfare training on the tennis courts of the Hilton Hotel in Kuwait City.

The other two journalists placed with 1st Battalion, Ron Synovitz of Radio Free Europe and Joe Giordono of *Stars and Stripes*.

Nitai Schwartz and Garth Stewart, who in Kuwait made clear to me their opposition to the war.

British tank crews wait for their turn at a firing range set up in the Kuwait desert.

The men of 1st Battalion being informed by their commanding officer, Lieutenant Colonel John W. Charlton, that the time had finally come to go to war.

Major George Fredrick, one of the officers with whom I shared a tent in Kuwait.

'Big Country', the M88 I travelled in for the first part of the campaign.

Sergeant Norman Weaver, the commander of the M88, just before the Black Knights entered the demilitarised zone that spanned the Kuwait–Iraq border.

The company prepares for the move into the demilitarised zone.

The US military vehicles that the M88 passed in the final approach to the Iraqi garrison at Tallil.

Iraqi prisoners captured around Tallil airbase. The US soldiers were shocked by how many of the Iraqis had fought back in that battle.

Private Roman Komlev, the Russian-born assistant driver of the M88.

Me, unknown soldier, Captain Bill Young and Lieutenant Colonel Charlton after the fighting at Tallil.

A US soldier takes a photograph of an Iraqi pick-up truck that had been destroyed by a Bradley shell in the recent fighting.

A dead body in the back of the pick-up truck.

Myself during the time the Black Knights were stationed around Samawah, sparring with paramilitaries and under threat from sniper and mortar attack.

The view through the hatch in the middle of the M88 during the sandstorm which engulfed us on the fifth day of the invasion, and reduced visibility to less than ten yards.

The Black Knights advance to Dragon 4, 2nd Brigade's regrouping base south of Karbala.

Myself with Private Roman Komlev and Sergeant Weaver at Dragon 4.

Private Jason 'Red' Carter, the driver of the M88, showing off an AK-47 that had been taken as a battlefield souvenir from a dead Iraqi soldier.

Captain David Waldron, the commander in charge of the Black Knights.

Myself during a nerve gas scare, after the Americans had destroyed a tanker containing chemicals which it was then realised might be blown towards the camp.

Sergeant Ray Simon manning the radio in the back of the CP.

The crew of 'Band Aid', the company's tracked medical emergency vehicle.

Passing over the Euphrates. Since the invasion had started the US army had skirted the west bank; now finally the river was being crossed, and only Baghdad lay before them.

Band Aid during the advance to Baghdad.

Sergeant Trey Black, the commander of the CP, manning the vehicle's .50-calibre machine gun.

The final stretch of road to Baghdad. The Black Knights were now at the very front of the advance, under attack from the Republican Guard and Saddam-supporting paramilitaries.

Sergeants Miguel 'Moe' Marrero and Jerold Pyle and the Abrams, 'Big Punisher', in which they led the Black Knights' advance into Baghdad.

Black Knights Map

1. The United States 1st Battalion, 15th Infantry Regiment, is encamped at Tactical Assembly Area Hammer, located in the Kuwaiti desert thirty miles from the Iraqi frontier. Among its 850 soldiers, all part of the 3rd Infantry Division, is a company made up of ten Abrams tanks and four Bradley fighting vehicles known as the 'Black Knights'.

2. On Wednesday, 19 March the battalion is ordered to move towards the Kuwait–Iraq border. It crosses into Iraq shortly after dawn forty-eight hours later. In coordination with units from the 3rd Brigade, the battalion attacks strategic objectives at Tallil, a settlement just south of Nasiriyah. The Black Knights find themselves at the centre of the bitterest resistance as the unit helps seize control of the local Iraqi garrison headquarters.

3. The battalion receives instructions on Sunday, 23 March to advance along the western bank of the Euphrates River to join the forces of the 3rd Infantry Division's 2nd Brigade based around Najaf. It is intended that the battalion will be amalgamated into that unit for the next planned attack, past Karbala and into the outskirts of Baghdad, which at that point is intended to commence in the next few days. However, near the Iraqi city of Samawah, 1st Battalion comes under mortar attack, and its orders are changed to suppressing Iraqi paramilitary resistance in the area.

4. 1st Battalion, and with it the Black Knights, on Wednesday, 26 March finally reach the forces of 2nd Brigade at a regrouping area codenamed Dragon 4, located just north of Najaf. The Battalion is instructed to join the battle against paramilitaries in the area and participates in an operation against a Republican Guard unit.

5. On Wednesday, 2 April the United States military launches its attack towards Baghdad. Its forces sweep through the Karbala Gap and secure a bridge over the Euphrates to the north of the city. The following day, the Black Knights lead the stage of the American advance which bursts through the Republican Guard's final defences and into the very outskirts of Saddam Hussein's capital, seizing a key road junction to the south of the city.

6. On Tuesday, 8 April the Black Knights are again leading part of the American advance. 1st Battalion has been instructed to rejoin 3rd Brigade, and this time the company is fighting its way towards the centre of Baghdad from the west of the city.

7. 1st Battalion, and with it the Black Knights, are in the heart of Baghdad when Saddam Hussein and his Ba'athist regime abandon the city on Wednesday, 9 April. The unit is then engaged in the job of restoring order by limiting looting, as well as trying to prevent the mounting guerrilla attacks being aimed against Iraq's new rulers.

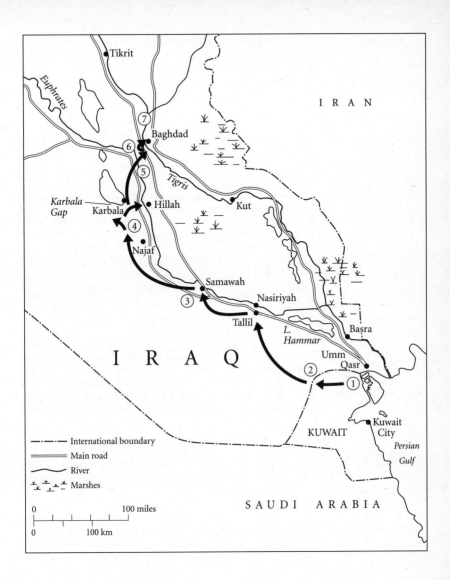

Operation Iraqi Freedom

1. 19 March: Military hostilities start when US forces bomb sites near Baghdad University where Saddam Hussein and his sons are believed to be sleeping.

2. 20–21 March: Ground war begins when thousands of American and British troops cross the Kuwait–Iraq border. Units from the British Army and American Marine Expeditionary Force drive north towards Basra. The US 3rd Infantry Division (Mechanized) divides its forces into three: one brigade heads towards Nasiriyah to seize key objectives just outside the city at Tallil; one brigade is directed towards Najaf; and a third brigade is ordered to travel the furthest west into the desert in order to adopt a position north-west of Najaf and south of Karbala.

3. Night of 21 March: Baghdad is ablaze after a massive bombing campaign titled Operation Shock and Awe is launched on the city.

4. 24 March: US troops become bogged down by Iraqi paramilitary attacks around Najaf, Samawah and Nasiriyah, resulting in days of frustration and growing apprehension among the American soldiers as the invasion stalls. News spreads that eleven US troops are missing – including servicewoman Jessica Lynch – following an ambush around Nasiriyah, and morale is further hampered by a vicious sandstorm on 25 March that reduces visibility to less than ten yards.

5. 26 March: One thousand US soldiers parachute into the Kurdish-controlled north of Iraq, joining Kurdish military fighters and several hundred American Special Forces already operating in the area.

6. 3 April: After first regrouping its forces and racing through the feared Karbala Gap, the American 3rd Infantry Division seizes a key road junction on the southern outskirts of Baghdad and launches an attack on Saddam International Airport.

7. 7 April: British forces gain control of Basra, Iraq's second largest city, as soldiers from the 3rd Parachute Battalion of 16th Air Assault Brigade capture the old quarter and with it suppress the last vestiges of large-scale military resistance.

8. 9 April: Saddam Hussein's regime abandons Baghdad after American troops advance to the very centre of the city. Images of Saddam are destroyed across the capital.

9. 11 April: American troops and Kurdish fighters capture the northern city of Mosul, one day after taking Kirkuk.

10. 14 April: Tikrit is entered by forces from the 4th Infantry Division, which had crossed the Kuwaiti border six days earlier with orders to travel north at great speed to secure the town, and US Marines. The fall of Tikrit, Saddam's birthplace and the spiritual heartland of the Ba'athist regime, means the American-led coalition's final major military objective has been secured.

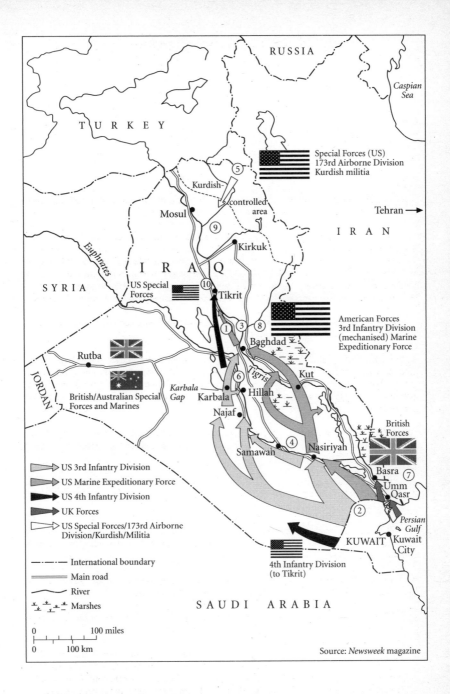

RUSSIA

Caspian Sea

T U R K E Y

Special Forces (US)
173rd Airborne Division
Kurdish militia

⑤

Kurdish-
controlled
area

Mosul

⑨

Tehran →

I R A N

Kirkuk

Euphrates

I R A Q

SYRIA

US Special
Forces

⑩ Tikrit

American Forces
3rd Infantry Division
(mechanised) Marine
Expeditionary Force

① ③ ⑧

JORDAN

Rutba

British/Australian Special
Forces and Marines

Baghdad

Tigris

Kut

⑥

Karbala Gap

Karbala   Hillah

Najaf

④

Samawah   Nasiriyah

British
Forces

Basra

⑦

US 3rd Infantry Division

US Marine Expeditionary Force

US 4th Infantry Division

UK Forces

US Special Forces/173rd Airborne
Division/Kurdish/Militia

Umm
Qasr

②

*Persian
Gulf*

KUWAIT

Kuwait
City

— · — · — International boundary

Main road

River

Marshes

4th Infantry Division
(to Tikrit)

SAUDI   ARABIA

0   100 miles

0   100 km

Source: *Newsweek* magazine

Preface

This book is about the soldiers of 1st Battalion, 15th US Infantry Regiment, 3rd Infantry Division, the men whose professionalism and bravery kept me alive during the time we spent together in the Middle East in March and April 2003. It was a privileged position in which I had been placed: watching from their centre battles in which I was not a combatant, not even a citizen of the country with whose army I travelled. My aim has simply been to explain what happened to those who were on that journey. It was a period when I lived in the back of an armoured vehicle, surrounded by tanks crewed by men trained to be among the very best at the task – killing – which is the ultimate requirement of the job of being a soldier. Michael Herr, in his Vietnam War book *Dispatches*, wrote, 'War stories aren't really anything but stories about people anyway,' and this book is above all a story about the people I grew to know during that time.

It is not intended as a gung-ho glamorisation of battlefield heroics. I saw far too many dead bodies lying by the roadside for that. Equally, this is no exposé of drugged-up GIs smoking opium through their gunbarrels or cutting off the ears of their victims. It is not a *Bravo Two Zero*, with men being tortured and running for their lives from Iraqi soldiers. I did not pick up a gun and fight off hordes of troops breaking through the American lines.

The story in these pages was instead determined by the events that occurred around me, and my desire to be an honest witness to them. It is about the real price demanded of the American soldiers you saw streaming across deserts on news bulletins and in newspaper photographs. It is about the thousands of dead Iraqis, civilian and military, left in their wake – so many dead, in fact, that by the end American troops had to dig pits with bull-dozers to bury the bodies, as they were beginning to rot in the heat and humidity. It is about what decisions made by diplomats and politicians actually mean for those on the ground. It is about the fact that in a war you do get shot at, you do see people killed, you are scared. It is about the jokes, the excitement, the friendships, the brutality, that bind those who take part in it together.

I am sure there are parts of this book the soldiers I was with will not like. I am sure there are conclusions they will disagree with. But this is meant to be their story, and I trust that they will recognise that I have tried to tell it as objectively as possible. There was a moment, when I talked to the American troops in the days after they had returned from the Middle East to their homes in the States, when I realised how damaging the actions I observed had been for those ordered to carry them out. My hope is that by describing what happened, candidly and unflinchingly, I can help people understand what it was really like to be in Iraq during those long, hot days of fighting.

I owe a debt of gratitude to the information officers at the Penta-gon, at the 3rd Infantry Division's bases in Fort Stewart and Fort Benning, and at the Ministry of Defence in London, who all with great diligence helped me check pages of facts about what piece of equipment does what and which unit went where. However, I am not a military historian and this book is not intended as a military history. It is primarily based on what I saw with my own eyes or heard from other eyewitnesses I believe to be reliable. The vast majority of the information it contains comes from the notes I made each day, the interviews I conducted with officers and men caught up in the fighting, and a journal I wrote up every evening. Great pains have been taken to avoid mistakes, but ultimately all I can know with any certainty is what I witnessed at first hand in the confusion of the battlefield.

At the *Daily Telegraph*, Sir John Keegan, Patrick Bishop and Michael Smith wrote articles which provided indispensable context to what I had seen. Ben Rooney, who wrote the newspaper's Gulf War II book *War on Saddam*, took considerable time and care to ensure that this military novice did not mix up his 155mm Paladin howitzers with his 120mm mobile mortars. Toby Harnden, the paper's Washington bureau chief, has always been there to provide advice and to gee me up when I felt I would never meet my deadline. I would like to thank my bosses, the *Telegraph*'s editor Charles Moore and foreign editor Alec Russell, for having the faith in me to send me out to Iraq in the first place, and then for encouraging me to write this book. It is impossible to express enough appreciation to everyone in the foreign desk team – Francis Harris, Sebastien Berger, Joe Jenkins, Paul Hill and Patsy Dryden – for being such a pleasure to work with.

I really could not have done this without my agents, James Gill and Michael Sissons, who guided me through the maze of the publishing world. At HarperCollins, Richard Johnson and Robert Lacey were skilful in their editing and generous with their help and advice. I would like to thank everyone who has offered suggestions on how best to tell my story, particularly Joe, John, Pin, Alice and my stepfather Norman, who all went through the manuscript and offered guidance on improvements. Judy helped me with the linguistic accuracy of spoken American English with greatly appreciated dedication. Thanks to my friends and family for truly being what both those words imply.

Oliver Poole
August 2003

ONE

'You're Fucking Dead'

January 2003 – Monday, 10 March 2003

I was standing on a dirt track outside an Iraqi army garrison at Tallil, a town just south of Nasiriyah. A picture of a stern-looking Saddam Hussein in military fatigues guarded the barracks' entrance. Tallil had been the centre of the first battle that the United States Army had fought in Iraq after crossing the Kuwait frontier twenty-four hours earlier. The last spluttering of gunfire had faded away just over an hour ago, and smoke still rose from the destroyed buildings around me.

A young man was showing me his photographs, flicking through the shots displayed on the pixel screen on the back of his digital camera. 'Only cost me four hundred bucks. Got it from some Indian in a shop down an alley in Kuwait City when we were there last year. Fantastic pictures. Can you see the depth of field in that?'

The picture was of an Iraqi soldier lying by the side of a road. His skin was hanging off in flaps, his clothes reduced to cinders. 'I saw the truck he was in get hit,' said the young man, a private in the United States military. 'Man, he was on fire when he got out of that vehicle. Now look at the clarity of that image. I was in a moving vehicle when I took it, and it looks like the camera was on a tripod. This is a great piece of kit.'

The next picture showed the same Iraqi. He was sitting up now, reaching out with his hands to hug the legs of a medic who had just given him treatment. 'Makes you proud to be American, the way we look after them,' the private said. 'They'd never treat us like that. Now follow me, sir. I want to show you something down here. It's our own mini highway of death.'

We walked a short distance to the remains of an Iraqi pick-up truck that had drawn a small crowd. It had been hit head-on by a tank shell. An American soldier wearing an anti-biochemical-weapon suit was having his photograph taken in front of the wreckage. The air was thick with the smell of burnt flesh. I looked inside. All that remained of the two men in the front were a few shards of bone. The two in the rear seats had been reduced to skeletons. The skin of the three perched in the back had been burnt to ash, the one furthest away fixed in the moment of death like one of the figures found at Pompeii, his arms thrown back and his head tilted in a scream that he had never been able to finish.

It was now well past mid-morning, approaching noon. It was getting hot, and the dirt on the soldiers' faces was lined with trickles of sweat. No one had slept for more than a few hours in the past three days. One member of the tank crew that had destroyed the pick-up was recounting how it had been hit. 'So this is it, I guess,' the soldier with the digital camera said.

Suddenly there was a deafening explosion, and we forgot the bodies in the burnt-out truck to stare at the town in front of us. An ammunition dump had been located and destroyed. The force of the blast was so powerful I had felt the air push against my body. A pillar of thick smoke rose up into the blue sky, forming a black cloud that slowly spread above us.

I had been amid the ruins of an ancient empire when I learnt I was to be sent to witness the power of a modern one. Two thousand years ago, in a desert on the other side of the world from

Iraq, a tribe near the Pampa de Huayuri, a plain in the south of what is now modern-day Peru, had fought the first battle of centuries of fighting that would see it expand from a few settlements in the Nazca valley to dominate the entire region. Its cities flourished, drawing in migrants wanting to share in its success. Its armies were unbeatable, its culture and style aped by its neighbours. To give thanks to their gods more than thirteen thousand geometric lines and stylised pictures were etched onto the surface of the surrounding desert, some of the lines stretching nine miles and the drawings more than a thousand yards in length. It is these that are the reason for the modern world's continued interest in the civilisation, the wonder being that they could not have been seen by those who made them, but only from the air. On the ground, nothing more than the occasional indentation can be made out as the setting sun casts shadows over the desert. Then a cataclysmic drought lasting decades struck. The Nazca people either starved or abandoned the area to search for new land to farm their animals and crops. By AD 800 the culture had effectively ceased to exist.

When I visited the region in January 2003, little remained but a jumble of collapsing monuments, viewed by the majority of the area's present-day inhabitants as fit only for unchecked commercial exploitation. One representative from UNESCO was struggling to keep at bay the developers determined to build houses on top of the antiquities, while also trying to rein in the local mafia who were systematically robbing grave sites and taking tourists directly across the ancient lines in four-wheel drive vehicles.

It was after a depressing day visiting these desecrated remains that I received a call from the *Daily Telegraph*, the newspaper for which I worked as West Coast of America correspondent, informing me that I would be accompanying the United States Army to report on its latest combat operation. The fevered speculation about whether there would be a war in Iraq appeared to be coming to a head. For months the United States had been insisting action needed to be taken to stop Saddam Hussein, the Iraqi President, who it maintained both sponsored Islamic terrorism and was continuing to acquire weapons of mass destruction for purposes hostile to the West. Debate was still continuing in the United Nations Security Council about the role of UN weapons inspectors, but American support for the military operation appeared to be gaining unstoppable momentum. Tens of thousands of troops had already been dispatched to Kuwait, and the *Telegraph*'s Washington bureau chief was confidentially predicting the war would not only begin in a matter of weeks, but would be over by Easter. Now the Pentagon had announced that special training courses would be held for the reporters who would cover the conflict. The armed forces wanted to make sure that, before they were dispatched to the battlefield, the press pack knew the nature of military life and were aware of the grim realities of the dangers posed by chemical and biological weapons. It seemed that the countdown to combat must have begun in earnest if the American government was willing to go so public as actually to instruct the media in preparation for it.

For the international community and the people in the Middle East this meant a ratcheting-up in the rate of the march to war. But for me it had a more direct upshot. I was going to boot camp.

A large part of my time on the journalistic equivalent of basic training was spent worrying about the effect going to war would have on my sperm. There just seemed to be too many threats lurking in the Persian Gulf that could make it inadequate for any subsequent reproductive endeavours. Firstly, there were the American uranium-tipped shells our military instructors kept talking about. There was no danger, they promised, as long as the target was not actually still burning, in which case the radioactive particles could be active. But don't things normally burn when they've been reduced to a distorted version of their component parts by a tank round, I asked. Well, yes, they admitted. And the effect? Some people say it can cause mutations in any future offspring, but there's no conclusive evidence, came the less than comforting answer.

Then there were the inoculations the military was offering us: anthrax and smallpox. There is no medical proof that these have any significant long-term side effects, or so we were re-assured in an hour-long briefing. But afterwards in the barracks in which we had been corralled, the journalists' talk was of Gulf War Syndrome and how they had interviewed veterans from the 1991 Iraq conflict who blamed the cocktail of jabs they had been administered, as well as the active uranium particles floating around, for their symptoms. These included physical exhaustion, muscle wastage and infertility. I resolved to investigate the viability of making a deposit at a sperm bank when our training period was over.

Indeed, this whole war thing was clearly going to be a dangerous business. A few months earlier I had told my editor I was keen to cover the United States invasion of Iraq, quietly confident in the assumption that there was absolutely no way the American army could possibly take the risk of putting a reporter such as myself anywhere near the front line. My closest experience of combat had been witnessing the carnage of Norwich High Street after closing time during a stag weekend the previous summer. During my stint in America for the *Telegraph* I had been based out of Los Angeles, meaning that I knew more than I had ever wanted to about Liz Hurley's baby and the perils for celebrities of being caught shoplifting, but nothing about the kill range of an artillery shell or the dangers posed by a recoilless rifle. At the time of year I was at boot camp I would normally have been preparing to cover the Oscars. It seemed inconceivable that anyone in their right mind would let a battlefield novice like me anywhere near to where people would actually be pulling triggers. However, here were colonels and majors happily telling the sixty newspaper, magazine and television reporters gathered at Fort Dix, a bleak air force base in the barren industrial wasteland of New Jersey, to put their minds at rest about the opportunities they would be given to cover military developments. They were going to be right there with the troops in the heart of the fighting.

The Pentagon had come up with a new concept called 'embedding'. Almost every battalion in the US Army engaged in combat in Iraq was to have a journalist assigned to it to cover the battlefield heroics that were confidently being predicted. The reporter would live and travel with the unit, sleep in its vehicles, eat the same food, share the same dangers. The soldiers would be told every conversation would be on the record, whether it was a briefing from a colonel or a one-on-one chat with a private. There would be no censorship, we were promised, other than the perfectly acceptable restrictions of not naming casualties – so that their families could be notified first – and of not giving any clues about forthcoming attacks. As it seemed I would be right in the middle of those attacks, it was hard to have any objection to not tipping off the enemy ahead of the action.

In class after class instructors detailed the array of weaponry likely to be deployed against us. We learnt how to escape if your convoy comes under attack (don't walk into the crossfire between two vehicles, a zone which in military terminology is 'the corridor of death'), how to react if under machine-gun fire (stand up, run for seven seconds, hit the deck for three seconds, repeat until in a safe spot or hit), and what to do in the case of a nuclear strike (not much, except meet your maker – but I suppose it was of some use to know that the water inside your flask would still be drinkable, even if the container itself should not be touched). We were sent on a route march on which we were subjected to fake gas attacks and ambushes. At one point a squad on our left opened fire with blank rounds; like sheep, we headed towards the nearest wood line on the right to take cover. It took us straight through the middle of a simulated minefield, and a sergeant gleefully walked up and, pointing at each of us individually, said, 'You're fucking dead. You're fucking dead.'

One afternoon we went through rudimentary first aid, the medics demonstrating how to use a credit card to cover a pierced lung and the right way to pile someone's intestines onto their stomach after they had spilled out. The next day we were advised on how to avoid being kidnapped or becoming the victim of a terrorist attack. A military anti-terrorism expert, his neck muscles so pronounced his shirt could barely contain them, paced in front of us detailing how our paranoias could best be put into practice. 'When you move into a new neighbourhood you should not only be able to identify your neighbours by face and name, but you should know their cars, where they work, how many kids they have, their basic routine,' he instructed. 'You can never be too safe. I personally use scissors to cut up into little pieces every letter or document I'm going to throw into the trash so that no one can check my personal information. My wife constantly complains that I'm mad, but you cannot be too careful, as there are people out there trying to kill us.'

He and his crew conducted a mock kidnapping of one of the reporters. A German television correspondent – one of the few other non-Americans invited to the camp – had been smoking a Marlboro Light outside her barracks when she was seized and bundled into the back of a van. Two days later we were shown a video of her interrogation. She was under spotlights, pushed up against a wall. Her eyes had been covered with goggles, the lenses of which had been taped over to stop her seeing where she was being taken. 'My parents wouldn't like it if you hurt me,' she said on the tape. 'I am the only child.'

When the video was finished the anti-terrorism expert rebuked us. 'We could've snatched several of you. You should always be prepared. Remember, there are people out there who want to kill you.' Later I mentioned to the German reporter how genuinely frightened she had looked. 'These people are maniacs,' she replied earnestly.

It was all sobering stuff. In combat, we were informed, 25 per cent of people lose control of their bladders or bowels when they first find themselves under fire. We were told that the shock of experiencing bullets whistling past your head gave you the sensation that time was either slowing down or speeding up, made you have a heightened awareness of detail, caused your mind to start fixating on unimportant concerns, prompted temporary amnesia, and – just in case you had any doubts – resulted in the experiencing of 'sheer terror'. However, nothing was as scary as the details of the effects of a chemical or biological attack. This was not only a possibility, but at the time seemed a likelihood. Every day the American government appeared to be producing more and more evidence about supposed Iraqi stockpiles, which was then confirmed by my own government in Britain. Few doubted that if Saddam Hussein did have such resources he would be happy to use them. Although reporters would be responsible for providing their own equipment, including helmets and bulletproof vests, the US military had insisted that it would issue us its own standard anti-biochemical weapons gear. This consisted of a suit, a gasmask and three packets of antigens that, if they could be administered in time, would hopefully negate the effects of inhaling nerve gas.

Descriptions of how all this kit should be used in an emergency dominated the week I spent at Fort Dix. The basic rules were simple, putting them into practice considerably more difficult. Firstly, you had to make sure you got your mask on within nine seconds of an alert being sounded, or you risked breathing in some of the gas. If you were too slow with your mask and could feel the first symptoms of exposure, the emphasis was on getting your antigen injection in before the nerve agent started messing with your motor-neurone system. Otherwise, in a matter of moments you would not have enough control over your hands even to be able to get the injection close to your body. In the parlance of the military this state was known as the 'chicken dance', as the flopping victim gyrating on the ground in backbreaking convulsions was reminiscent of a chicken whose head had accidentally been pulled off while its neck was being wrung. It was a condition which our instructor described as 'a whole world of pain'.

There was a bewildering array of details to remember. Some kinds of poisonous gas smelt like burnt almonds, others – almost charmingly – like freshly cut grass. Then there were the blistering agents that caused the skin to bubble and burst, and the largely self-explanatory choking agents which, at least, took only a few minutes to kill you.

The antigen injections came in packets of two doses, to be administered one immediately after the other. The first injection – the needle of which would automatically pop out and could pierce clothing – was a complicated anti-gas cocktail. It had never been tested in combat, as no American soldiers had ever been gassed. But it was suspected of having widespread side effects, one of the other reporters helpfully informed me, and among them, inevitably, was infertility. The second injection was essentially an incredibly potent dose of Valium, which acted as an instantaneous relaxant. It sounded like exactly what I would need if everyone around me was doing the floppy chicken.

In the off-base bar to which we went most nights to play pool and eat some proper food instead of the army ration self-heating meals we had been issued, the conversation invariably focused on the dangers that we might all soon be facing. It was felt that the training course, one of four being organised by the American Department of Defense for a total of more than two hundred journalists, had made clear the range of hazards while giving little time to practise how to respond if they ever actually occurred. A number of the journalists admitted that, after realising quite what might be involved, they now planned to quietly back out of the opportunity to go to the Gulf. Others were sceptical that the access being promised by the Pentagon would happen in reality, and therefore whether the opportunities for a painful death being described to us each day would even be a factor.

The American press did not have a good track record with the military. It was true that reporters and soldiers alike became misty-eyed when talking about Ernie Pyle, the World War II correspondent whose dispatches from the front with soldiers fighting in Normandy, Sicily and the Pacific had made him a household name in the States. His pieces were admired for their focus on the minutiae of the troops' existence – the letters they wrote home, the holes they slept in – and he had been driven by an unstinting admiration for the common soldier, as well as a determination to keep as far away as possible from his suicidal, alcoholic wife. Even General Eisenhower had taken the time to congratulate him for bringing the realities of army life to the people back home. However, the real point of reference was Vietnam. Ask military men from that era, and they will be united in the belief that it was the media that lost them that war by poisoning public opinion. Every time American soldiers have been sent to fight since, reporters have been kept as far away from combat as possible. In the 1983 invasion of Grenada there was a near complete news blackout, enabling the American forces to avoid acknowledging friendly-fire casualties, the unintended bombing of a hospital and the embarrassment of soldiers being provided with military charts so out of date they had to rely on tourist maps. Six years later a press pool was set up for the invasion of Panama consisting of a select group of reporters who would file dispatches to be shared with the rest of the world media. Not one of them was allowed in until the main thrust of the fighting had abated.

By the 1991 Gulf War reporters were largely confined to hotels and were hand-fed sanitised military updates. Half a dozen sent to live with the troops as part of another pool scheme were banned from using satellite phones amid official warnings that they attracted fire from Iraqi jets. One of the most lasting images of the Vietnam War is a photograph of a naked girl screaming as she runs, her flesh melting, from a South Vietnamese napalm attack on her village. By the liberation of Kuwait, media access had deteriorated so much that the most familiar image was a TV screen dominated by the imposing figure of General Norman Schwarzkopf pointing at a map.

'I was in Afghanistan, and they promised things were going to be better then,' said Carol Morello of the *Washington Post* as we ate dinner one night. 'But what was the reality? They wouldn't let us report the names of the units involved in combat, let alone anything like casualty figures. At one point a group of correspondents were locked in a warehouse and prevented from reporting on a "friendly fire" incident nearby that had left a number of American troops wounded. Other times we were told not to report events because of "operational security" reasons, only for the actions to be announced by the Pentagon at a briefing in Washington a few hours later. I suspect it's going to be the same again this time.'

Her view was a widely held one. Indeed, one of the reasons I had been able to badger my way to being selected as the *Telegraph*'s front-line reporter was that few held much hope of the 'embed' scheme ever being effectively implemented in practice. The more experienced hands remembered 1991, when those on the pool scheme with the American units had found that even when they were in a position to file, their articles had been delayed for days, sometimes even weeks, before military censors would let them be transmitted. It had been the reporters working independently, driving across the border in their own Jeeps and free of any military shackles, who had been able to provide the most vivid and analytical stories. The last thing they wanted this time was to sacrifice that freedom on the off-chance that the American military might for once decide to keep its word.

Yet there were reasons why it was conceivable that the Pentagon might live up to its promises in a new Iraqi conflict. This time it had its own motivations for wanting to do so. I might have misjudged quite how far the military would go in putting reporters in danger, but living in America for nearly eighteen months meant I had been better placed than those in London to sense that there was a shift in the air. The majority of victories in the First Gulf War are barely known to the public, as they were never captured by print reporters or TV camera crews. No soldier likes to believe he has won glory on the battlefield and then, on returning home, discover that people have no idea what he has achieved. This time the US military, particularly the army, which felt its exploits in 1991 had been unfairly eclipsed by the Marines solely because the Marines had journalists on hand to write about their actions, wanted to make sure its triumphs were told to the world.

Keeping the journalists away also risked surrendering the fight for public opinion to enemy propaganda. Officials were worried that Saddam could commit an atrocity, for example killing civilians or bombing a school, and then blame it on the Americans. As Bryan Whitman, the Pentagon's deputy spokesman, had told the assembled press: 'Saddam Hussein is a practised liar. What better way to combat disinformation on the battlefield than to have you report objectively about what the situation really is?' The rantings of Muhammad Said Al-Sahhaf, the Iraqi Information Minister who would come to be known as 'Comical Ali' for his absurd briefings about the humiliations wreaked on the American advance, were subsequently cited by the pro-press Pentagon advisers as proof of their foresight and wisdom.

If the war had gone differently, and reporters had witnessed at first hand a major defeat or numerous American casualties, their military hosts' attitude might have undergone a rapid reversal. As it was, at no point did anyone ask to look at anything I filed before it was transmitted. There were times when no one would tell me the exact composition of men and equipment in a unit for 'operational security' reasons, and it was often difficult to gain details about casualties. However, my experience ultimately was one of amazement at the amount of freedom I was given to wander around and ask whatever questions I liked to whomever I chose. There was no minder and no censor. The greatest restriction on my movements proved to be my own fear of exposing myself in spots where I was worried about getting killed, rather than anything the US Army did to try to limit my independence.

There was however one other factor motivating the American authorities to embrace a closer relationship with the press. In unguarded moments Pentagon officials would privately admit that they were betting on journalists 'going native'. The war in Afghanistan had illustrated that the military could no longer control the battlefield – correspondents were often on the ground before American combat troops – or the flow of information, as satellite communication was now so easy and inexpensive. Planners had concluded that if you couldn't simply stop journalists, it was at least worth trying to ensure that they told your side of the story and not the enemy's. What better way to do that than by placing them in units, so they formed a bond with the soldiers, and as a result found it harder to write negative things about them? The army knew it would be a challenge for any of us to maintain objectivity about the troops with whom we were living. Few of the assembled press pack had ever been on a battlefield before. We could end up so in awe of the weaponry we were witnessing, and so in debt to those we were relying on for protection, that it would prove emotionally impossible to express criticism.

Looking around at some of the journalists I was drinking with in the bar beside Fort Dix, it didn't seem the Pentagon had made a bad wager. Already many of our number had begun to adopt the jargon of the military. A reporter from the *Wall Street Journal* was saying he had 'good intel' on a Korean barbeque place. Another described a Leatherman pocket knife as 'really high speed' (air force-speak for top grade). Some had even begun to greet each other with the shout 'Hoo-ah', the military's multi-purpose signature response that could act as a hello, an affirmative to an order, or simply a rabble-rousing cry of bellicosity. Later, in

Kuwait, I came across many of the same group of people again, some of them wearing complete military fatigues. When, during a briefing in New Jersey, I had made a cheap joke questioning the legality of the conditions under which suspected terrorists were being held at Guantanamo Bay in Cuba, one reporter had berated me for my anti-American views. In the bar I could hear groups laughing and joking with their military instructors about how quickly the Iraqis would be annihilated.

I was only too aware, however, that I was as likely as anyone to fall into the Pentagon's trap. I had been one of those kids who had run around with an imitation gun fighting make-believe battles. At school it had been a requirement that you join the army cadet force for a year. It had not been the most glorious moment of my educational career. At one point I had failed the test on stripping and reassembling the SA80 rifle more times than anyone in the county since the examination had begun. It was a tour of service which concluded with me and a few others being thrown into a military prison at a British camp in Germany to which our school unit had been taken on manoeuvres at the end of the summer term. Our crime had been returning a quarter of an hour late from a trip off-base. Inside the jail we met a nineteen-year-old private who had been locked up for a week and given a toothbrush to clean all the walls and floor of his cell. It was not a sight that endeared the army to me. But I knew that I had secretly enjoyed running around shooting blanks and planning ambushes. It had been a buzz riding in a tank. I liked going up in helicopters. Now, excitement was growing inside me at knowing that all those games were going to be turned into reality, and I was to witness the spectacle of war for real.

Though I did not like to admit it to anyone, a part of me wanted to test myself by seeing how I would react under fire. I suspect almost all men secretly wonder how they would behave if they found themselves in the midst of a battle, that most extreme and masculine of all arenas. It would be the ultimate examination of my mettle. An indication perhaps that if it had ever been required I could have achieved what my grandparents' generation did: faced my fears, done my bit and successfully defended my country. I sincerely hoped that I would not flinch when the first bullet cracked nearby. I really had seen far too many war films.

However, in the back of my mind was the gnawing suspicion that my behaviour would not prove to be the stuff of the 'Commando' comic books I had grown up on. That I would be shaking in fear, shocked by the brutality of what was happening, stunned that people were actually shooting at me. I did hope I was not among the one in four who actually shat themselves, but it was always a possibility. There was one thing I knew above all else, and that was that I had no desire to get killed. I was young, I had plans. I did not want to find myself in the situation of having to lose even the tip of a finger.

One of the American reporters turned to me in the bar on the final night of our training and said, 'You know, when I was growing up, I used to read all Ernie Pyle's writings. Now I'm going to be doing what he did. Isn't that cool?' The problem was, I could never quite forget how Pyle's stint in the field had ended: he died in April 1945 on a small island off Okinawa, shot in the head by a Japanese sniper.

By the time I got to Kuwait my obsession with the potential dangers to my groin had worsened. Just before leaving London, where I had spent a week being briefed by my office before flying on to the Gulf, I had got together with some friends in a Brixton pub for a little send-off. The bar was run by an Israeli who had arrived in Britain fresh from completing his national service. To my increasing concern he rolled his eyes and shook his head in dismay when I revealed that the flak jacket I had just purchased did not have a groin guard.

'That is very bad,' he warned me. 'I know many friends in Israel who lost their nuts in explosions. Maybe four, five of them suffered in such a way. I visited them in hospital afterwards. No nuts. Not pleasant.'

He walked halfway down the bar and stood beside the jukebox. 'Mortar goes off here and you are dead.' He walked to the far end. 'It goes off here and no nuts.'

I had thought I had everything that could possibly be needed. The four weeks between being dismissed from boot camp and landing in Kuwait City were one long shopping spree. For a reporter, one of the advantages of going to war is that it is about the only time your publication considers money no object. The office had bought me a satellite phone through which it was intended I could call the foreign desk in London and also file articles over the internet via a data cord that linked it to my laptop. I had become a regular at the army surplus store in Santa Monica, the city next to Los Angeles in which I lived, where the shelves heaved with helmets made from bullet-resistant Kevlar, camouflage webbing belts, and handheld satellite-tracking navigation devices known as GPSs. In the Californian sunshine I would lug bags filled with survival equipment back to my small apartment. On the way I would pass a stall set up by the local 'Free Speech Society' at which an elderly man, shouting through a loudspeaker and brandishing handfuls of leaflets, was vigorously propagating his belief that the entire terrorist threat to the United States and the approaching military intervention by America in the Middle East was being manipulated by the 'Indio-British Conspiracy'. This was apparently a shadowy group of ardent imperialists in London and high-caste elites in India who wished to resurrect the British Empire at the expense of America's present domination. To my concern, he always seemed to be surrounded by a cluster of potential adherents flicking through the printed material on offer.

Everywhere I went, the topic of conversation seemed to be the approaching war. Being California, the biggest Democrat stronghold in the United States, reaction was rarely positive. A group of party girls I knew who lived in Hollywood were busy preparing placards for the anti-war marches planned throughout the state – it seemed to me as much for the social opportunities these events would provide as out of any overwhelming political conviction. My neighbour would knock on my door whenever a new hardening of the American attitude was reported, a thirty-two-inch television tuned to CNN visible in her flat across the corridor. 'It's only because they tried to kill his father and he wants their oil,' she would maintain about President George W. Bush's real motivations. Yet elsewhere in the country polls were rising in support of conflict. By the time I flew out on Sunday, 17 February, 60 per cent supported war, up six points from a month earlier. It seemed that as the likelihood of American soldiers going into battle grew, so did the numbers rallying around the flag. Among those who voted Republican, 82 per cent agreed with military intervention. A look at Fox News, the twenty-four-hour cable news channel that had raced ahead of CNN in the ratings battle by pursuing a consistently jingoistic line, provided a window to the sabre-rattling attitude of many in Middle America. One of its commentators called on the US to go and 'splatter' the Iraqis. A flickering Stars and Stripes appeared on screen as images were shown of navy ships sailing off to war. Before commercial breaks, announcers would exhort viewers to 'Stay brave, stay aware, and stay with Fox.'

Across the United States the real fear of the Arab world that had arisen after the 11 September terrorist attacks showed little sign of abating. The army surplus store had run out of duct tape, the durable sticky tape that the military had instructed me was an indispensable part of any reporter's survival kit. An intelligence tip-off – the same one that resulted in tanks being dispatched to Heathrow airport – had just caused the terrorist alert system established by America's recently formed Homeland Security Department to rise to orange, meaning the threat of a terrorist incident was considered 'high'. The resulting panic meant that across the country people were stocking up with duct tape, bottled water and plastic sheeting (which the government had instructed them to stick over their windows to protect their families from a chemical attack). One day as I searched through the items at the army surplus store an excessively fat man had come in asking if they sold grenades, as he wanted to make sure he could take out any 'sand niggers' if the need arose.

'There are too many crazies in this country,' the store manager confided to me. 'Every day we have people coming in and asking for weapons to protect themselves from terrorists. It's like they all think they're going to be in the middle of a war right here in their neighbourhood.' I had learnt that he was a refugee who had fled from Burma after his family had been arrested and interrogated by the ruling junta. When not at work he coordinated the local branch of Amnesty International. At its entrance the store had a lifesize model of a soldier about to bayonet some invisible enemy. Behind the counter was a picture of a skeleton shuffling a pack of cards under the logo 'We Deal. You Die'. When I asked how he had ended up working at such an unlikely establishment for a self-confessed pacifist, he had told me that his Burmese features were often mistaken for Middle Eastern. 'It's not so easy to get work these days,' he explained.

My body armour had to be bought in Britain. Its sale had effectively been stopped in Los Angeles as local hoodlums kept snapping up bulletproof vests and wearing them to commit crimes. Their victims had started suing the businesses that sold them, and no one was willing to risk stocking such items. The place to go to in London was a shop called Spymaster, located in a listed building in Mayfair. Customers had to be buzzed through the front door by a receptionist after first establishing the company they represented. Inside were glass cases filled with what appeared to be cast-off props from a James Bond film. There were recording bugs the size of pinheads, tape players disguised as briefcases, dummy Coca-Cola cans with detachable tops that acted as secret hiding places. A man in matching black pinstripe trousers and waistcoat and sporting shiny black leather shoes came forward to discuss my requirements.

'I think we have just what you need, sir,' he informed me, before disappearing into the back and returning with an array of bulletproofing. 'Now, what size exactly are you looking for?'

The first jacket he suggested was not what I wanted, being bright blue, which despite its clarity in establishing one as non-military was a colour we had been told at boot camp would attract any sniper in the vicinity. 'It is very popular with the journalistic client,' my stylist said, looking disappointed. The trick, we had been instructed by the Americans, was not to dress exactly like a soldier, so as to avoid looking like a combatant, but at the same time to wear nothing that could give away the location of the unit with which you were travelling. Finally we compromised on a two-piece set: a camouflaged flak jacket, and underneath it a detachable black harness holding the bulletproof plates. 'It's very you, sir,' he said as I tried it on. 'I'm so pleased we could find something suitable.'

I went down into the basement to use the bathroom. A guard dog was tethered to one of the walls. Looking into the rooms on either side, I could see boxes overflowing with a variety of electronic equipment. In an underground garage there were a couple of all-terrain vehicles and a three-wheeled sports car with a melded airstreamed body and what looked like a small jet engine poking out of the back. 'It's for a specialist market, sir,' I was told when I asked who would buy such a thing. 'Very effective, though, for those who find they need it.'

But still this groin problem was worrying me. Late at night in my Kuwait hotel room, as the continuing United Nations deliberations pushed back the possible start of a war, I scoured websites for someone who could Fed-Ex a Kevlar version of a cricket box to me. I had investigated the sperm bank option before leaving the States, but it had proved prohibitively expensive for someone on a reporter's salary. Prices seemed to start at around $1000, and for that I still had to sign a waiver saying that if I was killed my deposit could be sold to a fertility clinic. I had been momentarily excited when I discovered that a sperm bank in San Diego was offering a special discounted 'patriot's package' for servicemen off to the Gulf, but the receptionist had informed me that while it had proved 'very popular' with the men in uniform (although in most cases apparently at the behest of their wives and girlfriends), I could not be classed as a potential combatant. Finally, after discussing my angst with one of the other journalists staying in the hotel, I was directed to try bulletproofme.com. It was a revelation. Twenty-four hours later a custom-made groin protector was winging its way from a factory in America to the Gulf. The future of my family's lineage was looking a little bit more secure.

There had been one troublesome conversation in London. I had been in a nightclub in South Kensington with my friend Chris. It was an unlikely spot to talk politics, sipping martinis while around us lithe girls gyrated to hip-hop. But he had turned to me and said: 'Look, mate, just want to check; you are against all this war shit, aren't you?'

Embarrassingly, it wasn't something I had given a huge amount of thought to. I had been so preoccupied by the prospect of reporting on such a huge story, and so busy preparing for it, that there had been little time left to dwell on the rights and wrongs of what was actually happening. The truth was that my only conviction was an overwhelming desire for the war to go ahead, and that was for the most selfish of reasons: I wanted to be able to cover it.

I did have my doubts about whether invading a Middle Eastern country was the best way to ensure that fundamentalist Islamic suicide bombers decided to stop targeting London and Washington DC. Yet I was no peacenik. The idea of pre-emptive wars of deterrence was questionable, but the evidence being released to the public to show that Iraq had weapons of mass destruction, and was prepared to use them, seemed overwhelming.

I had talked to Iraqis who had been forced to flee their country, and was only too aware of the hardships involved in living under a military dictatorship as brutal as Saddam's. At an Arab conference near San Francisco held during the Afghanistan War I had found myself surrounded by Iraqi exiles. They had detailed their individual stories of imprisonment, torture and disappeared family members. To me it seemed only right that their countrymen should have the same opportunities to prosper as an accident of birth meant those of us in the Western world had, and I told my friend so. Nothing inflamed me more than the presumption that somehow dictatorships were an acceptable state of affairs for those living in the Middle East. There was no apparent way Saddam Hussein could be toppled bloodlessly, and it seemed to me that in the long run the war would save lives by ensuring that no one in future could be killed by his regime.

'Maybe, but people can't be forced to be free,' Chris had said. 'If they want a new government, they've got to do it themselves. Bullyboy America can't just decide to wade in and tell people in another country how they should be living their lives. People will resent them being there, which will lead to even more anti-Western feeling. A whole lot of blood will be shed for nothing.'

'At least they wouldn't be getting tortured or murdered at the whim of a madman,' I retorted. 'This war may give people the chance to live without fear, to make some money, have a bit of a laugh. I know that with it come McDonald's and oil contracts. I'm not completely blind. I know what's wrapped up in the package. I know that part of the problem is American support for dodgy regimes. But they're not planning to turn the Middle East into a new Raj. This is the US of A, not Nazi Germany we're talking about. People there really believe in all this freedom, democracy and diversity stuff.'

Influenced by my time living in the States, I had become convinced that America felt guilty about its own riches and comfort, embarrassed by what it saw as its excessive blessings, and so tried to ease its sense of unworthiness by trying to replicate its good fortune elsewhere. That was why it kept interfering in other countries' affairs. It was not just an obsession with security or economic opportunities, but a desire to forge other countries in its own image. Then their inhabitants could be as lucky as those living in the United States believed they were, simply for being American.

'Saddam publicly executes political opponents and zapped the Kurds with poison gas,' I said. 'He gets off on attacking his neighbours. Compared to that, the rest doesn't really matter, does it? It's just the price that has to be paid for these people to have the chance to live safely. Let's see if they welcome the Americans' arrival. That will show us whether this war is right or wrong: whether the people in Iraq greet it as a war of liberation, or just see it as another unwanted Western invasion to be opposed.'

We ordered two more thimblefuls of overpriced drinks. 'Look,' Chris said, 'Americans may *think* this is all happening to make things better for people in Iraq, but actually what they're doing is saying "We're going to determine how you're permitted to behave." They just don't get that not everyone wants to live like they do. They're pushing so hard around the world at the moment that it risks forcing people into extreme positions, even if they didn't originally want to be extremists. Good intentions, even if they exist, don't matter a toss. It's results that matter. You can't destroy a country and expect its people to thank you for it.'

Then we got up to make our way onto the dance floor to see if we could find some action. He turned to me. 'You'll see,' he said.

It was a fortnight after my arrival in Kuwait City that the assembled journalists were told they could finally join their designated units. Talk in the UN, and a heavy snowstorm on the east coast of

America that prevented the military anti-biochemical weapon kits earmarked for the media being sent to the Gulf, meant that to start with our experience of the build-up to war was one of lazing around in the luxury of five-star hotels. The main bureau of the army's press operation had been established in the local Hilton. The outside of the building was rapidly being turned into a military installation, with concrete blocks to keep out suicide bombers, armed checkpoints, and guard dogs that sniffed at every person and bag entering the complex. It was enough to make you feel nervous. Inside, however, was an Epicurean fantasy. Shallow canals of water fanned around seating areas lined with sun loungers shaded by umbrellas made from palm leaves. Smooth black pebbles were scattered on tabletops beside artistically twisted branches resting in glass vases. A harpist played in the lobby. Staff in apricot jackets waited at every corner for an opportunity to serve you.

It was in one of the conference halls in this oasis of calm and tranquillity, its spacious ceiling illuminated by discreet lighting, that we lined up to receive our inoculations. Staring at the person in the queue two in front of me, I realised he looked familiar. A quick check with the man behind me, an English reporter with Reuters TV, revealed that it was Oliver North, the former Marine colonel caught up in the Iran–Contra scandal which at one point had undermined Ronald Reagan's entire presidency. He had now been hired by Fox News to act as their embed correspondent with the US Marine Corps.

The army nurses who were administering the jabs had just clocked who he was. A squeal of excitement went up from a particularly plump one. Work was forgotten as the half-dozen medical staff in their tan combat fatigues buzzed around asking for North's autograph and to have their photograph taken with him. A doctor gripped his hand in a lengthy handshake. The centre of all this excitement was lapping up the attention. Though clearly no longer in his prime – he was fifty-nine – he was still a tall, muscular figure, his hair now grey but those distinctive eye-brows as dark as ever. 'Be careful,' he said to the plump nurse who had won the struggle for the honour to administer his jabs, 'there isn't much room left on that arm. Most has already been scarred by injections received in a lifetime in the service.' A Swedish journalist who was next in line gave a long sigh. 'How the Americans love a celebrity,' he said to me. 'Who cares if it's one who was accused of being a traitor to his country?' It was not a concern that was particularly preoccupying me. I was too impressed by the fact that, when I had to fill out the waiver about any possible side effects of the inoculation, Colonel North had given me his pen and then told me to keep it as a present.

During those days in limbo in Kuwait City there was little to do but lounge by the pool. There was certainly no alcohol, as it had been banned by the government, and many of the reporters were reduced to huddling around the hotel 'bars', sipping non-alcoholic beer in the hope of some sort of Pavlovian response, before retiring to their rooms at 10 p.m., their systems overcome with exhaustion at having to cope with the unfamiliar sensation of an enforced period of abstinence. Kuwait itself seemed remarkably calm for a country in which an army was gathering. There were the Emirate's soldiers clutching machine guns at the entrance to all the hotels, and the troops stationed in armed vehicles at the main roundabouts, but otherwise business gave every appearance of continuing as normal. The airlines reported that there had been no exodus of the population. The local stock market was even undergoing a mini boom at the prospect of all the contracts for reconstruction that it was expected would soon be available in Kuwait's northern neighbour.

One night I went with a group of journalists to a meeting of the National Democratic Movement, an organisation established to promote the spread of democracy in Kuwait. There was little talk of extending the franchise, but a lot about revenge and economic opportunities. 'We have waited thirty years to be able to expand into Iraq,' one delegate told me. 'Now we will finally be able to do so. And to see the end of Saddam Hussein at the same time makes it doubly satisfying.' A number said they knew of friends who were flying back to the country to make sure they did not miss a moment when the time came to start striking post-war business deals. One financial expert told me he thought the whole conflict would be over in twenty-four hours. No one seemed to think his forecast ridiculous.

Yet there were reminders that all was not normal. The Kuwaiti Department of the Interior had started sending morale-boosting text messages in Arabic and English to the general populace. 'Be strong and we will defeat our enemies' popped up on my mobile phone one morning. 'Always maintain vigilance against possible dangers' on another. A number of the predominantly Indian taxi-drivers said they had sent their wives and children back home for the duration of the conflict. As I drove along the system of motor-ways that ringed the city, I would pass long convoys of American military vehicles carrying equipment north.

Memories of the events of 1991 remained strong. In the hotel I was staying in, the Radisson SAS just along the coast from the Hilton, the main lobby was decorated with photographs of the destruction it had suffered during the Iraqi invasion. There was a picture of the reception area reduced to a mess of broken glass and bricks, the concierge's desk smashed in two. The floor of the laundry was shown piled high with the charred remains of burnt clothing. One photograph depicted the clock next to the lifts that had been discovered stuck at 5.37, the time it had been broken on the day the Iraqi soldiers were given the order to seize what they could, destroy as much as possible and then flee back across the border. On the side of local buses was an advertisement paid for by an Arab organisation featuring a kneeling American soldier hugging some Kuwaiti children. 'We will never forget,' the slogan pledged.

When I signed up for my Kuwaiti mobile phone service, the assistant – her hair covered in a silver headdress and surrounded by a haze of perfume reminiscent of Roman Catholic incense – told me that all the talk of a new war meant that she had started to suffer nightmares about the previous one. 'I was fourteen then, and we couldn't get out of Kuwait City. I know war is not a nothing, some matter to laugh about. It was awful. Always there was shooting, people frightened. The worst was at the end when they left; they lit the oilfields and it was always black. At ten in the morning it was black, when you wiped your nose it was black. My father still cannot breathe properly even today. I hope the American and English people realise that war is an awful thing. Even if it is quick, people die, lives are ruined. This is not just something to want to watch on television.'

It was Monday, 10 March when the media finally started to move to the military camps that were spread across the desert to our north. There were eighty-three of us being sent to live with the 3rd Infantry Division. A similar number were to go a few days later to join the American Marines, while considerably fewer would be joining V Corps Logistics, the unit responsible for ensuring supplies for the combat forces, and the 101st Airborne, which in the event of war was expected to be kept in reserve in Kuwait. A few days earlier we had all gathered in another luxurious Hilton conference room to be addressed by the 3rd Infantry Division's commander, Major General Buford 'Buff' Blount III. What had struck me was that beyond Reuters, Sky TV and the BBC, there were hardly any other British news organisations present. *The Times* had been given an embed spot with the US Marines, but I would be the only British daily newspaper correspondent reporting from inside the American army. There was a smattering of reporters from a few other European countries as well as Japan, but otherwise the Pentagon had clearly decided that it was best if the gamble of letting reporters live with troops in the front line was kept a primarily American affair.

Buff Blount had been notably confident about the whole operation. 'We are cocked and ready to go,' he told us. 'We have
thermal capability and great weapons systems that can hit several
tanks at one time from miles away, as well as eighteen multiple
rocket systems, all prepared to be sent into action. Chemical and
biological weapons will have minimal impact on us as we can
fight through any biochemical strike. We can protect ourselves,
decontaminate our troops and then keep on going.' The prospect
of such a scenario did not sound as reassuring as I guess he had
intended it to be.

On the day of departure we had been told to gather at the
Hilton at 6 a.m. The scene was chaotic. The American military
press office was staffed by half a dozen overworked information
officers. Even with the help of the division's soldiers there was a
lot of queuing as we were issued with chemical gear and then
taken out to the hotel's championship-standard tennis courts for
a last-minute refresher on how it worked. I was shocked by how
militaristic some of the American press corps were looking. One
reporter was in complete army kit, with only the small word 'Press'
on a green badge on his left shoulder, the position where soldiers
are required to sport their unit's name, distinguishing him from
the surrounding troops. On his right shoulder was a patch bearing
the Stars and Stripes. Another had his name sown on his camouflage fatigues in the same spot as the soldiers. His hair had been
shaved in a cut that resembled Robert De Niro's in *Taxi Driver*,
and he was already ranting about how great it was that he would
be getting to Baghdad before the Marines, how spineless the
French were for opposing the war, and how he hoped the US was
going to seize lots of oilfields to cover the cost of the impending
conflict.

Mostly, however, everyone was preoccupied with how thrilling
it all was. The journalists were joking about gimp suits as they
tried on the plastic biochemical protection gloves and gasmasks.
There was well-intended mickey-taking about who wasn't going

to make it back, based on people's ability to open the can that stored the gasmask cylinder without cutting their fingers. After a late lunch – a final treat of a club sandwich accompanied by orange juice freshly squeezed by a Filipina armed with a giant press – we were herded into four coaches and started the journey towards the border.

Soon we had left Kuwait City behind us. The road gradually narrowed till, with dusk approaching, we were on a barely tarmacked track marked with deep potholes. Then the drivers were following wheeltracks in the sand. There were no buildings in sight, just an expanse of desert; no bushes or trees, only dunes and the occasional manmade banks of sand known as berms. One of the buses peeled off, then another. The one I was travelling in was told to wait while the officer in charge guided the fourth one to its destination, a camp a short distance up a path that led off to our right. I climbed to the top of one of the berms. In the rapidly disappearing light I could make out the shape of some parked tanks and armoured personnel carriers. We were passed by a stream of trucks and Humvees, the wide-set, open-top four-wheel drives favoured by the American military. A pair of Chinook helicopters rattled overhead.

When we set off again the driver got lost in the darkness. On the GPS of the journalist next to me I could see a mark indicating the route we had taken. We were literally going round in circles. A correspondent from Reuters joked that the US Army wanted us to think it had more equipment than it did by making us pass the same lot twice. Finally a Humvee came out to guide us to our destination. It had a large American flag tied to its radio aerial. 'Follow the flag,' our driver was told.

Shortly after 10 p.m. we were instructed to get out. All lights had been banned this close to the Iraqi border, but it was possible to detect the outline of a few tents and vehicles. Major Mike Birmingham, the information officer responsible for the 3rd Infantry Division's embeds, divided us up into groups. I and around twelve others were taken along a twisting path flanked by rolls of barbed wire to a nearby command tent. The colonel of the division's 3rd Brigade, the unit whose base we had arrived at, sat us down and gave a brief welcome speech. There was a moment of confusion when we were split up once more and assigned to individual battalions, and it was discovered that my name did not appear on the pre-prepared list. After a brief discussion it was decided that I should be sent to the one that had the fewest journalists going to it. Soldiers appeared out of the night, threw my bags into the back of a truck and drove me and two other journalists towards the spot where 1st Battalion was encamped.

More than a month later, when I saw Major Birmingham again, on the tarmac of Baghdad International Airport, he confided to me why I had been absent from that roll. He had made a mistake when dividing us up as we were getting off the coach. Exhausted after days of frantic organisation, he had mistaken me in the darkness for someone else. Being from a British paper, and therefore of little importance in the eyes of the American military, I was meant to be at the back, with the banks of artillery. In the confusion he had sent another journalist to that location, and I had been directed towards the headquarters tent to join the 3rd Brigade's combat team, a front-line unit and thus a far more coveted position. When I arrived at 1st Battalion a soldier asked which of the three journalists present was from the *Wall Street Journal*. None of us was. Its reporter was by that time probably stuck with the artillery somewhere far to the rear.

The unit commander, Lieutenant Colonel John W. Charlton, known to everyone simply as 'the colonel', came into the tent in which the three of us had been billeted. He detailed the nature of the battalion with which we were now to live. It quickly became clear that there was little chance of the coming weeks proving dull. The unit had spent a total of nine months perfecting its combat skills on the training grounds of northern Kuwait. As a result its tank crews and infantry personnel were among the most honed in the US Army. High command had determined that if an invasion was ordered, the battalion would be transferred between brigades so that it would be at the forefront of almost all the main attacks planned on the route from the border to Baghdad. Firstly, the colonel's men would be part of 3rd Brigade for an assault on a military base at Nasiriyah, the first Iraqi city the army would target once war had been declared. It would then move north-west to join the forces of 2nd Brigade, which would be gathering south of Baghdad for the march on the capital. 'You're part of the team now,' the lieutenant colonel told us. 'We're going to see some amazing things. We will go into battle together, and more than once. I hope you enjoy the ride.'

Before flying out of London I had watched the debate in the chamber of the House of Commons in which MPs voted on whether in principle they supported a war in Iraq. Sitting in the Visitors' Gallery, I had heard politicians talk of 'war drums rolling', an opponent of the conflict described as 'a toady of Saddam Hussein', and the insistence that now was the time to make sure the Iraqi regime was 'disarmed by force'. At the time, what these words meant in practice had seemed a distant concept. Now it was all very real. A twist of fate had determined that I would be nowhere near the tail end of the gathered army, as I had confidently expected, but right at what the American soldiers termed 'the tip of the spear', among the units that would lead the charge into Saddam's forces. That night, as I lay on the green canvas camp bed with which I had been provided, I found myself thanking my good fortune that my groin protector had arrived in time. It looked as if it was going to be needed.

TWO

'You Will All Be Heroes'

Tuesday, 11 March–Monday, 17 March

The hardship of life in the desert was brought home the day after my arrival, when the battalion was engulfed in a sandstorm. One minute I was standing in the chow tent in the stillness of the evening air, chatting to a group of soldiers and happily tucking into the thin beefsteak with rice that was our dinner. The next, the setting sun had disappeared behind a wall of sand and the officers were shouting at the men to get back to their sleeping areas while they still might be able to find them. The wind that minutes earlier had been almost non-existent was now blowing so strongly that the air around us was filled with the sound of rattling canvas. Visibility fell to less than ten yards. Still clutching my food, I found the other two journalists assigned to the unit and we staggered backwards through the gale to our tent. The air inside was thick with a fine yellow dust that hung like fog. We strapped scarves around our mouths to try to keep our lungs clear, and put on goggles to shield our eyes. The wind soon reached forty miles per hour. Outside we could hear soldiers whooping and shouting as they ran around the surrounding tents to secure them with sandbags. There was a crash as the pegs gave way on a tent nearby and it was sent rolling across the parade ground. I stepped through the partition that separated our sleeping area from the rest of the tent in which we had been billeted and found three soldiers sitting in a group, two of them seeking refuge after being unable to reach their own sleeping areas because of the storm. 'Welcome to hell,' one said to me, a smile cracking the dust that caked his features. Piles of sand had begun to accumulate on every surface, spilling off desks and forming valleys in the creases of the kitbags lying underneath.

An hour later, Lieutenant Colonel Charlton came in to check we were all right. 'I wanted to make sure you'd found your way back from the mess hall safely,' he said. It was not a joke. A few days earlier a soldier had been lost for five hours after losing his bearings coming back from the latrines in a storm. Many had started taking their GPS units with them if they had to go out when the winds hit. The colonel perched on the edge of one of the canvas cots and sparked up a stubby cigar. 'I can't wait to leave this place,' he said. 'The sooner we can get out of here and advance across the border, the better. Every time we hear of something in the UN, we just think "Oh, shit," as it means another delay. It's all beyond our control, and that's what's so frustrating.'

It would be his duty to lead into battle the 850 soldiers of 1st Battalion, which for the purpose of the Iraqi campaign had been given the title Task Force 1–15, and his job to make sure it had enough ammunition, food and water. He had to determine a battle plan that maximised the technological advantages offered by his troops' equipment and minimised their exposure to danger. It was clearly a responsibility that was weighing upon him. He had only been appointed to the position, his first battalion command, in July, and now, at forty-two years old, was to lead men into war for the first time. But then, no one presently in the United States Army had ever been involved in an operation like the one proposed in Iraq. The last time American tanks had successfully invaded a country by land and seized its capital, the final objective had been Berlin, not Baghdad.

'We're short of a lot of vital equipment,' Charlton confided to us. 'They're telling people at the top that we have it, but it's all piling up in Doha [the American Air Force logistics base north of Kuwait City], and it isn't getting out here fast enough. We need engine grease, some types of ammunition; you can never have too much food and water. But on the other hand, we need to get going soon. The weather's only going to get hotter. We arrived here last summer, and it was hitting 120 degrees. People were drinking water all day and still they were barely pissing. Those are no conditions in which to be fighting.

'Morale is holding up, but these delays are not good for people. Soldiers are missing their families. Hell, I'm missing my wife. I've got two sons who are growing up without me seeing them. We were here six months last year, went back to the States for only forty-four days over Christmas, and then straight out again. It's tough on the troops. Two weeks ago we were at least in Camp New York [the permanent military base located near the Iraq border], where we had proper food, computers and tents for everyone to sleep in. Then we got the order to move out and establish a temporary camp in the desert. We find ourselves here, where you can only get a real shower once a week, there's one fresh meal a day, and there isn't even anywhere to go and buy tobacco. Sometimes I feel more like fifty-two than forty-two.' He eased his five-foot-ten-inch frame back a little and ran his hand over his closely cropped brown hair to shake out some of the sand. 'I don't want to mislead you. There are problems, and weather like this isn't helping.'

When I had woken shortly after dawn that morning, I had for the first time been able to grasp the scale of the American mobilisation. Stepping through the flap that acted as a door to the tent which was now my home, I had been greeted by the sight of an array of weaponry stretching to the horizon. In the distance were the giant aircraft hangars in which were based the Apache and Black Hawk helicopters that swarmed like insects in the sky above. In front of them spread the companies of tanks and fighting vehicles of the 3rd Brigade that would lead the invasion on the ground. Around them were clustered the domes of small, tan tents. Through their entrance flaps could be made out the shapes of soldiers escaping the rapidly rising heat. Some were writing letters, others reading magazines, many just lay against their kitbags to grab a few moments more rest. A number of clothes lines had been rigged up between vehicles, and from them hung fatigues in the dull yellow, brown and black that made up the US Army's desert camouflage. Opposite my tent stood the battalion's dark-green tactical operations tent. Through its canvas came the constant wheeze of the military radio spewing out updates to the unit's orders. Behind was the command tent. There was a plastic window in its side, and it was possible to see a giant map of Kuwait and Iraq dotted with symbols of enemy and coalition units.

To my left had been erected a twenty-foot sign that towered over the tented city around it. On it was painted the battalion coat of arms, a shield emblazoned with a Chinese dragon. Underneath was the unit's motto. It simply read: 'Can Do'.

A line had already formed for breakfast outside the chow tent on the other side of the hundred-square-yard parade ground which marked the centre of the battalion's encampment. The food was pretty basic. The morning meal was a version of the old C-rations, a dollop of synthetic eggs and reprocessed meat that came in tins heated up by the cooks. The culinary highlight of the day came every evening, when fresh food was prepared and ladled onto paper trays carried by the soldiers. This at least contained vegetables and some salad, the only natural source of vitamins available.

There was no set lunch. Everyone had to resort to the self-heating meals which would become an all too familiar part of life over the coming weeks. Known as MREs – 'Meals, Ready to Eat' – they came in a durable plastic bag about half the size of a phonebook that contained a small heater and half a dozen foil packages of pre-prepared food. The heater was ignited by pouring in a trickle of water that set off a chemical reaction. Some of the meals, such as the Chilli Macaroni or Beef and Mushroom, were pretty good; others, such as a catastrophic attempt at a curry called Country Captain's Chicken, barely edible. All had ten-year sell-by dates.

Many of the soldiers had their own individual recipes which they swore by, developed over months of practice tastings, in which processed cheese would be melted into casseroles, or orange drink flavouring added as a seasoning to rice. Though some spent considerable time trying to persuade me of their concoctions' virtues, few as far as I could see had anything to recommend them other than offering a little variety. Real excitement for me came when I opened a package and found it was one of the few that contained a little bag of chocolate M&Ms or Skittles. There was also always a plastic packet that held a paper napkin, salt and pepper, a baby bottle of Tabasco sauce, and damp-resistant matches. The cardboard packages containing four cigarettes that had last been a feature of American ration kits in the Vietnam War were much missed by the time we reached Baghdad and personal stocks of tobacco had begun to run low.

The latrines were even more Spartan than the catering arrangements. Poles had been stuck into the sand, and water bottles cut in half and taped to the top of the tubes, into which the troops urinated. Scattered around were a few wooden lavatories. The 'Shit House Rules' scrawled on the front in black marker-pen were pretty simple: 'No Pissing (Use Piss Tubes) and No Trash'. Once a day a contingent of soldiers would be required to pull out the barrel from underneath and set it on fire with diesel fuel, sending dark clouds of smoke billowing across the encampment. There were also a few makeshift washing areas, where padded ground-mats had been tied to posts to make enclosed circles. To shower you had to pour the contents of a bottle of drinking water over your head. The soldiers often left the bottles out in the sun before-hand to warm them. There was no running water. A truck housing real showers stopped by once a week, but the hot water it provided was barely more than a trickle.

The sandstorms, I was told, were a regular hazard, the result of weather conditions which each spring created atmospheric pressure that forced hot air downwards. The worst had lasted almost a week. During the day temperatures reached ninety degrees. At night it became so cold that some of the men would sleep in woolly hats. The soldiers had been living with variations of these conditions on and off for nine months. It was no wonder that the last thing they wanted was any more delay to the start of combat.

'No one understands what it's like here,' said a tank crew-member, twenty-one-year-old Robert Holewinsk, as I was being given a tour of the battalion's equipment. 'When we were here last summer I took pictures and showed them when I got back home, but still no one could get it. Most people just think, "Oh, those troops are in the desert waiting to go to war." They probably imagine us in barracks, kicking back, watching TV. Well, it isn't like that. If this is delayed to next autumn because of the French, I have to sit through another summer of this. I don't know if we can all take that. I'm from San Diego. I'm a surfer. I should be out there riding some waves, not stuck here forever.'

His crewmate pointed out into the distance across the bareness of the desert. 'You know, sir, that there is only one tree out there? It's located a few miles south, on the way to Kuwait City. Everyone slows down to have a look when they pass it. Isn't that pathetic?'

There was one question everyone wanted answered above all others: 'Any news of when we go?' When I told them about any bad developments – the possibility of a wait for another United Nations resolution, or that the French had promised to veto any moves that would approve a war – the reaction I got was vehement in its outrage and disappointment. What news the soldiers did have about events in the outside world was often inaccurate. One day I met a young private who was sitting looking dejected by the operations tent. 'Have you heard?' he asked me. 'The Germans have sent troops to guard Saddam Hussein. We're never going to get out of here now.' Another day there was a new morsel of information that rivalled interest in developments at the UN. A rumour had swept the camp that Jennifer Lopez, the pop singer and actress, was dead, killed in a car crash near New York. A while later I came across the tank driver who claimed to have been the one who made up the story. 'There was nothing else to do. I was bored,' he said when I asked why he had done it.

It was surreal listening at night to the BBC World Service on my short-wave radio and hearing debates about whether there was going to be a war at all. If you were where I was, surrounded by soldiers who had spent months training in preparation for a fight, unable to walk far without passing another convoy bringing in more equipment, there was little question that the decision had already been made, and indeed made a while ago. You only had to see the detail of the military maps to be left in no doubt about the degree of preparation already completed. Over the previous twelve years American aircraft and satellites had photographed every inch of Iraq and mapped out every building, government facility and terrain feature. Areas that had drawn some intelligence officer's suspicion were indicated as potential bunkers or gun posts. Good assembly areas for units to regroup or set up defensive positions had been marked, as were civilian buildings such as mosques, hospitals and schools that should if at all possible be left unscathed. It was an open secret that the troops had already been briefed on the battle plan. As one of them put it to me: 'What is the similarity between a condom and the US military? When it's deployed, it's damn well going to go into action.'

Task Force 1–15 was only a small part of an army of almost 130,000 troops gathered in Kuwait for that action, but its fourteen M1A1-Abrams tanks and thirty M2 Bradleys were a force to be reckoned with in themselves. In the 1991 war a single American battalion had wiped out an entire Republican Guard brigade. The Abrams was the world's most sophisticated tank, its 120mm main gun accurate at a range of two miles. This meant that the moment an enemy learnt the Americans were in the vicinity tended to be the moment when they died. It had a top speed of forty-one miles per hour, stood eight feet high and was thirty-two feet in length. As the army handout on the tank clinically described it: 'The Abrams is particularly suitable for attacking or defending against large concentrations of heavy armour forces on a highly lethal battlefield.' What this meant in practice was that it could blow up almost anything, while most of the weaponry available to the rest of the world would simply bounce off its armoured sides.

The Bradley looked like a tank, but was actually a heavily fortified taxi. It had its roster of weapons: a 25mm Bushmaster cannon, a TOW II missile system and a rotatable 7.62mm machine gun; indeed, in the previous conflict more Iraqi armoured vehicles were destroyed by Bradleys than by Abrams. However, its main purpose was to ferry units of infantry into battle. Besides its three crew – a commander, driver and a gunner – there was space in the back for seven passengers, or 'dismounts' as the military called them. It was in Bradleys that the infantry made its way to war, crammed onto the metal benches in the six-foot space in the rear, too tightly packed to stretch their legs, let alone stand up. It was, as one infantry sergeant described it, 'a coffin on tracks in which we only see daylight when they want us to kill people'. Once the back door was shut the only light came through the thin slits of half a dozen periscopes affixed to the vehicle's sides.

As well as the Abrams and Bradleys the battalion had barrages of mortars and artillery. The mortars were fixed to the back of converted personnel carriers so they could be whisked into and out of a combat zone. The artillery no longer consisted of fixed field guns but was now mounted on tracks, the Paladin 155mm howitzers resembling tanks but with vastly longer and wider barrels. Alongside them travelled an armoured carrier filled with shells. As in Nelson's navy, these were ferried from the shelf to the gun by hand, passed along a line of men, the last of whom jammed it into the breech of the barrel. The most fearsome part of their arsenal was known as a 'copperhead', a shell which guided itself to a target that spotters in the front line had fixed with a laser sight. Each cost $25,000. One loader described it as 'like throwing the equivalent of a Mercedes Benz each time at the enemy'.

There were convoys of support vehicles: fuel tankers, lorries filled with ammunition, trucks carrying food and water. There was a mobile medical unit, mechanics, radio communication experts, cooks, intelligence officers, anti-biochemical attack teams. There were at least a dozen scout vehicles – Humvees fixed with machine guns that would fan out in front of the advancing column of tanks. The battalion had its own bridging equipment. Rockets were towed on trailers. A barrage of Patriot missiles offered protection against missile attack.

This accumulation of weaponry had been stationed at the battalion's camp in Tactical Assembly Area Hammer, around thirty miles from the Iraqi frontier. Adjacent to it were another infantry battalion, an aviation regiment, a field artillery unit, an engineer battalion, a forward support battalion responsible for logistics, and at their centre the brigade headquarters, the tent to which my group of journalists had been taken on our arrival that first night. There was also a brigade field hospital and a biochemical decontamination centre, both of which appeared to be primarily staffed by female soldiers, to the obsession of all the men stationed nearby. There were rumours that a few of them were engaging in a bit of freelance prostitution, as some of the men were withdrawing large amounts of their pay despite there being little to spend it on. In the Afghanistan campaign a similar situation had apparently resulted in some women having to be shipped back to the States. No one, either officers or men, seemed particularly appalled by such a possibility, although I never heard of any female soldiers having to be sent home this time.

Despite the distance from the border and the fact that hostilities had not begun, everyone was very conscious of the possibility of a chemical attack. The order had been given a week earlier that gasmasks should be carried at all times. It was guidance that I adhered to. Already I would go nowhere without first making sure that the green cloth bag containing my mask and nerve-gas antidotes was strapped around my thigh, just in case Saddam decided to start the war first.

The soldier delegated to show the three reporters assigned to the battalion around was Rodrigo Arreola, a forty-year-old Latino with a jaw as chiselled as a comic-book superhero who as the battalion sergeant major was the unit's most senior NCO. My two fellow journalists were Ron Synovitz, forty, who worked for Radio Free Europe, the American government radio station that broadcasts from its headquarters in Prague to Eastern Europe and increasingly the Middle East (including Iraq), and Joe Giordono, a twenty-eight-year-old photojournalist for *Stars and Stripes*, the daily newspaper produced by the US military for its servicemen, who was based in Japan. Although they insisted that in the best tradition of American commitment to free speech neither organisation was subject to overt editorial control from its paymasters, it meant that I was the only one among the three of us whose paycheque was not ultimately dependent on the incumbent of the White House.

At first the idea of having a guide to show us around the camp had made me slightly uncomfortable. But it soon became clear that Sergeant Major Arreola had little interest in monitoring our activities. His main concern seemed to be that we wouldn't get run over by the lorries and Humvees that were crisscrossing the camp, and although he selected the platoons we talked to, once we were doing so he quickly disappeared to chat with his mates. He seemed to determine which units should be interviewed as much on the criteria of these social opportunities as anything else.

He took us on the first day to a tank unit, officially called Bravo company, B/1–64 Armour, but which since before the last Gulf War, for reasons now lost to collective memory, had always been referred to as the 'Black Knights'. The soldiers were talking about a wrestling match that had been staged the previous day between members of the company's tank crews and infantry units in an attempt to relieve the boredom. To their satisfaction, the tank men had 'slammed' the opposition. Sergeant Major Arreola took us to an Abrams on which the promise 'Big Punisher' had been stencilled in black paint on the gun barrel. Sitting on top beside the .50-calibre machine gun was its commander, Sergeant First Class Jerold Pyle Jr. Inside reading *The Eyes of Orion* by Alex Vernon, an account by five tank lieutenants of their experiences in the 1991 Gulf War, was his gunner, twenty-nine-year-old Staff Sergeant Miguel 'Moe' Marrero.

As with everyone I talked to during those first few days after arriving at camp, they both seemed more than happy to be interviewed. I had worried that the soldiers would be suspicious of me, a journalist in their midst, one indeed who was not even from their country. However, from the start they seemed pleased to have someone to talk to who was non-military, someone whose arrival meant a break from the mind-numbing routine of cleaning and preparing equipment that took up most of their waking hours. And then of course there was the fact that I was British. Everyone I talked to in the US Army could not speak highly enough of Tony Blair. He had been the first to stand beside America after 11 September, and now he was standing beside their nation again. This unstinting support meant that I was immediately perceived as being on the same side. As Sergeant Pyle said that afternoon, 'It could feel lonely out in this desert if you Brits weren't here with us.'

He guided me inside the turret to peer through the gunsights. The view was so clear I could almost lipread what was being said by soldiers talking 150 yards away. The inside of the tank was cramped, an area of little more than five foot square into which the barrel would jump back three feet when the gun was fired. The walls were utterly bare, the grey paint slightly peeling. When the hatch was closed it quickly became insufferably hot. Little plastic fans the crew had bought at an American department store had been stuck to the sides in an attempt to combat the heat. Sergeant Pyle, a thirty-nine-year-old veteran of the last Iraq conflict, sat in the hatch above me, his voice almost soporifically calm, his eyes shining intently above a light brown moustache.

'Everybody just wants to go home,' he said. 'We know we have a job to do, but we want to get on with it so that it's over sooner. You can't help being a little apprehensive at the thought of what might be waiting ahead, but no one doubts they can do this job. They just want to do what they've been trained for and get back to America.'

I wondered if he had been surprised that the Iraqis had run during the previous Gulf War. He stared at me. 'Oh no, they didn't run. They fought,' he said. 'The Republican Guard fought hard. On a morale level they were almost close to us. It's just that we beat them. There were big battles, but they lost, and they lost badly. But make no mistake, they fought – and I'm sure they will again this time.'

I would mainly come across the colonel at mealtimes. We would stand in the mess tent and discuss the world outside the army. He seemed almost relieved to have someone who was not a subordinate to chat to. He talked about how much he enjoyed living in Germany when he had been posted in Europe. Of holidays he had taken his family on to Paris, Prague and Venice. Occasionally he would mention the approaching conflict. 'Saddam Hussein is an idiot,' he said. 'We beat him twelve years ago but he couldn't stop trying to piss us off, so now we have to do it again. No one wants to invade, but because he's dumb we have to go in and take his country from him.

'I hope they won't put up much opposition,' he said of the Iraqi soldiers. 'Nobody wants to kill anyone if they can avoid it. I hope they realise we come to liberate them from the control of an evil, evil man, a man who has tortured and murdered his own people. The civilians should hopefully welcome us, and it would be beneficial if some of the regular army capitulates so at least it can help us police the country once it's over.

'But I tell you one thing: if they do fight, they will suffer. Our plan is ambitious. We need to cover large distances fast, and we will be ruthless with anything that stands in our way of doing so. Those are our orders, and we will fulfil them. All our soldiers know they will be backed by the best the United States military has available. With our equipment compared to theirs, it will not be a fair fight – but I don't want a fair fight. This will not be another Somalia. I want to make sure all my men come back alive.'

One morning I mentioned that I lived in Los Angeles. 'Los Angeles!' he smiled, lighting another cigar. 'I used to live in Los Angeles. I was only nineteen, and for a summer did a job working at a car dealer in Westwood. It was a really smart one, selling sports cars to movie stars and studio executives. It was my job to take the cars to be smog tested. I felt pretty good, I can tell you, driving around in a fancy car. Then at night there was always a party to go to. People thought I was a rock star because I was in a Rolls-Royce. Those were good days. Fun days. All a long time ago now.'

Weeks later, after Baghdad had fallen, I found myself chatting with the colonel's staff officers about their commander. To my surprise, few had a kind word to say about him. He would never confide details about his personal life to them. Not even his most trusted second in commands knew anything about his time in Los Angeles or his holidays in Europe with his family. Instead what they knew was the sharpness of his tongue and his intolerance for any form of failure. To me he had always been as helpful and charming as could be expected of a professional soldier ordered to accommodate the media in his unit. But with his men the colonel believed the military should be kept to military matters. He knew as little about their lives as they did about his. Knowledge of wives and family risked allowing personal emotion to interfere with what was required of him and his subordinates. They might not have liked it, but it got the vast majority of his men safely through a war, and achieved all the objectives assigned to their task force. His officers described him as a 'bastard' and a 'son of a bitch', but they also gave him the highest compliment a soldier can give another: he had proved to them that, without a doubt, 'that man can fight'.

There were so many units now gathered in northern Kuwait that space on the few available training grounds was at a premium. On Saturday, 15 March the battalion's master gunner, Staff Sergeant Travis Roark, the man responsible for distributing ammunition to the units, known by his radio call-sign 'Mike Golf', bounced into our tent. 'Live firing if you want to see it,' he burbled, the words coming so fast that each one was almost swallowed by the next. 'Maybe last before we cross the border. Got some space through arm-twisting a friend. First for a while. Lots of bangs.'

The four of us squeezed into his Humvee and we set off along a path through the sand dunes. 'Good you guys are here. Tell people what it's really like,' Mike Golf was saying, barely concentrating on the road ahead. 'Army life's not too bad. Been in it my whole life. Been more constant than any of my marriages. Well, my first divorce was because of the army. Too much time away. Second divorce was probably also because of the army, truth be told. I've just got married for another time but only seen her six weeks in the year we been wed. That's the army again. Still, wouldn't want it any other way.' The words stopped tumbling out for a moment as he leaned forward to stare out of the side window. 'My God, will you look at that? That is one sweet baby.'

A Bradley was pulling alongside us, its speed hitting almost forty miles per hour. The vehicle was newly delivered and its driver was putting it through its paces. There was nothing else in sight, just us and the Bradley going hell for leather across the desert, both kicking up plumes of sand. We hit a bump and took off. 'Hee, hee, hee,' shouted Mike Golf. 'Yep, when I was growing up in Kentucky I used to do a lot of dirt racing. Let's take this guy.' I turned to my right and saw Ron inspecting his Kevlar helmet to see if there was a dent from where he had just ricocheted off one of the metal support struts holding up the Humvee's canvas hood. We braced ourselves as Mike Golf pushed the accelerator to the floor.

The training site, I discovered when we got there, was British. 'Good guys, the Brits,' Mike Golf commented. 'Always there when there's a fight. Like that.' I was intrigued by the Americans' attitude to the British forces. It seemed to be the only other army they had any respect for. The Russians were animals, the Italians slap-dash, the French partisan, the Canadians non-existent, but in my whole time with the US Army I never heard a single word against Britain's soldiers. The general opinion appeared to be that they were fantastically brave, as they went into battle with what the Americans considered terrible kit. US troops would marvel to me how they had come across British troops in Kosovo or Bosnia and found that they did a great job while not having working radios or even machine guns that could be trusted. Compared to what they were used to, it seemed to the Americans that the British Army was collapsing through lack of funding.

When later there were incidents of British troops killed by 'friendly fire' from United States personnel, I asked an American soldier how such things could possibly happen. 'Because you don't have the equipment that we have to let everyone know where you are,' I was told. 'It doesn't cost much, but it would enable every-thing to be integrated so our forces would know exactly where your guys are at all times. The British have done a fantastic job here, but lives would have been saved if someone had spent enough money to protect the men who had been ordered into danger. I don't understand how people in England allow it to happen. But then, the rest of the world seems happier to accept its soldiers having to deal with that kind of shit than we are.'

After days surrounded by the predominantly Southern drawls of the Georgia-based 3rd Infantry Division, it felt slightly incongruous to find myself amid the Britishness of Her Majesty's Forces at the tank range. The dirty yellow British Challenger 2 tanks were lining up for their turn to fire. Troops with the insignia of 7 Armoured Brigade, the 'Desert Rats', on their shoulder stood in groups watching the arrival of our little American contingent with some suspicion. Alongside the British tanks, squaddies were zeroing the sites of their machine guns and rifles at a series of paper targets. I wandered over to introduce myself, and received a less than warm reception.

'Ahhh, a member of the press. Just what we always want to see,' one of the officers said sardonically. 'You arrive with our American cousins? We always enjoy their company here at our range; they're never more pleasant than when they want something from us.' Unlike the men of the 1st Battalion I had been with, not one of the British soldiers was willing to give his name. Ron was asked for ID as he tried to take some radio recordings, and was then hassled off the site. It had not taken me long after moving to the United States to realise it is a sense of cynicism, not irony, that Americans lack compared to us.

I had more of a welcome from a group of British soldiers brewing coffee behind one of their tanks. They were pleased when they discovered I could tell them the latest football results. None of them seemed particularly enamoured with finding themselves in Kuwait.

'We're an instrument of the British government, and if they tell us to do a job, we'll do it,' said one sergeant, his balding scalp pink from the sun. 'But if you ask me, I can't see why we've been sent here. This is America's fight, not ours. We shouldn't be getting drawn into it.'

The guy pouring the coffee nodded agreement. 'Let the Yanks get killed if they want to. But not us.'

One of the tanks on the range fired a shell. The ground jumped beneath me and I flinched from the physical pain the noise caused to my ears. Swinging round, I saw another tank fire. There was an orange flash almost as big as the vehicle itself, and then smoke falling back towards us. My ears were ringing. The British tank crew seemed completely unfazed.

'It's all about power politics, isn't it,' the sergeant was continuing. 'Tony Blair wants to be seen as an important man, so we get sent out here to keep Dubya happy. Tell me, why are we here? What are we doing that makes Britain a safer place? It's a fucking joke.'

It was not a question that the American troops would have needed to ask. One of the things that struck me as I talked to the 1st Battalion's soldiers was the almost universal belief that by taking out Saddam they would not only bring the gift of 'freedom' to an oppressed people, but even more importantly would make the United States a safer place for their children to grow up in. Again and again I was told that invading Iraq would stop weapons of mass destruction getting into the hands of terrorists, and therefore would help prevent another catastrophe on the scale witnessed on 11 September 2001. Saddam loathed the United States, he had weapons terrorists wanted, so if action was not taken he would give them to those who also wanted to hurt America. To most it was an article of faith, one they perhaps needed to hold onto to steel themselves through the months of discomfort they had already experienced and the danger that was now approaching. Many would state as a matter of fact that the Iraqi government had been involved in the destruction of the World Trade Center through, in some unspecified way, having given help to Osama bin Laden. This was an error that, whether as a result of ignorance or to encourage disinformation, I never once witnessed anyone correcting. They might not like being stuck in the desert, but the vast majority of American soldiers were in no doubt about the righteousness of their cause – and that cause was to protect their homeland from its enemies.

One night as I stepped out of my tent to brush my teeth I met one of the colonel's staff, Captain Bill Young. We talked about the prospect of war, he occasionally stopping to point out the little bursts of flame that flared for a moment high in the sky as a jet ignited its thrusters. I asked him why, beyond the obligation to follow orders, he felt he was here. He reached into the shoulder pocket of his fatigues and produced a photograph of his newly born son. 'Why am I here?' he said. 'I'm here for him.'

Earlier that day a shaven-headed sergeant in charge of a mortar team had run up to me and pushed something into my hand. His name was Sergeant States ('That is as in United States, sir'), and it was a small sticker bearing the coat of the arms of the New York Port Authority, the force that policed the World Trade Center site. 'I just wanted to make sure you tell the people why we're here,' he told me. 'My brother-in-law works for the Port Authority and he lost many good friends. That is never going to happen again. When we go north I'm going to stick one of these on the barrel of the gun so we don't forget what it is we are achieving.'

Eighteen months earlier I had been on one of the first planes allowed to land in New York after the destruction of the World Trade Center. When I had lined up with my fellow passengers to board the American Airlines flight at Heathrow, the captain had individually checked our passports. Once in the air, no one had been allowed to stand without first getting the permission of one of the flight attendants. Anyone wanting to use the toilets was accompanied to the rear of the plane by a member of the cabin crew, who would then wait and walk them back to their seats. We were not permitted even to retrieve anything from the overhead lockers without notifying someone first. When we landed at JFK airport the woman sitting next to me had burst into tears. 'I thought I was never going to get home alive,' she sobbed.

As my taxi crossed Brooklyn Bridge onto Manhattan Island I could see the smoke still rising from where the Twin Towers had once stood. Later, as I walked down to the site, which was already being referred to as Ground Zero, the streets were lined with thick grey dust that had been deposited when the buildings had fallen. At the front of the New York Stock Exchange on Wall Street it was almost an inch deep. The advertising hoardings for that day's *New York Post* had a simple message. There was a picture of Osama bin Laden under the headline 'Wanted Dead or Alive'. Peeking through the wooden boards that had been erected around the crater, I could glimpse the remains of the metal skeleton that had reinforced the bottom few floors of one of the towers, and which was now the only part still standing. It appeared pale and ghostlike, its top fragmented and gently swaying in the breeze. Stuck to postboxes and lampposts were hundreds of hastily-printed-out posters bearing the names and photographs of those missing, along with pleas from their families for anyone who knew of their whereabouts to get in touch. In a park near my paper's New York office a shrine had been set up around a statue of a horse and uniformed rider. Flowers had been piled up into banks on either side and dozens of candles lit. The surrounding paving stones were covered in handwritten poems and messages by New Yorkers trying to come to terms with what had happened to their city. A few called for retribution, but the vast majority were pleas for peace and an end to violence in the world. 'Our grief is not a cry for vengeance', read one. 'Hate breeds hate. Forgiveness is peace' another. A poster written in red, white and blue ink said simply: 'In their memory may one world unite together in love'. In those first few days after the tragedy, the gut reaction of many of those who had seen at first hand the suffering conflict could bring was of the need of the world to embrace its common humanity.

At the *Telegraph*'s New York office the staff were exhausted and still partly in shock. Even though there was some joking about how the bars at the weekend had been filled with men and women determined to get laid, memories of what they had seen still dominated. The paper's local correspondent had been on the way to buy an engagement ring for his girlfriend when the first plane hit. He had spent the next few hours watching bodies fall from the sky and running down a street to escape the clouds of dust and debris.

That night I met a friend for a drink. He had been staying at the Marriott World Trade Center, the hotel in the first tower to be hit, and was in an adjacent office block when he had heard the crash. 'We were all evacuated and stood on the road outside. Then the fire engines started to come past. There was an endless line of them. One after another, going to save people trapped in the burning towers. We all cheered as they drove up the street. None of us knew we were cheering people on their way to their deaths. I could see their faces in the windows, and I was shouting along as heartily as everyone else.'

In the following weeks I travelled across the country filing pieces on how the national psyche had been affected. In previous visits I had always been struck by how open America was, the simple hospitality that meant relative strangers would invite you into their homes, the almost complete lack of security at the airports and main buildings, so unusual to someone who had grown up in London during the height of the IRA bombing campaign on the British mainland. Now people were frightened. Everywhere houses and cars sported the American flag, so many that flag factories were working twenty-four hours a day, seven days a week and still failing to meet demand. I was near the Sears Tower in Chicago, the tallest skyscraper in the United States, when a rumour spread that a plane had been detected heading towards the building. Despite reassurances over the Tannoy system that it was a false alarm, the street filled with panicked office workers. In Oklahoma City I visited the memorial park built beside the remains of the Alfred P. Murrah Federal Building, the complex bombed by Timothy McVeigh six years earlier. People were crying because it reminded them of those who had lost their lives in New York and Washington. Before a flight to Reno in Nevada the pilot gave a little speech over the intercom. 'Welcome to our flight today, and I hope it's a pleasant one,' he said. 'During our time in the air I want you to treat this aircraft like your home. By that I mean that I hope you will defend it like your home. That if the need arises you will sacrifice your lives if necessary to make sure that we win a fight to retain control of this airplane.'

A year later I took the journey in reverse, travelling east across the country and ending up in New York for the first anniversary of the attacks. People had become more settled by then, but the memory of what had happened was still only just beneath the surface. It was not only events like the panic buying of duct tape that illustrated the continued unease. In a bar in Los Angeles, the girl I was with noticed that a bag had been forgotten by a man who had just walked out. Instead of picking it up and running after him to hand it back, she worried with the barman about whether there could be a bomb inside. Every time you now boarded a plane your luggage would be laboriously checked, and little swabs taken to test for explosives. Passengers would thank the ground staff for putting them through such an inconvenience.

Fear, as I would witness again during the war in Iraq, is the most barbarising of emotions. A growing number of Americans were now willing to turn a blind eye to what had to be done in order to get back the feeling of security they had lost: the men locked up without charge in a military base in Cuba, the extension of government snooping into e-mails and phone lines, the prospect of military courts, the airborne drones carrying out assassinations in foreign lands. It was broadly accepted that their President was right when he said a message had to be sent in the crudest terms to anyone threatening the USA; the nation now wanted action taken on its behalf. The Taliban, anyone associated with al-Qa'eda, and ultimately Saddam, were to be crushed. Much of the rest of the world may have had experience of terrorism and war within its borders, but modern America had not. The sense of invulnerability had gone, and it appeared to be proving impossible to recover that lost innocence.

As I made my way back across America for the anniversary I encountered my share of crazies. On Telegraph Avenue in Berkeley, California, a man wearing a T-shirt bearing the slogan 'Beam Me Up, Jesus' told me the whole attack had been the work of aliens. 'After Flight 93 came down in Pennsylvania, they saw a craft buzzing around. Now, what was that? All earth air traffic had been grounded. And in the World Trade Center, where are all the bodies? They were transported out first to be experimented on,' he explained to me. In Lynchburg, Virginia, a fundamental Christian evangelist told me it had been 'a warning from God. This is the time to pray.' He worshipped in the church at which the Reverend Jerry Falwell was pastor. Falwell had gone on television forty-eight hours after the Twin Towers fell and said New York had been hit because its tolerance of homosexuality, abortion and 'liberal positions had caused an angry God to remove his protection from the city'.

It was not only the extremists who had been struggling to understand and explain what had happened to their country. In Pleasant Grove, a small farming town in Kansas, a cowboy called Steve 'Smitty' Smith tethered his horse and told me: 'After September 11, I looked at a map to work out where all these places in the Middle East were. It took me an hour to find Israel, it's so small. But you need to know these things. Now we realise that what happens in those places I found on that map affects all of us, even the lives of us right here in Kansas, where we all thought nothing bad could ever happen.'

In New York, thousands had gathered from across the country to pay their respects. A group of Hell's Angels had ridden from California on their Harley-Davidsons, raising money on the way. One man interviewed by my colleague Sam Leith had carried an eight-foot crucifix from Illinois in tribute. 'It's the least I could do, although as a professional chiropractor I must admit I'm worried about what it has done to my back,' the pilgrim told him. I saw him again that evening on the subway. He had unscrewed the two parts of his cross to get it through the turnstile, but then dutifully reassembled it to take it down the escalator.

When I visited Ground Zero it was remarkable how much had changed from a year before. The remains of the metal skeleton had gone. The crater where the buildings had stood had largely been filled, and the area cleared of rubble. The wooden boards surrounding the site were covered in handwritten messages from visitors. Souvenir sellers had moved in with their T-shirts bearing an image of the World Trade Center or the slogan 'Let's Roll', the last known words of Todd Beamer, one of the passengers on Flight 93 who tackled the terrorists before the aircraft crashed into a field in Pennsylvania. More than a hundred people were listening to a man who was reading out the 'Portraits of Grief' from the New York Times, a series of obituaries on all those who had died that had been appearing since the tragedy. That night in a bar near Times Square I watched most of those present rise from their seats to hear the President's televised commemoration speech. In the days and weeks after the original attacks, posters and flags had appeared across the United States bearing the pledge 'We will never forget'. So far, it is a promise that – for better or worse – America has managed to keep.

Yet not every soldier in the battalion saw the approaching conflict in simple terms of right battling wrong. There were indications that some at least held doubts about the operation they were involved in. One afternoon, the heat reaching into the nineties and the air shimmering above the desert plain, two members of a mortar team showed me around their vehicle. I climbed in through the back, squeezing past the dark metal of the gun tube poking out the top of their adapted armoured personnel carrier. The 120mm mortar could fire off sixteen rounds in a minute, a rate that would require one of the crew to pour water over its barrel to stop it overheating. On the ceiling at the front of the vehicle were stuck pictures of naked girls, the majority from Spanish-language pornographic magazines. The two boys, nineteen-year-old Nitai Schwartz and twenty-year-old Garth Stewart, were keen to tell me that they did not want to fight. Nitai, fresh-faced, with an impish grin, little more than five feet seven inches in height, was born in Israel but had lived in the US since he was a child. 'I'm Jewish, and I was raised to hate Arabs,' he told me. 'To think they were evil, and that they were nothing but terrorists trying to kill us. But then I came out here to Kuwait and I found they were really nice people. They were hospitable and treated us kindly. I'd thought they would all be what I was raised to think they were, but they weren't. Now I realise I have no reason to fight the Iraqis. They're posing no threat to us. And I tell you, some others think the same. There are others disenchanted like us about what's happening here. If we could, most would vote just to go straight home to their families. Why should America be here? It's not our continent. We shouldn't be involved.'

'I have no beef with the Iraqis. This is Bush's war,' said Garth, a taller, more fleshy youth. 'It's all for political reasons. We're just tools in his game.'

Nitai agreed with this. 'People say we live in interesting times, as if that's a good thing,' he said. 'They're fucked up. We'll do what we're told, we're soldiers and we signed up so we have little choice, but I don't like it.'

It was hard to tell how many others felt the same. No one else

I talked to told me they did. Most seemed to take the opposite view, like the twenty-year-old driver of an adjacent Bradley who had proudly proclaimed: 'I signed up to serve my country. I am a very strong American. I do not believe America would do anything wrong.' However, those holding anti-war views would be likely to keep them quiet. The question was whether exposure to combat for a cause they didn't believe in would make them more likely to express their opinions publicly, or whether they would abandon them as the sense of loyalty and pride in their unit's achievements grew in the face of shared dangers.

The young mortar crew showed me the cramped area surrounding the gun barrel in which they lived. I pointed at the girls on the ceiling. 'I know it looks like they're of a sexual nature, but they're not,' Nitai said. 'Actually it just means when you're out there and things are happening you can look up and relax.' I asked him if he had a girlfriend of his own. He looked at Garth. 'I did, but when we came out here for so long she ended it with me. Said she couldn't wait.'

They had heard about the anti-war movement back in the States, and it worried them. 'The thing that gets me is the thought of all those people back home watching this on TV and laughing at us, saying, "Thank God we're not those sons of bitches,"' Nitai said. 'What if this is like Vietnam, where we go back and they throw rocks at us?'

As I left he stuck his head out and called after me. There was a girl in America, not his ex-girlfriend but a different one, who he wanted me to e-mail on his behalf to ask her to write to him.

The next time I saw Nitai was two days later, when a group of soldiers had been gathered next to the parade ground to practise the procedure for a medical evacuation by helicopter. The chopper had wobbled to the ground in a swirl of dust and the troops were taking turns to strap each other to stretchers and be carried on board. Nitai was cracking jokes as he was bussed forward, the soldiers carrying him running in a crouch, in an image eerily reminiscent of newsreel footage of the Vietnam War. Some were taking photographs of the scene. The sergeant in charge of the medivac had listed the possible dangers: don't get your head caught by the propellers, make sure your casualty is tightly bound so he doesn't suffer more damage, if you're loading injured PoWs first strip them naked to ensure they aren't carrying any kind of bomb.

I had got a reply from Nitai's friend, who was called Amy. She said how pleased she was to hear about him, that she would send a letter soon, and that everybody wished all the American troops well. The other soldiers jeered a bit at him for having contact from a girl, but he just shrugged his shoulders. 'I suppose you have to get something good out of this,' he said.

Sunday, 16 March, our sixth day since arriving at the camp, brought with it a change of mood. The sense of frustration and exhaustion evaporated as news of fresh orders spread among the soldiers. George Bush, Tony Blair and José Maria Aznar, the Spanish Prime Minister, were in a meeting in the Azores to determine what should be done following the collapse of the diplomatic process. They had hoped for a second resolution by the United Nations Security Council to establish an international mandate for war with Iraq, but that had been derailed by the opposition of France and Russia. The activity at the US Army camps in northern Kuwait indicated that the pro-war nations had already decided what to do next. The tank crews were being told to remove the uranium-tipped shells from their casings, the order was given that the charcoal-lined biochemical-weapon protection suits should be unpacked from their air-sealed container bags, and equipment and ammunition ordered weeks ago had begun to arrive from Doha by the crateful. Tents were starting to be dismantled. A group of soldiers were even taking the 'Can Do' sign to bits. Camp was to be struck, and we would be moving to our final pre-invasion position just south of the border.

Major George Fredrick, the most senior black officer in the battalion, had been sleeping in our tent since his was blown away in the sandstorm. He was grinning with expectation. 'Roomies,' he said, giving his usual welcome as he pushed back the tent flaps to get to work, 'you can smell the excitement in the air.' Outside we heard him giving full voice to the 3rd Infantry Division's military song:

> I am just a dog-faced soldier with a rifle on my shoulder
> And I just eat raw meat for breakfast every day.
> Just feed me ammunition
> And keep me in the 3rd Infantry Division.

Just before noon a service was held by the army chaplain in the parade ground. It was one of four to be held throughout the day, and with war now imminent around a third of the soldiers were expected to attend at least one. 'You know the phrase "There are no atheists in foxholes"?' one of the lieutenants said to me. 'Well, here you discover what that means in practice.'

The chaplain, Raymond Folsom, was a Southern Baptist, and the stole of his vestments was coloured a wealth of yellow, orange and red, a present from a village he had been assigned to during an aid mission to Central America. His altar was a cardboard box resting on the flap at the back of a Humvee over which a green cloth had been placed along with a cup and crucifix, their silver plating dulled by exposure to the elements. Another box covered with a camouflage mat stood in front of him as a lectern, and on this he rested his Bible. Five men from A Company had been press-ganged into forming a makeshift choir. They were pretty ropey – certainly unable to hold a tune – but at least they led the singing, a job that was needed as the congregation was embarrassed about giving a hearty rendition of the hymns. The Sunday before, a white bird had flown overhead in the middle of the service, an event which had amazed everyone present, as other than the occasional small, dirt-coloured finch, it was the first bird that any of them had seen in weeks. There was considerable interest as to what feat the chaplain would achieve this time.

The previous evening he had come to our tent to introduce himself, and had told me that he was concerned about casualties, and also about the stress such a length of time in the field was putting on many of the soldiers' marriages. More than half a dozen had ended in divorce after the earlier six-month training period in Kuwait. Back home was his own wife, a beautiful Jamaican who from the photograph he showed me was clearly considerably younger than his fortysomething years, and their eight children, including two sets of twins. 'She was a gift from God,' he told me.

Reverend Folsom was not an overtly pious man. He had been a regular soldier before he had heard his calling, and his humour was as earthy as that of the men in the flock he served. Yet his eyes glinted with evangelical fervour as he talked of instances of God acting in the world. He was clearly excited at the fact the coming invasion would take him past some of the Old Testament's most holy spots. Near Tallil would be Ur, the city where Abraham was born and where he first felt the touch of God and began the trek which ultimately took his family to Israel. North of Najaf was the settlement of Kufah, where Noah is believed to have built his ark. We would be passing through a landscape where prophets had witnessed the word of the Lord on isolated rock outcrops, where pilgrims had died from thirst and starvation as they sought to spread the message of an unforgiving God. The chaplain had plans to baptise new converts in the Euphrates, that most Biblical of rivers, when the unit bridged it en route to Baghdad. Already five soldiers had volunteered to receive their initiation into the ranks of the army of Christ.

Each night when the colonel and his staff staged their daily meeting the chaplain would be invited to address them at the end with a modern-day parable. Such a prominent role for religion in the decision-making process was not considered unusual. Many of the men in the 3rd Infantry Division were drawn from the American South – the centre of the Bible Belt – as the unit's permanent camps were located in Georgia. Crucifixes could often be seen hanging beside dogtags, and the presence of God was regularly alluded to.

Reverend Folsom recounted to me one of the stories with which he had recently instructed the officer staff. 'Three men had died, and they were very bad men,' he said. 'Two of them were corporate types, dressed in a jacket and tie, the other a plumber in his overalls, but all of them had lived wicked lives. They found themselves in hell being greeted by the devil, who indicated three doors in front of them. They would, the devil told them, have to choose one, through which they would go to spend an eternity of suffering. Opening the first, they saw as far as the eye could see thousands of people standing on their heads on a concrete floor. Through the next were as many souls condemned to torment again, this time standing on their heads on a floor of nails. Through the third one there were again thousands of people, but they were just standing around up to their knees in human shit. The stench was disgusting, but they were having a great time nevertheless, laughing and drinking alcohol and slapping each other on the back.

'The two corporate men chose the first room, as they could not face nails, and the smell of the shit was just too overpowering for them. But the plumber was used to the smell of shit, so he was happy with the third room. The door closed behind him. He had spotted some of his friends in there, and they greeted him warmly and they all started to share a drink. Then the door opened again and the devil poked his head in. "OK everyone," he said. "Break over."

'It seemed worthwhile,' the chaplain said to me, 'to remind everyone at a time like this that however sensible a decision seems, and however much forethought you may put into it, you can still end up with your head in shit.'

At the Sunday service all the soldiers were carrying their M-16 machine guns, but many also were clutching their own Bibles, some embossed with gold. The chaplain held his arms out in front of him, sweat already dripping from his shaved head, and smiled. 'They said the wind would come back today, but look, the air is still. I prayed last night there would be no dust for when we gathered, and the storm has stayed away. See, your prayers can be answered.'

'Amen,' called back his flock, happy to hear of any indication that God might be looking out for their welfare.

Reverend Folsom cried out praise to Jesus for enduring sufferings for forty days and forty nights in the wilderness similar to those endured in recent days by the soldiers. He called on God's protection in times of danger. He told stories of Old Testament prophets who had lived near to where the army would be advancing. 'Pray, as many times Israel won its battles because they prayed. Because it is God who wins battles, whatever your technology. Pray for the people of Iraq. You, Lord, put people in their place and you take them down. Pray that it is without a shot fired. Pray for our safety.'

Some of the black soldiers started to roll their heads to the rhythm of his words. One called for a prayer for his family. Another that he might one day find his own 'special lady'. The chaplain was prowling across the sand as he preached. The choir broke into a rendition of 'Amazing Grace'. In the distance could be heard the sound of a tank convoy. An Apache helicopter flew overhead as the congregation was exhorted to raise their voices to offer the final verse as a prayer to God: ''Tis grace has brought me safe this far/And grace will lead me home.'

I did not take communion but Ron did, the wine replaced in consideration of local sensitivities by grape juice. He told me that as he waited to take the Eucharist he had heard the chaplain say to the soldier in front: 'Body of Christ. Blood of Christ. Soldier keep washing your feet.' It was a piece of advice that I would later realise I should have heeded more carefully.

The next morning the colonel summoned his troops. The meeting in the Azores had finished, and President Bush had given Saddam a final ultimatum. He had forty-eight hours to leave Iraq or face the consequences. Soon after dawn, the sun only just above the horizon, the battalion came in its companies to the parade ground. They were silhouetted in front of me, the company battle flags held above their heads as they marched in formation, the soldiers with machine guns and grenade launchers slung on their backs. Their commander stood in the middle of the assembled men and called them to attention. His standard-issue 9mm Beretta pistol was in a holster strapped to his right leg, and his gasmask hung over his left shoulder. His eyes were concealed by sunglasses.

He told the men to break rank and gather around him. The front rows knelt on one knee, the rest stood in a semi-circle. There was to be no Shakespearian-style oratory in this pre-battle speech. Lieutenant Colonel Charlton knew his men, and he told them what they wanted to hear.

'I understand that some of you don't like this place we've got here,' he said. 'So I've been doing some real-estate shopping, and I think there are some better places up north we should check out. And after we check out those places up north, we're going to take a nice trip to a place called home. But first we have to do the job we've been sent here to do. You may see enemy units that will fight tremendously hard, so don't underestimate them. When you go in, you take the fight to the enemy. You go in there with both barrels and you let them have it. You let them know that they're taking on the US Army and you crush them.

'When you cross the border you will be part of a massive army. You will see thousands of vehicles attacking. You will see hundreds of aircraft overhead en route to destroy targets in Iraq. You will see Tomahawk missiles flying over us. And you will be part of that. One day down the road you can look back and say you took part in protecting America, in protecting our allies in the region, and in destroying an evil person who has killed thousands and thousands of his countrymen. So let's get on with this. If they want a fight, you finish it. And you finish it fast. Then we can go home. And you will all be heroes.'

THREE

Objective Liberty

Major General 'Buff' Blount was standing over a map of Iraq. He was a big man, both in height and across the shoulders, and the muscles which as a young soldier must have carried a full pack with ease still, at fifty-two years old, filled the loose desert fatigues he was wearing. There was none of the gung-ho attitude that typified the Hollywood image of an American commander. Instead, in measured tones he detailed to the attendant press corps the route his forces would take in the coming days, using a metal pointer to draw attention to a particular bridge or city as the plan extended to include it.

It was an extraordinary moment: the meeting at which it became clear quite how far the American military high command was planning to take the embedded journalists into their confidence. Before the battle had even begun the reporters placed with the 3rd Infantry Division were being told exactly how it was intended that Saddam Hussein would be taken down.

From the border the American Marines would push up past Basra, Iraq's second largest city and its military stronghold in the south, and across the Euphrates River, advancing along the main highways to tackle Baghdad from the east. The army would move up the west of the country, a route which would take it past the main southern cities of Nasiriyah, Najaf and Karbala. After the order was given to cross the Iraqi border, an order expected in the next seventy-two hours, the three brigades of the 3rd Infantry Division were to seize hundreds of square miles of territory in only a few days. Tactical objectives would be taken, but the cities themselves would not be conquered. The focus was on ensuring that troops and equipment swept northwards to Baghdad as fast as possible to bring about a quick end to the regime. The 3rd Brigade, the unit my battalion was part of, would head straight to the outskirts of Nasiriyah, a city of about 300,000 people on the Euphrates to the west of Basra. The other two brigades would go deeper into the desert, one arriving outside Najaf, the other pushing even further out in a route that would take it far from any cities or towns until it arrived, hopefully unimpeded, almost two days later below Karbala, the last major settlement south of Baghdad.

There would then be what Buff called a 'tactical pause', a few days in which the soldiers could rest and regroup while the air force 'softened up' the Republican Guard units stationed in defences described by Saddam as a 'ring of steel' around his capital. Next would come the final advance to Baghdad itself. The city of five million people would be encircled and a stranglehold imposed by the American forces. How long, one of the reporters asked, was it expected to take the Americans to make the 350-mile journey from the border to the Iraqi capital? Buff paused and looked down at the Iraqi units dotted across his map. 'Around seven days,' he told us.

The three journalists with 1st Battalion had been informed when we woke at sunrise on Wednesday, 19 March that we had an appointment with the general that morning. The winds that the chaplain had claimed responsibility for delaying had finally arrived, not blowing as strongly as during the storm that followed our arrival, but enough to send the sand horizontally across the desert in white clouds. The previous day had been sunny as work on collapsing the camp continued in earnest. Giant pyres had been lit as everything that was not needed was set on fire. Lines of tents disappeared. Food and water were piled high on tanks and armoured cars. No one knew when new supplies might arrive, so they were going to take as much as possible while they still could. Companies began to resemble gypsy caravans as ration boxes and bags filled with personal belongings were strapped to every available surface. Little now remained of the camp. Even the wooden latrines were being broken up and burnt.

We met the rest of the reporters placed with 3rd Brigade at the unit's headquarters. A number had been having a difficult time. While we had been provided with a tent, and even some electricity that had enabled a temporary office to be set up in one corner, others had been moved from vehicle to vehicle, never staying more than one night in one place and with no facilities to power their equipment. One group had barely been allowed to talk to the men, having been confined to a small area and told not to wander around, their battalion commander suspicious of their presence and unwilling to reveal the forces at his disposal.

We made our way to Major General Blount's briefing in a 1st Battalion Humvee driven by a young captain. All around were signs of an army on the move. Convoys of fuel trucks snaked through the sand. Lines of tanks emerged suddenly from the dust clouds before disappearing just as quickly back into the gloom.

The captain had a portable CD player and speakers suspended in the webbing on the ceiling of his car. He put Ozzy Osbourne in, and we shouted out the lyrics when 'Warpigs' came on:

> *Generals gathered in their masses*
> *Just like witches at black masses*
> *Evil minds that plot destruction*
> *Sorcerers of death's construction*
> *In the fields are bodies burning*
> *As the war machine keeps turning*
> *Death and hatred to mankind*
> *Poisoning their brainwashed minds.*

And then the cry '*Oh Lord yeah*,' to which we all punched our fists in the air.

'I think it's going to have to be KISS as the soundtrack when the time comes to cross the border,' the captain ventured.

The inside of the general's command tent had been padded with layers of synthetic white cloth to try to keep out the sand and dust, giving it the feel of a decontaminated laboratory. It was hard to hear what anyone was saying above the constant whirl of extractor fans that sucked out any rogue particles that had some-how still managed to intrude. Everything was starkly lit by banks of fluorescent lights. Around the table bearing the map of Iraq were lines of benches at which soldiers worked away on laptops. In the corner was a television tuned to Fox News.

The briefing left me in no doubt that the American army had reached a subtle level of media management. On the one hand it provided invaluable information to the gathered journalists, information which in the coming weeks would enable them to place the localised actions they were witnessing in a larger context. However, by giving details in advance, and then making it clear that none of them could be used before the events described had happened, the US military prevented any of the journalists from publishing educated guesses about its intentions. Located as they were in the front line, some of the reporters' speculation could have been far too accurate.

There was still a risk that one of the reporters would publish the actual details of what had been determined. The BBC had hired a former member of the SAS to drive the Jeep holding their equipment. After the general had finished he looked be-mused. 'I just can't believe it,' he said. 'I can't believe that they think no one is going to muck this up for them.' When I met Major Birmingham, the division's information officer, at Baghdad airport a month later, I asked him if anyone had. To my surprise no one had broken the embargos or spilled any oper-ational secrets, testament to the correspondents' desire not to risk anyone's life – not least their own – for the sake of an exclusive.

As we prepared to leave we were informed that not only could none of the information be published in advance, but we could not even indicate in any articles that an off-the-record briefing from the general had ever taken place. I thought that was pretty stringent, and said so to the ex-SAS driver. 'That,' he told me, 'is so that if you're captured the Iraqis don't think you know much. Therefore they should hopefully decide it isn't worth seriously interrogating you.'

Back at 1st Battalion's camp the last tents were being dismantled. It was a desolate scene, the soldiers with green scarves wrapped around their mouths and noses as protection against the sand that had made their eyes red from exposure. The time had come for me to be moved to the company with which I would be travelling into Iraq. The colonel had determined that it would be the Black Knights, the tank and Bradley unit I had been introduced to when I met Sergeant Pyle. Joe was to go with the scouts, the Humvee-driving reconnaissance soldiers. Ron had asked to be at the rear with the battalion headquarters, which he hoped would offer a wider range of radio clips. I would hardly see either of them again. From that day onwards I would be almost exclusively surrounded by soldiers.

That morning I had received two e-mails from my newspaper. One was from the editor, addressing all his correspondents in the region. 'Everyone should and will be brave, but no one should be reckless,' it said. 'Good luck!' The second informed me that the newspaper had taken out death and disability insurance on my behalf. I noted that my death was worth £250,000, the loss of a single limb £180,000, and of hearing in one ear just £45,000. Insurance coverage of £1 million had also been taken out to pay for a team to rescue me if I was kidnapped.

A sergeant came over to help me carry my belongings. He was in charge of the transport in which I would be based, the company's M88, a heavily armoured maintenance vehicle required to go into the heart of any fighting to provide help to tanks broken down on the battlefield. It was armed with a .50-calibre machine gun, its three-inch-long bullets powerful enough to penetrate an armoured personnel vehicle. The M88 was more than twelve feet high and thirty-four feet in length, and moved on tank tracks to ensure it could go over anything that the vehicles it looked after were able to traverse. On the front was a digger and on the top a small crane that enabled it to lift thirty-five tons. I was pleased to have been placed in it. Its armour was thick enough to protect those inside from the majority of the enemy's weaponry, and that made me feel safe. On the front someone had put up a sign christening it 'Big Country', a homage to its power and size.

The sergeant, Norman Weaver, arrived as I was struggling to collapse my camp bed. Grabbing a piece of metal, he beat a small clasp open on the side and then effortlessly snapped the two sides together. Taking it with me would prove pointless, as I would never sleep in it again. However, in the hope of some future comfort we lugged it with the rest of my stuff over to where the company was based. Sergeant Weaver carried the green kitbag holding my body armour and most of my equipment. It was very heavy. Two thirds of the way across the camp even his bearlike frame began to feel the weight. 'Leave it here,' I suggested. 'We can come back and get it together.' He declined. 'I'm the kind of guy who doesn't like to be beaten,' he told me.

The battalion had manoeuvred into formation and was awaiting the order to advance towards the border. The wind had begun to die, and vehicles could now be made out arrayed in a horseshoe shape across the desert plain, the Black Knights located halfway down the right-hand side. My bags were tied with the rest of the baggage on the roof of the M88. I climbed through a hatch in the side, the door so heavy I was almost unable to open it, and viewed my new habitation. Boxes containing tools and spare parts were piled around me. Some had spilled open, and their contents were scattered across the lightly corrugated metal floor. Pornographic pictures were stuck to one of the walls. Everything was covered in a thin layer of sand. There was a lightly padded black seat in the middle on which Sergeant Weaver would stand, the top half of his body extending through the turret hatch above. This enabled him to grasp the handle of the vehicle's machine gun. At the front were two more seats, for the driver and his assistant. If they were required to go anywhere at night one of the pair would drive, the other would watch through night-vision goggles. As there were no thermal sights built into the vehicle, the driver would rely on his partner to tell him, through the internal intercom system, what was coming up ahead.

I placed my computer and most important possessions amid the heap of boxes at the back. Above me was a small hatch through which I would be able to see what was going on. A teenage boy was staring at me from the driver's assistant's seat. I smiled a hello. To my relief he smiled back. The whole of the vehicle's interior must have been little more than eight feet long, and it was not high enough to stand up in. It was in this space that four of us were going to have to live, sleep, work and travel. I hoped they did not mind too much the imposition of my arrival.

A red-haired youth came up to the side door, a pair of glasses dominating his face, and looked at me. 'Howdy, I'm Red. 'Cause of the hair. Not too imaginative, the army,' said Private First Class Jason Carter in a strong rural accent. He was twenty-one years old, and had grown up on a farm hundreds of miles from the nearest city in the depths of Illinois. 'So, are you some kind of reporter?' The other crewmember, the one who had smiled at me inside the M88, was Roman Komlev, who at eighteen was the youngest soldier in the company. He had arrived in the United States as an immigrant from Russia six years before, speaking not one word of English. Also a private first class, he continued to stare silently at me, though in an intrigued rather than a hostile way. I got out and smoked a cigarette. Others in the unit wandered over to check me out. Most seemed benign. The crew of the adjacent tank crew climbed down to greet me.

'Oh, I wouldn't shake his hand,' Red said to me as one of them approached.

'Why not?' the tank crew guy retorted, the faintest of moustaches attempting to grow on his top lip.

'Because you're a homo.'

'No I am not,' said the tank guy.

'OK – but everyone says you are. And you know you look gay.'

'Just because you've got red hair so all the girls won't touch you.'

I climbed back into the M88 as they began playfully wrestling each other. Unpacking my laptop, I started to type up that day's report. A lorry drove up, and out of the back was served the evening's food. Appropriately for the last hot meal provided to an American army going to war, it was a hamburger. On a tank on which had been written the promise 'Baghdad Bound', I saw First Lieutenant Michael Burns stencilling the name of his wife on the outside of a hatch cover. How was he feeling now the prospect of battle was so close, I asked. 'There is a time for talking and there is a time for doing. Now we put all the training into practice,' he told me. 'Let's bring this thing on.'

Night fell as I worked. Occasionally little groups of soldiers would come up to stare at me through the side door.

'How does he do that without being able to see the keys in the dark?' one asked.

'It's called touch typing,' Sergeant Weaver said. 'It's a skill. Very difficult.'

I felt pretty important at being the centre of so much interest. Red came up with some of his friends. 'Hey, reporter,' he called to me. 'Will you do something for us?'

'Of course.'

'Will you say: "No, this is a knife"?'

'Huh?'

'Just say, "No, this is a knife." It's from that *Crocodile Dundee* film.'

'But he's Australian.'

'Who cares? It'll be funny.'

They all doubled up with laughter when I said it. 'Hey, check out the proper accent,' Red called to some others. 'I get such a kick out of this guy.' I began to suspect it was going to be a long evening.

Shortly before midnight the order was given to start the engines. In front of us a line of headlights stretched as far as the eye could see, a procession of vehicles drawn from the American camps previously scattered across northern Kuwait, now heading as one towards the Iraqi frontier. The troops of 1st Battalion peeled off and took their allotted place in that giant convoy. They were going to be driving throughout most of the night. I unpacked my sleeping bag and spread it on the metal floor at the back of the vehicle. The crankshaft of the engine thudded beneath me as we rattled along the sandy track. Its regular beat was surprisingly calming. I put on my helmet to stop myself being injured as I was bounced off the metal walls by the bumps in the road, curled up in the space available amid the boxes of equipment, and despite my expectations fell immediately asleep.

When I woke it seemed as if we had not moved. The sun was up, and when I stuck my head through the hatch our surroundings seemed identical to those we had left behind. The same lifeless desert stretched on all sides. A similar selection of vehicles was gathered around our M88 in a formation almost exactly the same as that of the previous evening.

Red was lying on the digger at the front, looking exhausted. 'Mornin',' he said. 'Pretty nice ride for you. Pretty hellish for the rest of us.'

Sergeant Weaver was asleep on the roof. Roman was stretched

out inside. They had only arrived an hour earlier, having had to tow a broken-down tank for most of the journey.

'That fucking tank,' said Red. 'Always that one is giving us trouble. We couldn't go more than ten miles per hour the whole way. I could have hit that lieutenant [the commander of the broken-down tank, who had been sitting beside Red during the drive]. He was telling me what to do. "Faster. Slower." How to drive my own vehicle. Goddamn army.'

We were camped just outside the demilitarised zone, the stretch that ran three miles into Kuwait and six miles into Iraq which had been established along the border after the 1991 war. Behind us was the company's medic van, an armoured personnel carrier known among the soldiers as 'Band Aid'. The head medic, Sergeant James Swinney, was tucking into an MRE.

I had met Sergeant Swinney a few days earlier, when the PX truck had come to 3rd Brigade. The PX is a mobile shop stocked with luxuries such as chocolate, cigarettes, cans of Coke and baby wipes. Baby wipes were the most beloved of all these items for many of the soldiers. Often unable to shower and with water supplies rationed, they resorted to them in order to keep themselves comparatively clean. In the next few weeks I would become used to passing soldiers, their uniforms encrusted with dirt, some of them having just returned from brutally bloody missions, and smelling on them the sweet fragrance of the child-sanitising perfume lingering from their latest desert wash.

The PX only came once a week, and the queue for it had begun to form three hours before it opened. Joe and I found ourselves standing beside Sergeant Swinney as we waited in line. He spent most of the time regaling us with tales of his sexual exploits. Sergeant Swinney loved to talk about 'pussy'. Many times in our journey through Iraq I would find myself listening to how, when he was younger and wilder than the committed family man that I got to know, some poor innocent had found herself at the receiving end of his desires. Many of his tales were so explicit that soldiers would groan in horror at their detail. Few nationalities seemed to have escaped Swinney's clutches. Mexicans, Malaysians, Puerto Ricans and the occasional European had been notched on his bedpost. One evening on the outskirts of Baghdad he distracted a group of young privates from the dangers lurking outside by detailing to them the best way to lick a girl's arsehole as a surprise diversion while administering cunnilingus (not to be done for too long a time, was the crux of his advice, though the results, he insisted, were spectacular).

Unlikely as it seemed, his other passion was Walt Disney. He had an annual pass to Disney World in Florida, and at weekends would drive his family – he had married for the second time eighteen months earlier – down from the base in Georgia to enjoy the rides and restaurants. In his medical vehicle was a little portable DVD player, and at night, to escape the stresses of the military situation, he and his crew would settle down for a relaxing viewing of one of Disney's animated classics. *Beauty and the Beast* and *Lilo and Stitch* were among the favourites, though *Lilo and Stitch* had the advantage that, despite its being a cartoon, Lilo's older sister was hot.

One of the best times in Swinney's life had been his late teens, when he had been able to combine his two greatest enthusiasms and had worked as a lifeguard at one of the Disney resorts near Orlando. 'There was so much pussy,' he would say, a faraway look in his eye, 'it was like taking fruit from a tree.' After these easy pickings he had begun to go off the rails. A misjudged romance with a beauty queen had ended painfully when the girl had become pregnant and had been persuaded by her mother that she could do better out of life than end up with a lifeguard. Swinney had been heartbroken. Drugs and drink had followed to excess, ending with a motorcycle accident which had left scars that could be seen on his body to this day. Finally his father had taken him in hand. Enough lazing around in swimming trunks working on his tan, it was time to become a 'real man'. There was no choice given but to join the army. Swinney's background as a lifeguard meant he found himself in the medical corps. Now thirty-three, he was known to everyone simply as 'Doc', was universally respected for his expertise, and with the help of his two assistant paramedics was the first line of treatment for anyone in the company who was injured in combat.

Having finished eating, Doc was washing his face and pouring water over his hair to get rid of some of the sand. His hair was much longer than anyone else's in the unit, though the men were divided as to whether this was because he was too stubborn to do what he was told and get a haircut, or because he thought it hid the reality of a receding hairline. That morning he was as usual in a chirpy frame of mind despite, like the rest of the soldiers, having barely slept the night before.

'When this is all over, me and my wife are going to take you down to Florida,' he promised me. 'We'll go to Pleasure Island, the bar area at Disney World. It's so great there. You won't be able to help but get yourself a girl. There are bands and dancing. It's fantastic. Unless of course you go on a Thursday, that's gay night. But any other night, if you go home alone you must already be dead.'

The rest of the unit were awake now, and were busy conducting light maintenance on their vehicles. Sergeant Weaver and the M88 crew had taken the engine out of the broken-down tank and were overhauling it. The company's commanding officer, Captain David Waldron, known to everyone as the CO, came over to introduce himself. He was a tall, lanky man in his mid thirties, his appearance almost geekish with his tufty hair and his physique swallowed up by his baggy fatigues, eyes peering through a large pair of spectacles. He was the last man I would have pictured as a warrior at the forefront of an invasion, but subsequent events would reveal his indefatigable sense of duty in combat, and prove how wrong first impressions can be.

He spoke fondly of England. 'I play rugby, and played against

Myself interviewing
Captain James
Montgomery at the
base camp in Kuwait.

Right: The press pack
receives its final anti-
biochemical warfare
training on the tennis
courts of the Hilton
Hotel in Kuwait City. I
am in the foreground.

The other two journalists
placed with 1st Battalion,
Ron Synovitz of Radio
Free Europe and Joe
Giordono of *Stars and
Stripes*. This picture was
taken during the
sandstorm that engulfed
the battalion at the end
of our first full day in
the camp.

Nitai Schwartz and Garth Stewart, who in Kuwait made clear to me their opposition to the war. Stewart would lose part of his foot in Iraq.

Below: British tank crews wait for their turn at a firing range set up in the Kuwait desert. Unlike the Americans, few of the Desert Rats expressed much enthusiasm for the coming fight.

The men of 1st Battalion being informed at sunrise by their commanding officer, Lieutenant Colonel John W. Charlton, that the time had finally come to go to war.

My 'roomie' Major George Fredrick, one of the officers with whom I shared a tent in Kuwait.

Below: The M88 I travelled in for the first part of the campaign. Its strength and durability had led it to be christened 'Big Country'. Note the gasmask now permanently strapped to my thigh.

Sergeant Norman Weaver, the commander of the M88, just before the Black Knights tank company entered the demilitarised zone that spanned the Kuwait–Iraq border. I am sitting at the rear of the vehicle.

The company prepares for the move into the demilitarised zone.

The US military vehicles that the M88 passed in the final approach to the Iraqi garrison at Tallil. Note the artillery in the foreground, and the smoke from burning buildings in the distance.

Left: Iraqi prisoners captured around Tallil airbase. The US soldiers were shocked by how many of the Iraqis had fought back in that battle, the first they had engaged in during the war. Their officers had told them to prepare for widespread capitulations; instead they found themselves ambushed by an enemy many of whom – as this picture illustrates – were dressed in civilian clothes.

Private Roman Komlev, the Russian-born assistant driver of the M88. He had just been told there were snipers active in the area, and an American soldier had already been hit.

Below: Me, unknown soldier, Captain Bill Young and Lieutenant Colonel Charlton after the fighting at Tallil. Note that everyone is dressed in biochemical protection suits. Around our arms and ankles is tape that changes colour if nerve gas is in the vicinity.

Left: A US soldier takes a photograph of an Iraqi pick-up truck that had been destroyed by a Bradley shell in the recent fighting. There were seven bodies inside, and another Iraqi soldier lay dead on the ground, the RPG he had been preparing to fire fallen beside him.

Bottom left: A dead body in the back of the pick-up truck.

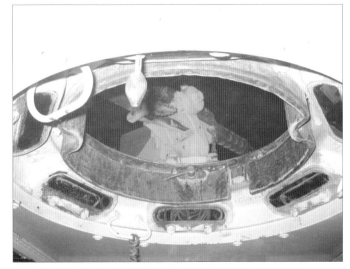

Top right: Myself during the time the Black Knights were stationed around Samawah, sparring with paramilitaries and under threat from sniper and mortar attack. There had been few opportunities to sleep in the previous days.

Middle right: The view through the hatch in the middle of the M88 during the sandstorm which engulfed us on the fifth day of the invasion. It turned the air a reddish-orange and reduced visibility to less than ten yards.

Right: The Black Knights advance to Dragon 4, 2nd Brigade's regrouping base south of Karbala.

Above: Myself (right) with Private Roman Komlev and Sergeant Weaver at Dragon 4.

Right: Private Jason 'Red' Carter, the driver of the M88, showing off an AK-47 that had been taken as a battlefield souvenir from a dead Iraqi soldier.

Left: Captain David Waldron, the commander in charge of the Black Knights. His men had been suspicious of his standoffish manner, but he earned their respect by his ferocity in battle.

Sandhurst there on a tour in 1994. They beat us, but it was such a historic place and everyone made us feel right at home. My wife loves England, always saying how much she likes the history and the accent, and has always wanted us to go and live there for a while. They have an American officer stationed at Sandhurst on an exchange programme, and she's keen for me to put myself up for the position. I may well do so. Fine country you come from.' I would discover later that he had vigorously opposed the idea of having a reporter embedded in his company, arguing that it could pose a distraction that would place his men in danger.

Under Waldron's command were ninety-six men, the vast majority of them in the ten tanks and four Bradleys that made up the company's attacking capability. Most of them were aged less than twenty-three, barely a handful had ever been on holidays outside the United States, and of those who had, in nearly every case it had only been a visit to Mexico. The sergeants were older, most in their late twenties or early thirties, and it was they who kept tight control over the day-to-day running of the unit. The head NCO, a figure known as the first sergeant who was equivalent to a sergeant major in the British Army, was forty-two-year-old Roger Burt, a linebacker-sized Puerto Rican who whenever I saw him had a wad of chewing tobacco pressed into the side of his mouth. It was he whom the enlisted men viewed above all others as their role model, one of their own who had risen to this pinnacle of authority.

These soldiers were not Marines, who prided themselves on doing push-ups until their knuckles bled or could run for thirty miles carrying 140-pound packs. Except for the infantry in the back of the Bradleys, the company was primarily made up of tank crews – 'tankers' as they were called in the American military – and their pride came from their vehicles and their adeptness in manoeuvring them in combat. They depended on their tanks to protect their lives, and their attitude towards them resembled that of an owner to a favoured pet. Crews would give their vehicle a name, would talk to it encouragingly when they were struggling to get over rough terrain. For them the thrill – the pay-off to all the driving and training – came in the opportunity to fire the Abrams' main gun. When the trigger switch was hit, the force of the blast would cause the tank to rock and the air to fill with the smell of cordite. 'It's like you've just had the greatest sex,' was how one gunner described it. 'You can't stop shaking afterwards from the excitement.' None could say often enough how much they loved the moments of action.

It was now almost mid-morning. I was lazing in the sun when Sergeant Swinney began to rush around the parked vehicles making sure everyone had their 'J-list', the army term for the anti-biochemical-weapon uniforms that had been issued. I called the office in London on the satellite phone. They told me that the previous night American bombers had hit a building near Baghdad University where intelligence had learnt that the Iraqi President and his sons had been sleeping. It was not known if Saddam had survived the 'decapitation attempt', but later it would be concluded that he might have been injured, but had not been killed. Iraqi forces had retaliated by launching four missiles into Kuwait, raising the fear of a possible chemical attack, although no one had been hurt and none of the rockets had contained any gas.

The movements of the men around me suddenly became more urgent. The original plan had been that they would have twenty-four hours to recover from the previous night's advance to the edge of the demilitarised zone before crossing the border, but following the Iraqi missile strikes the order had been passed down that 'G-day', the start of the ground offensive, would now commence at midnight.

Everyone was overexcited. From the moment I had joined the Black Knights I had been struck by how optimistic the men were. They were always joking about the battle ahead and talking about the great deeds they would accomplish. The atmosphere had already been lightheaded, but now, as they worked to finish their final preparations, many stripping down their machine guns and cleaning sand from the insides with toothbrushes, it became positively frenzied. Tank crews were talking about the tickertape parades they expected would greet them when they got back to the United States, and wisecracking about which Hollywood actors would play them in the film of their combat heroics. In order to record the moment for posterity video cameras were unwrapped from the plastic sheeting in which they had been kept as protection from the dust storms. Crews posed for photographs in front of their vehicles, their hands hung around comrades' shoulders or held in V for victory signs. By the time the order was given to move the last few miles into the demilitarised zone to take up their pre-invasion position less than a mile south of the frontier, it was as if they were a football team off to play in a cup final, not an army advancing to war.

The same tank that had had to be towed the previous night broke down again on the way. The maintenance crew went to work on it. I stood half out of my hatch watching missiles being fired, the trails of smoke from the Multiple Launch Rocket System batteries – known as MLRS – rising through the blue sky before disappearing into the lower atmosphere.

Suddenly there was a shout of 'Gas, gas, gas!' the warning for a chemical attack. I was confused. We had been told there would not be any more practice alerts this close to the start of the invasion. Everyone was running. Red and Sergeant Weaver leapt into the M88. I fumbled around at the back, taking my gasmask out of its case, trying to remember how I had been trained to put it on. Close your eyes, breathe out into the mask to clear it of any nerve agent in the air, hold your hand over the airway, breathe in to check there's a vacuum. I reached around to pull the two straps at the base below my ears. One of them tightened, but I couldn't find the toggle on the other side. Sergeant Weaver, mask on by now, was screaming for the hatches to be pulled shut. I knew all this was taking much longer than the regulation nine seconds.

It proved to be a false alarm, but we had not known that. When the all-clear was sounded, men emerged from their vehicles looking faintly embarrassed at the memory of the terror that had gripped them moments before. 'Fuck that. Fuck that,' said Red. 'I thought we were all dead.' One of the straps on my gasmask had got caught around the canister on the mask's left side, which was why I hadn't been able to pull it taut. Sergeant Swinney later confessed to me that he had been standing half bent over in the medic van, his mask on, one of the antigen needles held just above his right buttock as he tried to determine if he was feeling the first effects of exposure to nerve gas.

The scare brought with it the end of the football-team atmosphere. That night, as everyone waited for the war to start, was a long one. Sergeants walked around their units in the darkness, asking how their men were coping and warning them of the challenges they would have to face. Some of the soldiers prayed. Others wrote to their wives and families, handing the notes to friends for them to deliver if the time came when they would not be able to express the sentiments in person. Orders were issued for the troops to go to MOPP ('Mission Orientated Protective Posture') level 1, the stage on the military biochemical readiness scale that meant they had to climb into the jackets and trousers of their protective suits. Everyone knew it was unlikely they would come off before the war had ended, even though the charcoal-lined suits were stiflingly hot in the desert heat. Tape treated to become speckled with pink dots if a nerve-gas agent was in the air was wrapped around arms and ankles. All lights were now banned.

Roman climbed next to Sergeant Weaver and sat beside him on top of the armoured vehicle. Their bodies were silhouetted in the moonlight. 'I'm frightened,' the teenager said.

'It's OK to be frightened,' he was told. 'Everyone's nervous. Just do your job well and trust the rest of your unit. That's all we can do: our best. And if we do that, everything's going to be all right. You have to believe that.'

I slept fitfully for a few hours, at one point having a nightmare in which I was trapped in a tunnel and the call 'Gas, gas, gas' was coming. Waking up, I saw the imposing figure of Sergeant Weaver standing in his hatch, unable to sleep as his mind was filled with thoughts about the coming day. He looked down at me, his shaved head and dark moustache clear in the moonlight. 'Are you all right?' he asked.

'Of course,' I replied. The strange thing was that, whatever my subconscious may have been telling me to the contrary, I did feel remarkably unapprehensive. I was not thinking about getting injured, let alone about what the start of the war might mean for the Iraqis who stood in the Americans' way. I was confident in the ability of the soldiers I was with to protect me, and I had no doubt that somehow I would emerge unscathed, with a string of distinguished newspaper reports to my credit. Embarrassing as it is to recall now, at this time what I was witnessing seemed merely like some great theatrical spectacle being carried out for my benefit. I was excited at the prospect of what would happen next, and caught up in the momentum of events. It was only when I began to see dead bodies that it would all become shockingly real.

'Remember you can talk to me if you ever need to,' Sergeant Weaver said. 'You're now as much a part of my crew as the other two.' I thanked him, and I knew he meant it.

There was a short delay the next morning – Friday, 21 March – after we had driven to within sight of the ten-foot-high berm that marked the border between Iraq and Kuwait. A hole had been punched in it by military bulldozers, their crews now lying on the earth bank smoking. The first army units had crossed into Iraq at points to our north just after midnight, the Marines slightly earlier. Word came down that we were waiting for a TV news crew to finish setting up, as Ted Koppel, one of America's most influential news anchormen and host of the ABC show *Nightline*, wanted to do a live broadcast to the States while the first vehicles to cross the border at that spot went through behind him. I thought this was ridiculous – part of an invasion being held up so it could get on a news bulletin – but the soldiers seemed to approve of the idea. The members of one of the tank crews busied themselves making a sign emblazoned with a greeting for their wives that they planned to wave at the camera. As we finally pulled forward I saw Koppel doing his live stand-up, and beside him 'Buff' Blount, the general who had briefed us on the battle plan.

By now I was dressed in my army-issued anti-biochemical-warfare kit, in the desert camouflage sported by most of the American soldiers. On my head was my Kevlar helmet, covered in the same regulation colours. The outfit made a mockery of my earlier concerns about how to blend in with a combat unit while not looking too much like a soldier. I was now dressed almost exactly like everybody else, down to the US-issue boots I had picked up weeks before in Santa Monica. As the general passed I waved and shouted a hearty hello. He stopped, looked up and, thinking I was one of his men, gave a proud salute as we left him behind and drove on into what awaited us on the other side of the frontier.

Christal Swinney was tidying the bedroom of her two-storey home in Fort Stewart, the sprawling garrison near Savannah, Georgia, where the Black Knights were based, when the phone rang. The house had been provided by the army, and almost everyone on the street had a husband on active service in Iraq. They would knock on each other's doors when they heard details about events in the Gulf. Gossip from phone calls was quickly shared with friends, and developments reported on the news dwelled upon at the on-base shops, cafés and schools. Already neighbours were talking about the 'green suits', the officials in green dress uniforms whose job it was to tell families that a soldier had been killed in combat. On her letterbox Mrs Swinney had hung a yellow ribbon, a symbol of hope for a soldier's safe return from duty.

Earlier that day she had been downstairs watching the rolling news channels' coverage of the outbreak of the ground war. 'You'd see the pictures of all the American soldiers, and you wondered which were the ones you knew,' she would tell me later. 'I know people who slept on their couches because they didn't want to miss a moment of the television in case they saw a glimpse of their husbands and so would know they were safe. It was crazy; you could actually watch the war that they were fighting. After a week I turned off the TV.'

The Swinneys had been married less than two years. They had met on an internet chat site, exchanged a few e-mails and then gone out on a date. 'He wrote to me afterwards and said he thought I was beautiful,' Christal said. 'I wrote back and said I thought he was handsome, and we took it from there.' She had three children from a previous marriage, he one with his ex-wife. Just before Christmas their own baby girl, Sydney, had been born.

When the phone rang in her bedroom that first day of the ground war, she looked at the number and realised the call did not originate in America. She picked up the receiver, and at the end of the line was Doc Swinney. The company had been driving for six hours en route to Nasiriyah, the general attitude one almost of anti-climax. They had been hyped up at the prospect of crossing the border, but had been greeted by nothing more dangerous than a few camels and confused Bedouin nomads. A number of the soldiers were complaining that they were bored. They had come across burnt-out tanks less than a mile from the border, but these were relics from the last time America had decided it needed to act against Saddam Hussein. In 1991 the armoured vehicles of the United States Army had swept through southern Iraq, and across the land over which its men were once again advancing a battle had been fought, the evidence of which still lay untouched more than a decade later. There were no bodies; they had long ago been removed and buried. But there were dozens of wrecks, the debris rusted red but the black of scorch-marks still visible on their sides.

I had temporarily moved out of Big Country and into Sergeant Swinney's medic van at a fuel stop. The wires in the M88 that I needed to connect my laptop to the vehicle's battery had been severed in the previous day's gas scare, so I had begged my way into recharging it on the electrical converter set up in Band Aid. After I had called the office in London to be briefed on the general situation, Doc had asked if he could ring his wife. Like Sergeant Weaver, he had barely slept the previous night as he dwelled on the coming conflict. Now he wanted to tell his family how much he loved them, just in case something happened and he did not have an opportunity to do so again.

'He told me he was OK and everyone was doing well,' his wife would later say to me. 'I told him our baby girl was back here waiting for him. I told him we were all thinking of him. That I loved him, we were proud of him, and for him to be careful and come home safely.'

In the desert of southern Iraq, Doc Swinney was crying as he passed back the satellite phone.

That night saw the Black Knights' baptism in combat as a unit, their first experience of the excitement of battle and the fear of coming under fire. Sergeant Swinney would be at the heart of the fighting, performing heroics for which he would later receive the Silver Star for bravery. I would come across my first Iraqis, lines of frightened and despondent men forced to sit in the mud under the watchful eyes of their American captors. When it was over there would be a growing sense of confusion as exhausted soldiers came to terms with the reality of the dangers that now surrounded them, an ever-present awareness which none of them would be able to escape until they had left that country.

A number of vehicles had not even made it across the desert. The pressure for speed, to ensure that the attack came as a surprise to Iraqi forces who were expecting a slow advance up the highway past Basra, meant that anything which broke down was abandoned at hastily established mechanical repair stops. Dozens of non-tracked vehicles became trapped in the sand. At one point the battalion passed part of Major General Blount's staff stranded in the desert, the wheels of their vehicles buried to above the hubcaps and the crews sitting on top watching the rest of the column drive by.

As the sun set, the lights came on in Nasiriyah, the first town the soldiers had seen in three months. The American bombardment started at 7 p.m. Through night-vision goggles, the explosions of artillery shells and air strikes could be made out amid the buildings. Behind the spot where the Black Knights were stationed a missile battery opened up, sending a series of anti-personnel rockets streaming into the distance. There was not much noise from the soldiers now. In each vehicle crews studiously cleaned and checked their weapons. Sergeant Weaver sat talking to Red. 'I'll do whatever it takes to make sure I get home to my family,' he told him in a whisper. At around 8.30 p.m. the lights in the town went out, but the bombing continued.

The plan was not to enter Nasiriyah itself, but to seize the key tactical objectives in an area on its outskirts called Tallil. One battalion in 3rd Brigade would secure the nearest bridge over the Euphrates. Another would occupy the airfield, the second biggest military air base in Iraq. A third – the one I was with – would take on elements of the Iraqi 11th Infantry Division, attacking its garrison HQ located to the north-east of the airport. 'Objective Liberty' was the name the US military had given the site.

Before we crossed the border, American intelligence officers had indicated that they expected it to be an easy operation. Agents in Nasiriyah had reported that the soldiers in the 11th Division were mostly conscripts, and had little stomach for battle. Thousands of leaflets had been dropped throughout the area, carrying detailed instructions in Arabic on how to surrender to the invading forces. That night the company believed it would roll in and be greeted by white flags.

After the war was officially declared over, it would be claimed in some quarters that the expectation of easy victories in the south was an invention of elements in the media who wanted to discredit the American battle plan. However, in an address before the invasion was ordered, Major General Blount had said that he expected welcome parades in the south. When I had been briefed by the colonel and his intelligence officers just prior to crossing the border, it had been made clear to me that no significant resistance was expected before the US Army reached the Republican Guard units entrenched around Baghdad. It was calculated that the Shia-dominated south would be delighted to be freed from Saddam's dictatorial and brutal regime. It had risen against him after the 1991 Gulf War, and it was assumed that it would do so again. That was what the soldiers and NCOs of the Black Knights had been told, and that is what they were expecting.

When the order to start the attack was given at 10.30 p.m., the M88 was in the middle of the formation, bracketed in front and behind by tanks. As we advanced towards the city I was overwhelmed by excitement. Not that I was taking the dangers lightly – as well as my bulletproof vest and flak jacket, the groin protector was making its debut – but for the first time I was in the midst of an army setting forth into battle. When I had filed my latest article to the office I had learnt that something called 'Operation Shock and Awe' had been launched against Baghdad, a massive missile and bomber attack on key installations. British Marines had been fighting south of Basra at the port of Umm Qasr. Across the south of Iraq, ten thousand American vehicles were moving northwards. I was playing a bit part in an important historical drama. For most of the coming weeks the physical details – discomfort, lack of sleep, dirt, men shooting around me – would leave little time for such considerations. However, at that moment I was aware that history was being made, and it was impossible not to succumb to the exhilaration that came with it.

We crossed the desert plain, mounted an earth bank, and reached a highway. As everyone steeled themselves for the first contact with the enemy, catastrophe – at least from my journalistic point of view – struck. The driver of one of the tanks temporarily lost control of his vehicle and sent it through the central verge, ripping the tracks on the right side. The M88 crew sprang into action. I watched forlornly as the rest of the company disappeared into the distance, my mind dwelling on the images of warfare that I had spent so long preparing to see but might now never witness. I was filled with dread that Saddam would flee and the Iraqis surrender, now that the Americans had removed any doubt that they might have been bluffing.

The situation with the tank was bad. A large part of the track was ruined, and it was going to take hours to mend it. Its commander, Staff Sergeant Dennis Whelan, was bawling out the driver. 'You useless piece of shit,' he was shouting. 'I knew you were a lazy, stupid, good-for-nothing, but I thought you could at least drive in a straight line down a road.' Whelan was thirty-three, of Irish stock and proud of his temper. 'I'm going to leave you here when we finally go,' he told him. 'Let's hope the Iraqis capture you so you can ruin some of their equipment.'

The power of the United States was rolling past us: tanks and Bradleys, artillery accompanied by their mobile command units, medic vans with red crosses painted on their sides, convoys of scout Humvees with soldiers standing on the back seats clutching grenade launchers and handheld rockets. In wave after wave the units of the American army were advancing to take their first target of the war in Iraq.

For this small outpost of the Black Knights, however, the battle was merely to get a cup of coffee. Sergeant Whelan had, to everyone on the M88's amazement and delight, produced a packet of Starbucks Breakfast Blend along with a small percolator and announced it was time for a caffeine hit. 'You can never be too prepared,' he said, opening a little tin of fig rolls as everyone sipped their coffee from cups made from cut-in-half water bottles.

The broken-down tank's gunner was discussing the best camping spots in California with me. Sergeant Whelan was remarking how small Ted Koppel had looked: 'He seems a big guy on TV, but he was like a midget or something.' The driver was hiding in a darkened spot beneath the tank's gun, the barrel of which had the name 'Bulldog II' stencilled on it, trying to avoid being seen and thereby risking re-igniting his commander's ire. We waved at some of the military vehicles driving into Tallil. Over the military radio came a report that the bridge and airfield had been secured with little opposition. A machine-gun nest was located on the road to the Iraqi HQ. We watched as a five-hundred-pound bomb obliterated it. The force of the detonation was so powerful it created a perfectly shaped mushroom cloud that disappeared into the darkness.

I offered them the chance to ring home. Most of them were visibly emotional after they finished their calls. Even Sergeant Whelan's voice cracked, though I noted that he mainly adopted a similarly gruff manner for talking to his wife as he had for chastising his driver. At one moment in the conversation he had shaken his head in bemusement. 'Of course it's safe to go out of the house. The Iraqis are in Iraq, not the United States,' he had barked.

Sergeant Weaver took a break from working on the tank. He too called his wife, walking around the back of the M88 to gain some privacy. When he came back he wanted to talk about his family. 'We call each other our soulmates,' he said of his wife. 'I'm as much in love with her now as I was the day I married her.' When I had first met Weaver I had felt slightly intimidated. He was a big, strong man, around six feet, arms like tree trunks, confident in what he did and his command of his vehicle, seemingly able to survive for long periods on almost no sleep. However, as I talked with him on that highway I realised that despite his training and years of experience he was almost as nervous and uncertain about finding himself in a war zone as I was. He was only three years older than me, and, I was relieved to discover, equally determined to avoid heroics that could lead to the possibility of getting killed.

'I don't like being stuck out here by ourselves,' he said while we were waiting on the road. 'Who knows what's going on? I mean, look at that.' In the distance the horizon was lined with the headlights of dozens of vehicles crossing the desert. It had been a while since the last American unit had passed, and I realised we were very alone, out of radio contact with our company and with only one tank to protect us. 'That could be the Iraqi army counterattacking, as far as we know,' Weaver said.

Two days later I would realise how pertinent his concerns were. I heard on the BBC that close to where we were parked that night a convoy of maintenance vehicles had been ambushed after their commander took a wrong turn, separating them from the rest of their unit. Seven Americans were killed and six taken prisoner; a number of them were later paraded on al-Jazeera, the twenty-four-hour Arabic television news network. Among those captured was a nineteen-year-old private, Jessica Lynch, who was taken to a hospital in Nasiriyah to be treated for two broken legs and a broken arm. A one-time Miss Congeniality winner in a beauty contest at her local fair, she had enlisted primarily to pay for the college education she needed to become a kindergarten teacher. Back in the United States the fate of Private Lynch would become a symbol of what had happened to the hope of a short, neat liberation of a grateful Iraq.

Sergeant Weaver was back to talking about his wife: 'She tells me she's lost weight. She's a biggish woman, not that I ever minded it, but it worried her. Says she's got herself in shape for when I get back. We met at high school. Can you believe that? We've known each other almost all our lives. Didn't go out then, though, just became best friends, spent all our time together, hung out, studied. I even took her to the prom, but I didn't do anything. A kiss on the cheek when I said goodnight, nothing more. I've often wondered if I should have.' He smiled. 'You know, I've never asked her if she wanted me to. I should when I get back. Stupid to leave these questions unanswered.

'After we left school I moved away and joined the army, and we lost touch. Then I went back on leave a few years later, and we met up again by accident. I was in Wal-Mart, and she was working there and I was in the checkout line. She walked up and said to me, "You mean to tell me you're here and not going to say hello?" That night I turned up at her house uninvited, and then I took her out the next day. For four days straight we spent every moment together. I took her to a theme park, the strawberry festival. We held hands the first time at that strawberry festival. Kissed a month later. Been together ever since. It's almost perfect. I'm happiest being at home with her and the children, not doing anything special, just all being together. I miss that. Miss that more every time I'm away.'

The most serious argument in their marriage had come three years ago, when his first ten-year military term had finished. His wife, sick of the amount of time he was away on duty, warned that if he signed up again she would consider filing for divorce. She was struggling with the strain of bringing up their two children without a husband around to help. He signed up for another ten years, and she stayed. 'She knew I was doing it for our family,' he said. 'I'm a soldier, it's what I do to pay the bills. After this I'll leave with a good pension and we can build a good life to-gether. I knew she hadn't wanted our children to be raised with their father away so much, but she understood why I stayed in the army. She knew I did it for them. She knows how much I love her.'

It was almost dawn before we finally moved forward again,

driving past the clusters of American support units that now lined the highway. We arrived at a roadblock set up on the route to the Iraqi air base and army headquarters at Tallil just as news began to filter through that the Iraqis were fighting back in force. First light had brought with it an ambush on part of 1st Battalion near the garrison entrance. It was hard to work out what was going on, but the radio was filled with reports of enemy positions being identified and demands for them to be targeted. Two soldiers had been medivaced.

There was considerable smoke and gunfire in the distance. It appeared that some engineers, protected by a couple of scout vehicles, tanks and a Bradley, had been placing concertina wire across a road to the east of the garrison to act as a roadblock. It was against this group that the main counterstrike had been launched, although pockets of fighting were being reported across the area. Now that there was some daylight, the Iraqis could pick out where the American troops were located, and it was clear that they had wasted no time in pressing home that limited advantage. The United States Army was not receiving the welcome it had expected.

The lieutenant controlling traffic was adamant about not letting us through. 'I cannot let you pass. My orders say no one is to pass,' he insisted.

'But those are my boys up there, and I'm not with them!' Sergeant Weaver shouted back.

Around us were other vehicles that had been separated from their units during the night's operation. Directly behind was a truck loaded with artillery shells that had become unfastened and spilled over the highway. To our left was a medic van which had been delayed dealing with a trooper hurt in a minor accident.

On the bridge above was a small Iraqi army installation, now abandoned. It was fully light now, the sun a pale orb just above the horizon, and it had started to rain lightly. With one of the medics I climbed up the side of the embankment and we made our way through the barbed wire that marked the outpost's edges to have a snoop around. A small puppy, no more than four or five weeks old, that the soldiers based there had kept to entertain them, was yelping in one of the outhouses.

The living conditions were very basic. Four squat, one-storey, single-roomed buildings stood in a line, their walls constructed from bricks made of mud and straw, the roofs corrugated iron. Inside the sleeping area, posters had been hung on the walls in an attempt to liven up the barren setting: a football team, a calendar featuring Saddam and his sons, some quotes from the Koran, a poster in Arabic showing the markings of a variety of American missiles. Candles had been used for lights, and one rusting car battery powered a decrepit military radio.

The medic started playing with the dog, which rolled onto its back so its belly could be scratched. It followed us when we went down to rejoin the vehicles, and soon a group had gathered to feed the puppy bits of MREs as it barked and ran around in excitement. As with the Starbucks during the night, I found something unsettling about the scene. The activity was so ordinary, and the location so extreme. A group of young Americans were playing with a dog. Yet they had guns slung on their backs, were dressed in full anti-biochemical-warfare suits, and the sound of explosions had intensified as the firefight a short distance to the north-east reached its height. And where were the animal's former owners? The men who had eaten from the battered metal plates I had found piled beside a bucket half-filled with soapy water, and who had slept on the three thin foam mattresses under the posters in the dormitory. They could be dead, killed by the comrades of the youths now entertaining their pet.

Standing a short distance behind us I spotted two Iraqi prisoners of war being guarded by a pair of American infantrymen. One of the PoWs was sitting on the ground, staring at an oil slick on the tarmac, his face utterly despondent. The other, however, was standing almost to attention, tall and still proud in the dark green uniform of an officer in the Iraqi regular army. One of the American soldiers with them was a translator, and through him I asked the Iraqi officer why his soldiers had not capitulated as expected. He gave me a withering stare. 'Because this is our country,' he said. 'And we will fight to protect it. What would you do if you were us?'

An order came over the radio that it was now safe enough to advance. The barbed wire was pulled back and our small convoy moved forward. The surrounding fields were covered in a smattering of light brown grass, long stretches of which had been turned to mud by the rain and the tracks of American vehicles. A plume of black smoke blew across the horizon. Bursts of gunfire could still be heard ahead where the battalion had yet to fully secure its objective.

As we drove, the American army unfolded before us. First there were the outstretched necks of the rows of artillery. Then we passed through the rear of the combat units. Soldiers stared at us from the back of Bradleys, their faces blackened with dirt and smoke. There was the whoosh of a missile taking off to our left, close enough to make Sergeant Weaver recoil.

Then we turned a corner, and for the first time I was truly afraid. It was the result not of the sound of gunfire or the possibility of danger ahead, but of the sight that lay in front of me. Two Iraqis were crumpled in a hole in the dirt, their skin crisp and black. I had never seen a dead body before, let alone one left behind by combat. The fractured remains of a bone stuck out of a socket where an arm had once hung. A helmet had been fused to the top of one of the dead soldiers' skulls. Lips and eyes could still be made out on what remained of a face, but the eyelids had been burnt clean off, the corneas turned grey by the flames.

The details of weapons' ranges and blast zones had seemed so academic when explained to me at the camp in Kuwait. Now, for the first time, I fully grasped what this war would actually involve. That knowledge left me as frightened as anything I would experience in the coming weeks of fighting. From the hatch in front of me Weaver was also staring at the corpses. 'This is not good,' I heard him say, before he tightened his grip on the handle of his .50-calibre machine gun and we drove onward towards where the rest of the company was waiting.

We passed another Bradley, its infantry unit fanned out across a small field. Three Iraqis kneeled in a doorway, hands on their heads, their weapons thrown on the ground beside them. Ahead, more PoWs were lined up beside the road. Their hands had been tied behind their backs with plastic binders, and most stared in disbelief at the soldiers who stood guard over them. At least half seemed to be wearing civilian clothes. More tanks were now around us. An armoured personnel carrier, our company's radio command post, was among them. The staff sergeant, Trey Black, was standing in the turret manning the machine gun. 'Watch yourselves,' he shouted, 'there are snipers just in front.'

'Which side?' Sergeant Weaver called back.

'Both,' came the answer.

A badly burnt Iraqi was being lifted into the back of a medic van on a stretcher. Infantrymen were carrying out house-to-house searches. I began to spot people I knew – Major Fredrick, the chaplain, Captain Bill Young. I got out of the armoured vehicle and tried to determine what had happened. A group of soldiers were leaning against the side of a Bradley. 'The fuckers keep firing at us,' one shouted. 'This is bullshit.'

I saw Joe, the *Stars and Stripes* photographer, who had been caught in the middle of the fighting. He gave me a light for a cigarette. His hands were actually shaking. 'The last person whose cigarette I lit got shot,' he said. 'Jesus, it sounds like a line from a bad film.'

He had been with the scouts at the attacked roadblock, standing at the front of the vehicles when the shooting started as he prepared to take a photograph of the American soldiers at work. 'A few shots popped off in the distance,' he said. 'No one paid much notice, and then the sky was filled with incoming tracer rounds. Everyone was running and shouting and trying to get back to their vehicles, returning fire at targets on either side of the road less than a hundred yards away. Then, as the firing grew louder, there were three sharp, sickening screams. This scout, the one whose cigarette I had just lit, had been hit. A soldier appeared and covered him with his body while another administered first aid. I found myself in the Humvee, hid at the bottom, and waited for it all to be over.'

I saw the lieutenant colonel. He was standing outside his vehicle puffing on a small cigar, eyes hidden by his wraparound sunglasses. 'Busy day,' he said. What happened to the expected capitulations, I asked. 'Things shaped up just like our worst-case analysis with the enemy employing its defensive positions,' he explained. 'We didn't want to have to kill them, but the enemy gets a vote, and he decided to fight. And when they fight, they decide to die. It was surprising for a moment there, but when we realised what was happening I brought in everything: artillery, missiles, mortars, the lot. All hell was let loose down here.' No one knew exactly how many Iraqis were killed in Tallil, but it was estimated to be around 230, with twenty vehicles destroyed. More than 250 had been taken prisoner. As it would turn out, not one Iraqi unit would capitulate before Baghdad had fallen.

Captain Young was trying to understand what had occurred that day. 'Why are they fighting?' he asked me. 'Why are they fighting for such an evil man? Don't they understand we're Americans?' I left him monitoring the radio, listening to reports of small groups of armed men sighted skulking around our perimeter.

I knelt beside one of the groups of PoWs and tried to find any who spoke English. I wanted to find out who was fighting and why, whether the American soldiers were seen as invaders or liberators, whether Saddam was viewed as a hero or a tyrant. The soldiers guarding the prisoners were angry. 'You've got to understand that a few minutes ago they were trying to kill us,' one told me.

An Iraqi air force pilot named Saif al-Din informed me indignantly that every American who had crossed that border would die, as Iraqis would fight for every scrap of land. A captain called Ahmad insisted that everyone hated Saddam Hussein, but that it was the business of the Iraqis, not the Americans, to remove him. A young private with a droopy moustache said in broken English that he had been forced to fight. He raised his fingers to his head in the shape of a pistol and said someone had told him, 'Fight, fight American,' or he would be shot. A man dressed in civilian clothes, his long white robe stained brown from the dirt, was bellicose. 'America is an elephant and we are an ant. But still we are a proud people and we would rather die than suffer the dishonour of defeat.' An army major, Salam Shakir, simply asked me, 'Will they kill me now?' as he nodded towards the soldiers surrounding him. 'They know Geneva Convention, yes? They not allowed to kill me. They know that, yes?'

I was left even more confused about what was going on than when I had begun my questioning. It was a pitiful scene, the frightened men guarded by the nervous soldiers, all gathered in the shallow mud of a field across which many of them had been fighting each other.

The Black Knights had formed a defensive perimeter on an open stretch of land to the south of the garrison. Sergeant Swinney was leaning against his vehicle, looking exhausted. It had been his crew that had responded to the scout shot beside Joe. As the Iraqis hidden behind the berm had opened up, Swinney and his assistant, twenty-one-year-old Specialist Terry 'Frankie' Franks, had driven Band Aid alongside and then run forward to help the casualty. Doc covered him with his body and let loose with his M-16 while Frankie administered emergency first aid.

'I was like a man possessed,' Doc said proudly. 'Ask Frankie. I was shouting "You fucking this", "You fucking that", and firing at everything. He said I was so mad he was frightened of me. I must have fired more than 220 rounds – I wasn't going to get killed out there.

'Frankie was kneeling down beside me, applying bandages to the wounds, and bullets were landing at our feet. He looked up at me as if to say, "Can we get out of here now?", but I told him I had him covered, and started targeting rounds at the guys who were shooting at him. One bullet flew right over Frankie's head, hitting the vehicle just above him. If he hadn't been leaning forward to help the casualty it would've hit him, but he just kept doing what he had been taught to do and looking after that guy.' The scout had been shot in the abdomen, but no internal organs had been hit. He was critically injured, but would survive.

The US military estimates that on average it takes two thousand rounds to be fired for each enemy killed. Any firefight brings with it a terrifying number of bullets zinging around the heads of all those caught in its midst.

'At one point I saw something move in the distance and I was shooting away at it, then I realised it was a dog,' Doc continued. 'I couldn't believe I was wasting my time shooting at a dog when bullets were coming in on me. Then they were behind us, and I was shooting at them and I was shouting and swearing. I saw this motherfucker firing at us from behind a broken-down wall and aimed real long, like I was on the firing range, and the bullet hit only two inches from where his head was. Two inches. It was that close.'

Major Fredrick told me that for covering the injured man with his body Swinney was being put forward for a medal. When I asked Doc about this he shrugged, and with a genuine absence of affectation replied, 'I was just doing my job. It's my job to look after all the men I'm responsible for, and try and make sure that when they need me, they get home alive.'

He was disturbed, though, that many of the Iraqis had been wearing civilian clothes. Soldiers were talking about men producing weapons from beneath Arabic smocks, and of groups, none of them dressed in uniform, firing AK-47s. One told me about a tank that had been carrying a white flag, but had been swinging its barrel around as if to open fire, so he had destroyed it with a shell. Others described seeing Iraqi soldiers forcing civilians out of houses to act as human shields. Later there would be reports that Iraqis had been seen aiming at troops on their own side who would not advance.

The American soldiers had been given very strict rules of engagement before they crossed the border, and it seemed the enemy was using those limitations to their advantage. No one in civilian clothes, even if they were holding a weapon, was to be shot at until it had been established that they posed a clear threat. In practice this normally meant after they had actually opened fire. All efforts had to be taken to avoid damaging civilian structures, particularly mosques, hospitals and schools. If Iraqi soldiers had to be buried, it should be done with their bodies pointing towards Mecca. This was a civilised army, one made up of Americans, the message had been passed down, and it was to behave in a civilised way on the battlefield.

American intelligence officers had received information before the invasion was launched that Iraqi soldiers were carrying civilian clothes in their kitbags. At the time this was seen as an indication that they were poised to desert at the first possible opportunity. Now it seemed that a number of them had been waiting for the order to shed their fatigues to make it harder for the United States military to identify them. This was not the kind of enemy that the Americans had been warned to expect. It was not one in which company commanders marched forward and signed capitulation agreements, or even one that seemed to care about the distinction between combatants and civilians on which the American rules of engagement had been based. It was becoming clear that this enemy simply wanted to kill the soldiers who were invading their country, and saw no need to appear civilised about how they managed to do it.

Sergeant Weaver was dismantling and cleaning the M88's .50-calibre machine gun. 'Be careful,' he said. 'We've been warned to expect a counterattack.' The radio was still full of reports of small groups of armed men being spotted around our perimeter. He did not speak as he oiled the gun's component parts. Later he would tell me what thoughts he had been dwelling upon. 'You remember when we saw those first bodies on the road into the garrison?' he said. 'Earlier we'd been so excited at getting the order to go forward. Then I saw those dead Iraqis, and in a moment I realised life is precious. I knew they probably had a family, that having people who loved you wouldn't stop you getting hit. I suddenly understood how easy it is for everything to be taken from you.'

Others were similarly overwhelmed by the rollercoaster of emotions experienced during the previous twenty-four hours. Climbing through the side hatch of the M88, I discovered twenty-five-year-old First Lieutenant Davis Garabato, known as the XO – Executive Officer – because he was second in command in the company, lying on the floor staring at the ceiling of the vehicle. 'There'd been so much waiting and training that even as we'd driven around the objective area I hadn't appreciated that this was for real,' he said. 'Suddenly they started firing, and I realised it was no training exercise. And do you know what I was thinking at that point? I was thinking: "I can't believe they've taken on the might of the United States Army."'

It had been a long time since I had slept properly and I was very, very tired. My eyes were playing tricks on me, seeing shapes in the trees or the furrows of the surrounding fields that disappeared when I focused on them. My brain could no longer articulate the questions it wanted to ask. Some of the soldiers were talking about the possibility of a chemical attack, as the Iraqis would now know where we were. Somewhere out there were people occupied solely with working out methods to bring harm on the men I was with. I put my helmet back on, checked that my gasmask was within arm's reach, and sat beside the lieutenant at the bottom of the M88. Then, remembering what Nitai Schwartz had told me a few days earlier, I picked up one of Red's porno-graphic magazines and flicked through it in the hope that – as Nitai had promised – the sight of naked girls would make me feel less anxious at times of stress. I was relieved to learn that he had been right.

FOUR

A Kool-Aid Sky

The next day I discovered how I would react the first time I came directly under fire. There was none of the hoped-for heroism, though at least I was not the one in four meant to literally shit themselves. Instead I found myself scrabbling around at the bottom of the M88, holding my helmet to my head with one hand, and desperately searching for my bulletproof vest with the other. We had been stuck in a tailback of tanks and armoured cars when Iraqi mortar rounds came in, throwing the thirteen-ton vehicle just in front of us into the air. I stared horrorstruck as First Sergeant Burt stumbled amid the wreckage, blood spurting from deep wounds cut across his body by the shrapnel. It had seemed so unlikely even moments earlier. The plan was being kept to: the men of 1st Battalion were leaving the job of securing the area around Nasiriyah to the rest of 3rd Brigade and were pushing on to join up with 2nd Brigade in order to help lead the attack to Baghdad. Since mid-morning we had been on the highway, the atmosphere more relaxed as the confusion and fighting of the previous day was left behind. No one was sad to leave Tallil, from where there were still reports of an attack being organised against the American forces. Now we were driving north-west as part of what the BBC World Service news was calling the fastest and longest tank advance in history.

There had been warning signs that all was not right. A four-man unit of Iraqi paramilitaries riding on mopeds was captured with a radio on which it was suspected they had been passing information about the Americans' location. 3rd Squadron, the 7th Cavalry, a unit known as the 3–7 Cav that acted as the reconnaissance scouts for the entire 3rd Infantry Division, screening its advance and flushing out trouble, reported that it had been assaulted by waves of enemy troops. Their commander described 'almost suicide missions' in which Iraqis armed with AK-47 assault rifles ran up against tanks, which mowed them down. This happened near a small city called Samawah, seventy-five miles north-west from Nasiriyah and halfway to Najaf, that American intelligence had believed would offer no resistance at all. In the vehicles that made up the Black Knights, few were dwelling on such details. They had been told before crossing the border that after securing the garrison at Tallil they would keep advancing, and now they were. There seemed little to worry about. Everything was going according to plan.

The mortars opened fire a little after three o'clock. I was looking out of my hatch at the back of the M88 when there were three loud explosions in quick succession. Sergeant Weaver shouted 'Incoming!' Red and Roman prepared to evacuate, standing half in and half out of the vehicle as they waited to be told whether to run. The crew of the fuel tankers a short distance ahead had already done so, and were taking shelter in a ditch. We had been parked in a line on a road built along the top of a berm while the mobile battalion headquarters was moved to the front. First Sergeant Burt was standing on the road trying to marshal the company to one side so the command vehicles could drive through. We must have presented an inviting target, clearly visible for miles around, going nowhere, and perhaps too confident in the presumption that the Iraqis would be too scared to attack. The unit was strung out 'like ducks at the fairground', as Sergeant Trey Black would later describe it.

The mortars landed between the back of his armoured personnel carrier, which was the company's radio command point, and the front of Doc Swinney's medic van. It was Band Aid that had been thrown four feet into the air, destroying its engine. Sergeant Burt was blown off his feet by the blast. Blood flowed from wounds to his legs, arms and lower back. Only the fact that he was wearing a fastened flak jacket stopped him being fatally injured. Swinney ran to give first aid. 'Give me water,' Burt ordered, but no liquids could be given to someone who was bleeding severely, in case they needed to be operated on. 'Give me water,' he shouted again. 'I've got to get rid of this dip.' He wanted to spit out the wad of chewing tobacco that had been pressed into the side of his mouth.

I had not spotted any of the rounds coming in, though Sergeant Weaver would later say he caught a blurred streak of black falling from the sky moments before the detonations. However, I saw the blasts, and took in the damage they caused before the shock that had rendered me immobile passed and I was able to drop inside the vehicle to desperately get into my armour. I had no thought but to heed the voice in my head screaming at me to put on the bulletproof plates that would, like some magic amulet, guarantee my safety. Everyone waited for more shells to be fired now that the Iraqis had our location fixed. Orders were coming over the radio for people to stay in their vehicles and get them off the road, but the convoy had been pushed so close together that no one could move. The crews of the fuel tankers at first refused to get back into their trucks. They knew too well the effect an exploding shell would have on their cargo.

Finally the battalion began inching its way forward, and scattered across the surrounding fields. News was coming in of attacks on other groups of American forces behind us, and plans to keep pushing forward were being abandoned. Convoys were pulled off the main highway and sent on smaller, slower-moving roads to the south where there was less likelihood of an ambush. Fresh instructions came through to 1st Battalion: forget 2nd Brigade, focus on finding enemy mortar teams and securing the routes around Samawah. The 3–7 Cavalry would push on alone, taking the fight towards Najaf. The job of the unit I was with was to help secure the highway behind them. In little bursts of movement the vehicles of the Black Knights advanced towards their new objective, one group pushing forward, then stopping for another to leapfrog in front.

It was after 6 p.m. when the company drew up in formation in a field by a dilapidated industrial complex just outside the southern outskirts of Samawah. There were many scared men among those encamped that night. Sergeant Weaver, Red and Roman were all looking shocked at what they had seen. 'Anyone but the first sergeant,' Red was saying. 'He was meant to be the one looking after us. I thought he could never get hit.' Weaver took down the one-shot handheld missile launchers which had been stowed in the M88, methodically unwrapped them from their outer covers and positioned them in easy reach in case they were needed. First Sergeant Burt had been evacuated to 3rd Brigade's field hospital, where he was being prepared for a series of life-saving operations. Band Aid had been abandoned on the road. News was being passed around that there had been a resumption of fighting around Nasiriyah. Weaver asked for a cigarette. 'This is the first for ten years,' he said before lighting it. 'My wife won't like it, but I don't like this. That was scary stuff.'

There was a knock on the side door. It was Doc Swinney. 'Can I come in? I don't have anywhere to stay. I lost Band Aid,' he said. He had dislocated his shoulder when his vehicle had jumped from the force of the explosion. Inside, the five of us pressed into the available space, the only light coming from the pale green glow cast by a fluorescent stick snapped alight and stuck between two boxes. At Doc's request, Weaver popped his shoulder back into place. 'I didn't even realise I'd hurt myself until after we'd dealt with Sergeant Burt,' Doc said when he had recovered from the pain. 'You saw Sergeant Burt, right? That was bad. He was not in good shape. He was bleeding everywhere. When we carried him out of there, my helmet was underneath him, supporting his back, and by the time we laid him down, it was half filled with blood.'

Sergeant Weaver's face was hidden by shadow. 'The radio says this kind of thing is going on all over the place,' he reported. 'This is some welcome parade. It's worse than anything I saw in Somalia.'

'My friend,' replied Doc, 'this is the baddest shit any of us have ever seen. And you know the worst part of it? There's only one way home, and that's through Baghdad.'

The American army would find no warm welcomes in Iraq's southern cities until Saddam Hussein's regime was tottering in its strongholds in Baghdad. The Iraqi President had ordered members of his Republican Guard south to bolster the willingness of conscript soldiers to fight, a willingness that it seems was enforced by warnings that any deserters would be killed. The 1st Battalion's intelligence officers told me that a first lieutenant in the Iraqi 32nd Brigade claimed soldiers had been trying to 'escape', but had been stopped at gunpoint. A similar story had been related to me by one of the PoWs at Tallil. Human Rights Watch, a non-government organisation working in the region, would report that it interviewed an Iraqi soldier who witnessed ten deserters shot by a colonel. The bodies were left on a nearby hillside as a grim warning to all considering similar action.

Members of the Saddam Fedayeen ('the Martyrs of Saddam'), a paramilitary force originally set up by Saddam Hussein's eldest son Uday, but now under the control of his slightly less psychotic younger brother Qusay, had also been dispatched to hinder the enemy advance. It was they who were primarily responsible for the mortar and sniper attacks, and who harassed American targets from unmarked pick-up trucks and mopeds, dressed sometimes in their black uniforms but mostly in civilian clothes, to enable them to disappear effortlessly into a crowd. As many as a thousand Fedayeen were believed to be in Samawah. Among them were foreigners who had come to Iraq to fight the Americans, mostly young Palestinians from Syria, Lebanon and Egypt. One of them, captured after being shot in the arm, was found to have a Syrian passport on him. On the visa, in answer to the question asking the purpose of his visit to Iraq, had been written the word 'Jihad'.

The people who lived in the south had suffered brutal reper-cussions from forces loyal to Saddam, and the Ba'ath Party that he headed, when they had previously tried to revolt. Since 1991 there had been five rebellions in the region, all ruthlessly suppressed, with accusations of mass murder and widespread torture. Two brigades of the Iraqi 11th Division were still active on the east side of the Euphrates, their presence intended to prevent a Shia insurrection accompanying the American invasion. It was not an environment likely to encourage garlands of flowers being offered to an advancing army. Especially one from a foreign power that, following the libera-tion of Kuwait in 1991, had encouraged an uprising, then done noth-ing to protect those who took up arms from being slaughtered as Saddam reasserted control across his country.

Yet in the minds of the American soldiers strung out in the thin line of vehicles now stretching from Nasiriyah to north of Najaf another fear was growing, a far more terrifying explanation for why they were facing more determined opposition than expected. It might not be just because a small group of fanatics were using the threat of violence to force an unwilling people to take up arms. Few of the soldiers wanted to risk jinxing themselves by even mentioning it, yet a growing number would confide to me their gnawing misgiving that the invasion had not triggered a popular revolt against Saddam, as their leaders had promised, but had instead triggered an uprising against the United States Army. In the Iran–Iraq war, an outbreak of patriotism meant Shia Iraqis had united with the ruling Sunni minority and fought against their religious brethren in Iran. The question was whether a similar nationalism was arising again, whether the Americans would have to battle a nation of twenty-seven million people for every scrap of land. I could not forget the words of the first Iraqi I had talked to, the PoW standing proud at the roadblock at Tallil whom I had asked why there had been no capitulations: 'Because this is our country. And we will fight to protect it.'

It was the day after our arrival at Samawah that I heard the V-word used for the first time. Specialist Stazny, a mechanic in the armoured carrier which serviced the Bradleys, was staring at the houses that marked the edge of the city when he said to me: 'I sure hope we haven't just walked straight into a new Vietnam.'

Few things are more unsettling to a soldier than the appearance that his superiors do not know what is going on around them. The men I was with were only too aware that what they had been told to expect was not occurring. No longer were their tanks pushing forward. Instead the high command had determined that the southern cities could not, as originally planned, simply be bypassed, but instead had to be controlled so that supply lines would not be endangered. The hoped-for surrenders and Shi'ite uprisings had failed to materialise. The United States Army was going to have to overthrow Saddam the hard way.

The first day after the confusion on the highway, I had to focus my willpower before I could climb out of the M88. Dawn brought news of an American scout injured by a sniper, but I knew that I had to reclaim the outside world or I would become unable to function, too nervous to leave the safety of my vehicle. Luckily, my reluctance to look weak in front of the soldiers, the companions to whom I had insisted I would not be a burden and could cope with the awaiting dangers, was as strong as my fear of being injured. It propelled me into the fresh air with a smile fixed to my face, determined not to disgrace myself.

Nevertheless, I did not now go anywhere without wearing my helmet and flak jacket. They had joined my gasmask as the essential items offering a hope of protection against the people out there trying to kill me. That morning as I walked around the vehicles everything seemed almost normal: the same faces, the same American accents, and the same calming voice of the BBC on the radio. But this was not a simulation minefield; this was real. And the knowledge that the soldiers around me were as nervous as I was did not make me feel any safer.

Our surroundings did not help either. The arid desert had gone, replaced by an expanse of squalid scrubland. Clumps of crippled bushes provided the only distraction from dirt-covered fields. Any grass, if it had ever existed, had either gone into hibernation to escape the heat or died. On the horizon were bowed, windswept trees, and at the edge of the city a monotonous line of box-shaped buildings made from bricks as brown as the ground they stood on. Behind us was a cement factory, around which piles of twisted scrap metal were slowly disintegrating from rust. Wild dogs roamed the area, their barking filling the hours of darkness. Even the blue sky had disappeared, replaced by leaden stormclouds that seemed to press down upon us. Occasionally they would spit with rain, causing the tank tracks to churn the earth into mud.

Earlier that morning the M88 had towed Band Aid to our encampment. Doc Swinney was now standing beside what remained of his vehicle, detailing to a growing audience how it had felt when the mortar round detonated. The front panel of the medic van was peppered with shrapnel. One of the shells had bounced underneath and exploded into the engine, reducing its workings to so much mutilated metal. The engine compartment had absorbed most of the blast and saved everyone inside from serious injury. If it had gone off a second or two later, it would have blown through the floor of the main seating area, sending shards of metal towards the crew housed above.

'Next time I see any Iraqis they better watch out,' Doc was

saying. 'If they shoot at me again, I'm gonna make sure I kill those sons of bitches. Couldn't they see that this was marked with a red cross? They didn't give a shit. I tell you, I'm gonna take revenge on those bastards. I'm the meanest medic you're ever going to meet.' Later that day he was issued with a new vehicle. That night, he would tell me later, he dreamt that it too was being shelled by mortars.

Captain Waldron came to look for me. He had just returned from a meeting of the battalion staff officers and was angry at what he had learnt. His patrols had adopted a policy of searching every vehicle on the roads that crossed the surrounding fields. That morning they had found a twelve-year-old boy clutching an AK-47 machine gun in the back of a truck. The child was terrified. When questioned, he had claimed that a unit of paramilitaries had come to his home, forced the gun into his hands and ordered him to shoot Americans. Reports were coming in from across the area that soldiers were picking up armed Iraqi civilians who said Saddam's henchmen were roaming Samawah doling out weapons and making people head out into the countryside to kill US soldiers.

Journalistically, the frustration of my situation was that, with no transport of my own, and unwilling to stray too far from my armoured vehicle, there was no way I could independently authenticate these claims. Throughout my time in Iraq I was always struggling to grasp the whole picture while having only a few pieces of the jigsaw available to me. The latest reports of a supposedly terrorised population certainly fed the Americans' instinctive faith that their cause was right and the Iraqi regime's wrong, and therefore the information had to be treated with some suspicion. However, the evidence in its support seemed to be growing. The survivors of the 'suicide' attack against the 3–7 Cav had also been interrogated. They said they had been given AK-47s, herded into taxis at gunpoint, taken to the battle site and told to charge the tanks or be shot. It was a credible explanation of why they had been willing to carry out such suicidal tactics.

The captain told me that paramilitaries were harassing anything passing down Highway 8, the road skirting Samawah which, in his briefing back in Kuwait, Major General Blount had identified as the US Army's primary logistics route to Baghdad. Mortars and artillery were being located next to hospitals, schools and mosques. When a shell was fired at the Americans, their computers could use its trajectory to calculate the exact spot from where it had come, enabling them to respond immediately and annihilate the danger. Other targets were being identified by Special Forces operating within the urban area. However, to Captain Waldron's frustration, half the strikes he was calling for were being vetoed higher up the command chain as they would be too close to politically sensitive 'no combat zones'.

'I lost a scout this morning to sniper fire and my first sergeant was hit by a mortar yesterday. That means I'm taking it a little bit personally,' he said. 'How am I meant to protect my men when the generals are denying me the ability to bomb enemy positions? I'm meant to be in Karbala by now, and instead we're screwing around here. My sentries were so jumpy last night they were getting nervous about donkeys – and we're in tanks, for God's sake. We don't want to hurt people if we can avoid it, but now it has to be that if you've got a weapon, whatever clothes you're wearing, you've become an Iraqi soldier. You are immediately a credible threat and we can kill you. This rules of engagement crap is making me lose men. Go and write that up so something gets done about it.'

The crew of a tank that had broken down while crossing the desert during the run from the border to Tallil rejoined the unit just before midday. 'It's chaos out there,' its commander, Staff Sergeant Robert Byrd, told the group of soldiers who greeted him. 'Everyone's squeezing onto these little roads, and it's all clogged up. There are tankers and trucks trying to get stuff north and they can't even move. We started driving along the fields on either side, cutting in and out of the traffic when we could. We saw this officer, and he was shouting at us to get back on the road in case there were mines, and we told him: "Sir, if you want us to get up and fight those Iraqis, we got to get moving to our unit." This isn't working at the moment. It's time to stop trying to be Mr Nice Guy. They're bombing us; let's start bombing the hell out of them.'

'We're just taking hits and giving nothing in return,' agreed another tanker. 'Did you hear about those PoWs they killed?' He was talking about the American maintenance crew ambushed near Nasiriyah, the bodies of two of whom had been shown on al-Jazeera, appearing to have been executed with shots to the head. The soldiers were united in the belief that the young missing female soldier, Jessica Lynch, was being gang-raped by her captors. The tanker looked to where I was lying on an adjacent tank, my eyes closed. Thinking I was asleep, he lowered his voice and said, 'We should be killing everything. It's what they deserve. These people have no regard for human life.'

A slow fuse had been lit, one that would burn fiercely during the strain of the coming days. In Kuwait I had witnessed these soldiers regarding themselves as the rescuers of an oppressed people, talking about their simple desire to go home, expressing a trusting belief in the right of Americans to protect their own country from terrorists, laughing and joking while practising taking wounded to medivac helicopters. Now, these essentially decent men were being made savage by fear and anger. It was as if an edifice was slowly falling away. I watched the American soldiers slowly but steadily demonise the enemy, begin to express a hatred of the very sight of the country they had been sent to liberate. Iraqis became merely 'Hajji', properly the respectful term for a Muslim who had made the pilgrimage to Mecca, now slang for the anonymous Arab. Iraqi tactics that were seen as flouting the accepted rules of war – mistreatment of prisoners, violence against their own people – were dwelled upon, and stored up as justification for the death that would be rained down on the country. The process started with those first shots in Tallil, hardened in these days outside Samawah, and ended in Baghdad. By then, the soldiers I had travelled with for so far would shoot with abandon at houses containing weapon caches and smear faeces over the walls of a Republican Guard barracks.

In the M88, Roman and Red were sitting in semi-darkness. Both were reacting to the situation in their own fashion: Roman with barely concealed terror, Red with fury. Roman had hardly spoken since the mortar round the previous day. He was wearing a black balaclava that covered almost his whole face, exposing only a circle around his eyes. 'Isn't this getting to you?' he asked me. 'You don't even have to be here. Why don't you just go home? You can't even shoot at the people shooting at us.'

Roman was an only child, and his family had left St Petersburg when his father was hired by an American-based computer business. The previous October, a few months after he had joined the army and moved to Georgia, his dad had died of cancer, leaving his mother alone in their family home near Chicago. Roman was still waiting to receive his American citizenship. By joining the army the process would be speeded up – it was military policy that a letter of recommendation would be sent with a citizenship application for personnel who had performed well during their term of service. In my time with the US military I met Filipinos, Puerto Ricans, Mexicans, even a British citizen from Glasgow, all of whom hoped their enlistment would help turn their green card into a US passport. For Roman, however, it seemed that a larger price than he had expected was being demanded before he could become a full American.

On the first day after crossing the Iraqi border, while we sat beside Sergeant Whelan's broken-down tank, I watched Roman man the M88's .50-calibre machine gun, smiling to himself as he pretended, like a small child with a toy, to mow down hidden enemies in the darkness. Only a few hours later, in the centre of Objective Liberty, he was instructed to take the gun again after we had been told there were snipers in the area. Sergeant Weaver and Red had been required to jump out to attach a broken-down Bradley to the back. I had looked up through the hatch and saw Roman's knuckles go white as they gripped the gun handles. When he came down he was trembling. He was so nervous that if anything suspicious had even flinched while he had been holding that gun, I have no doubt he would have opened fire immediately, and only afterwards looked to determine if it was civilian or soldier. If I had been in his place, my reaction might not have been all that different. At the time I was huddled at the bottom of the vehicle, not willing to put my head outside the safety of its armoured sides even for a moment.

Sergeant Weaver stuck his head in, on the scrounge for more cigarettes. 'Just one more then I'll stop,' he promised. He tried to reassure Roman that he would be all right. 'Everything's going to be OK. The captain is in control.'

Roman looked disbelievingly at him. 'When I joined the army I thought it would let me see the world,' he said. 'But I didn't want to see this bit.'

Red was playing with an AK-47 found at Tallil which Sergeant Black had presented to the M88 crew. It had been hung in pride of place in the middle of the vehicle, and Red was methodically taking it to pieces and putting it back together again. 'I'm going to get one of these for myself,' he promised. 'If it was up to me, I'd nuke Baghdad and get it over with.'

A first lieutenant, Mike Few, came over looking close to tears. In his hand he had some coffee and a few pieces of chocolate which he placed on the side of the M88. 'I'm having a terrible time,' he said. 'My tank is breaking down. Those guys . . .' he indicated his crew, 'we're not doing well. Please can I call my wife on your phone? You can take these.' I had become slightly cagey about being a portable ring-home service, and had begun to claim that the only number I could ring was the office, but he was distraught and exhausted, so I let him use my phone, telling him there was no need for barter, it was the least I could do to help.

When he had walked off to make his call I turned and saw my three crewmates staring at me disappointedly. 'You have a lot to learn about the army,' Weaver said. 'We're taking that coffee, and from now on you're demanding a higher rate.'

The next day, at the moment when morale was probably at its lowest, the wind returned in its full fury, whipping the sand from the nearby desert and reducing visibility to little further than a hand's length in front of your face. The crew of the M88 had been instructed to pick up spare parts at the central mechanics base, a hastily-set-up structure a few miles from the front line across which were scattered the shells of dozens of wrecked vehicles. The damaged Band Aid had been towed to the site the previous day, and already it was being stripped of useful components, reduced to a bare frame as its workable parts were recycled.

As we toiled our way back towards the company and the first dust clouds beginning to sweep over us, a report came in of mortars being fired at another unit a short distance down the line. We were ordered to turn around. By the time we pulled back into the mechanics HQ, the storm had struck. All the working vehicles were ordered to take sentry duty at the perimeter, their crews taking turns to man the machine guns, squinting into the dust clouds in the hope of spotting a counterattack.

Further north-west, this was exactly what was happening to the 3–7 Cav. Iraqis were emerging from the cover offered by the storm to fire their guns and RPGs (rocket-propelled grenades) at the tanks as they passed through a narrow gully at the top of a hill. Nearer by, Lieutenant Colonel Charlton, the commander of 1st Battalion, was leading groups of Bradleys across the bridge at the centre of Samawah to try to draw the enemy into combat. But in the desert further east, where our M88 was stuck, the four of us inside were staring through the hatches at the sky in something approaching awe as it became a deeper and deeper scarlet, and the sand began to seep through every hole and fissure to cover the metal floor.

'It's like the orange of a burning candle hovering over us,' I said of the sky.

'No,' answered Sergeant Weaver, 'it's too bright for that, too fluorescent. It's like the colour of orange Kool-Aid. Something completely synthetic, nothing that is in any way natural.'

He took first sentry duty, his face covered in a scarf and goggles, the night-vision binoculars held to his eyes to try to detect the thermal shape of any Iraqi soldiers approaching through the haze. A sergeant, Bill Jones, only twenty-one, had sought cover with us. He had been the driver of the M88 before his promotion, which required him to take command of the company's equipment being repaired in the rear. As I struggled to keep the sand off my computer and write my daily story, the three soldiers – only two of them old enough to buy alcohol in the country in whose forces they were fighting – shared cigarettes and talked about the kind of war in which they now found themselves caught.

Bill turned to his friend. 'You bearing up?' he asked.

'I feel like we're getting our ass whipped,' Red answered. 'Wherever I turn there's someone trying to kill me. Damn this country and damn these people.'

'Roger that. Yesterday we were taking up one of the soft-top trucks and suddenly there were three Iraqis shooting at us. I was under that vehicle before I even knew it, and the staff sergeant was right there beside me, as scared as I was. The Bradleys came up and started shooting the hell out of them. We got 'em. Took 'em prisoner. But, God, I thought I was going to piss myself.'

Red tried to wipe some of the sand from his face. 'That's the problem with this pussy army,' he said. 'It's run by retards. We just wait to take hits. The Iraqis took those mechanics prisoner and shot some of them in the head. They start throwing shells at us and we can't even fire back in case it hits civilians. Damn that "hearts and minds" shit. Let's just bomb these bastards. Give as good as we get. Otherwise we're going to lose this war.'

Bill nodded at Roman, who was sitting in the assistant driver's seat staring at the sand clouds outside through a periscope fixed beneath the hatch. 'How you doing?'

'Not too good,' he said. 'I don't want to be here any more.'

'You'll be OK.'

'I don't know if I'll get out of this.'

'Yes, you will. We'll all get through this.'

'I'm not sure. And if we do, what will we be like? Will I be looking over my shoulder whenever I walk down the street, thinking someone's going to shoot me?'

Bill took on the responsibility he knew his rank demanded and tried to reassure the soldier beside him. 'Look, Komlev, you just have to think positively about things. Be brave. Are there places in Chicago where you're frightened to go?'

Roman smiled. 'Yes.'

'So would you not go there? Places in your own city?' He clearly expected to be told that there was nowhere on his home turf Roman would not be willing to visit.

But the Russian was laughing now. 'Of course I wouldn't. They're dangerous!'

All three of them were laughing. 'Fuck this bullshit,' said Red. 'Let's bomb everything and get the hell out of here!'

They began to talk about girls and sport, normal stuff that kids their age were gossiping about in bars everywhere. The challenge was to draw from Roman if he had ever had sex with anyone, and if so how many times. He was being very circumspect about the whole thing. 'I have many girlfriends,' was the most he would emit. 'Everywhere they love me. Too many to mention.' So do you prefer blondes or brunettes, Bill was asking. Big tits, small tits? 'All kinds,' was the simple answer. 'The important thing is they all love me.'

Red was far more open. He began to talk about a dream he

had had the previous night. 'I was dreaming about my girlfriend. She used to work in this little video store and I was walking in and could see her at the counter. She used to close up and put on a porno and we would have sex, and in my dream as I walked in she had this dirty smile on her face. Then Sergeant Weaver woke me up because we had to go and pull some stupid tank out of the mud or something. God I was pissed at him!'

It was getting dark, and the wind was still sending clouds of sand over us. There was thunder in the distance, then lightning. A bolt struck just in front of our vehicle, causing the ground to shake, and lighting up the M88's inside. 'Fuck, I thought that was a mortar,' Bill said. Then it started to rain. I climbed out and stood on the roof to let the thick drops wash the sand and dirt off my face.

Inside, Red was talking about his home town, Toledo, a town with a population of just eleven hundred (or as he said, '1,999 now') in rural Illinois. Roman had taken over sentry duty, and Sergeant Weaver was sitting on the metal floor blinking his eyes to try get rid of the particles of sand. 'We're hillbillies and proud of it,' Red was saying, his voice quiet. 'Where I come from, most people marry the first person who gets them laid. Most don't last. They marry straight out of high school, have a kid, he works his butt off, she starts partying the whole time, running up bills, and then they split.

'My best friend, Kenny, was going out with this girl, Lona. I liked her more than most of the other ones. They'd only been together a few weeks and we were at the mall and Lona and Sarah, the girl I was with, came running over and they were shrieking, "We just saw Kenny going into a jewellery store. We know he's going to buy her a ring. Go in there and help him choose."

'So I go in there and I'm saying, "What the fuck are you doing, man?", trying to persuade him not to do it. But he's like all manly and deep-voiced and saying, "I just got paid and I want to buy a ring." He spent $400 on that shit. We're all driving back drinking a few beers and I hear Kenny in the back, all quiet like, coming over all tender, and saying "Will you marry me?", and I'm just thinking "Oh shit." We got out and Kenny's hugging me and saying, "You got to be my best man." I was like, "Yeah, of course," but there was no way I was going to get involved in that bullshit. Then, as the wedding gets close they're getting all pissed at me. "Where are you? Why aren't you helping?" I was just hiding in my house, though of course I turned up in the end, did the toasts and everything. I had to really, he was my best friend. They didn't even get married in the real courthouse, 'cause it was getting renovated or something. It was in the annexe next door. In a corridor – people were walking right by during the service. The whole thing was such a joke. But you know what really pissed me off? After he bought that ring, a few days later he was asking me to borrow money. I ended up paying for part of that fucking ring. It was bullshit! That's why I joined the army. I didn't want to be in no trailer with some kid and some demanding bitch spending my money. There had to be something more to life than that.'

Most people in Britain or the United States had a far better idea of what was going on in Iraq than the average soldier who was actually there. Without twenty-four-hour news coverage, the troops on the ground were reliant on the occasional snippet of information passed down the line, either directly from one soldier to the next in a process of Chinese whispers, or via the military radio. Inevitably, bad news such as the taking of American prisoners or the extent of fighting around Nasiriyah moved the fastest. Few were aware that some US forces were less than a hundred miles from Baghdad, or that waves of Apache helicopters and B52s had been blitzing the Republican Guard. For most of the time, and for most of the people, knowledge of the battlefield was limited to what they saw around them, and what they were seeing then was a floundering invasion being harassed by a determined and evasive enemy.

The situation for the officers was almost as bad as for their troops. From my arrival at 1st Battalion I was tapped by its intelligence team, deprived as it was of computers or independent information, for details of what was going on in the outside world. Captain Waldron would ask for daily updates about what was actually happening around us in Iraq. I had always been happy to provide them. It may have conflicted with the impartiality required of a reporter, but it would have seemed churlish to refuse when so much assistance was being offered to me. However, I too was becoming increasingly isolated, the scope of my world growing ever smaller. I saw no one but the troops around me. The harsh conditions were slowly eroding my equipment. Originally I had been able to attach my satellite phone to my computer and access the internet. Now the cord had broken. The numbers on my phone were beginning to stick. My laptop had been covered with layers of plastic to try to keep out the sand. It was a constant struggle to recharge its batteries with so few power sources available. Often I was having to write my articles in my notebook, or if it was after dark and lights had been banned, I would have to relay them to my newspaper directly over the phone without notes. My grasp of what was happening across Iraq was becoming limited to what I heard on my shortwave radio – which worked only in bursts – or in little nuggets of information gleaned from the foreign desk in London when I rang in to check if there were any queries on my copy. Unable to file via e-mail, my articles were dictated word by word to copytakers based in Wetherby, just outside Leeds. I had begun my journalistic career as a trainee reporter on that city's evening paper, lived there for two years, and still had a number of friends in the area. It was always slightly surreal calling in and hearing the familiar lilt of the Yorkshire accent, the conversations filled with the reassuring sound of phrases like 'Thanks, love' and 'Be careful out there,' while around me I could see only the shapes of tanks and tired soldiers.

So the men of the Black Knights lived in their own little bubble, often not even seeing anyone from the rest of the battalion as they stayed in their assigned sector on the perimeter. But occasionally they would come into contact with other bubbles, other self-sufficient units carrying out their own orders, allowing them a glimpse of troops as confused about the general situation and nervous about what was really happening as they were. Everyone was just performing his assigned tasks in the production line of war, in the hope that concentrating on work would push away the worries, and trusting that someone out there had control of the overall picture.

One such moment of amalgamation came on Wednesday, 26 March, the fourth day since the company had been redirected to Samawah. The storm was still blowing, though less fiercely than the previous night, and the sky was no longer a reddish orange, but a more comprehensible pale yellow. That afternoon the order had been given that it was finally time to move forward again. Other units were to take over the responsibility of keeping the roads in the area free of paramilitary attacks. The vehicles of 1st Battalion were to be loaded onto a convoy of HETs, the heavy equipment transport trucks designed to ferry tanks and Bradleys long distances. I was placed with Roman in one lorry, Sergeant Weaver and Red in front of us in another. As I squeezed onto the bench at the back of the cab the driver and co-driver were bickering about food.

'I can't believe you've done it again,' said the driver, his skin creased by eczema. He was holding an opened MRE. 'You've got to stop searching out the M&Ms and leaving the rest.'

'I was hungry!' said his partner, a lanky black dude from New York. 'A guy's got to eat.' In a box between them were dozens of food packages, their sides slit open and the little meal packets spilling out. 'I get hungry. You know that. The chocolate keeps me awake.'

I asked them where they had driven from. 'Somewhere up there,' said the driver. And where were we going? 'Back up this road.' But where to? 'I don't know. We just drive until they tell us to stop. Then we come back to some other piece of desert, pick up some more stuff, and drive back up there again to another piece of desert. Up and down this fucking road all the fucking time. Don't know where we're going, don't know where we come from. Just drive through this fucking storm with this asshole taking all the best bits of food before I can get my hands on them.'

The black guy turned to me and shrugged. He lifted his left hand and brought the fingers up and down against the thumb to mimic a nagging mouth.

'Up and down this road,' the driver was continuing. 'No one tells me where we're going, what we're doing. Just drive, drive, drive. Waiting for someone to either attack us or for someone else to tell us that we can get some sleep.' There had been a sniper the previous day, firing at the tyres of one of the lorries. Everyone had been told to be prepared for the possibility of similar incidents during our journey. In the back, Roman and I leaned on our kitbags and grabbed some sleep. When I woke the storm had not abated, but it was dark outside. The tarmacked highway had thinned to the point that it was barely wide enough to take the lorry's wheels. The black guy was asleep. The driver was still talking, telling a story about his father. No one had been listening.

'He was in Normandy, you know. Parachuted in and they caught hell. Makes this look like a walk in the park. He landed miles from where they were meant to and he couldn't find any of his unit. Ended up trapped in a foxhole with two other Americans, surrounded by the SS. They were shooting and throwing grenades and the two other guys got killed. My dad was hit and surrendered and was taken to a PoW camp. It was tough on him. He lost both his legs because they never gave him good medical care for his injuries. He died when I was a teenager. It was the strangest thing. It was the middle of the night, I was in bed in the room I shared with my brother, and I heard my dad's wheelchair and the bathroom door open. The next morning I was wakened by my mother screaming. He'd died while using the little urinal the social services had given him. He was laid out on the bathroom floor. The strange thing about it was that we had all heard him go in there the night before. My mom, my brother, me, all of us had been awake. It wasn't the noise; he'd been quiet. I think we'd all just somehow sensed something important was happening. That we weren't going to hear that wheelchair no more.'

I slept again. A few hours later I woke once more. The two in the front were arguing about food.

'If you're hungry, eat one of the meals. Leave the chocolate alone,' the driver was saying.

'But I like chocolate,' his companion snapped back.

After midnight we received the order to stop and the tanks were driven off the back of the lorries. 'Your turn to drive,' the driver said to the black guy. 'There's another load somewhere behind us that we've got to pick up.' And then to himself: 'Up and down this fucking road, all we ever do. Up and down this fucking road.' The black soldier helped me carry my kitbag down from the cab. 'I'm gonna take that food when he's sleeping,' he whispered to me with a conspiratorial smile. 'A guy's gotta eat.'

The next morning, Thursday, the air was still and a blue sky had reappeared above us. The company drove its vehicles the last part of the way to the designated regrouping area, a stretch of land in the middle of the desert, 120 miles from Samawah, just north-west of Najaf and due south of Karbala. It was known as Dragon 4, and it was here that 1st Battalion would finally hook up with the units of 2nd Brigade that it would now be fighting alongside. The open countryside appeared starkly beautiful after the grim urban environment of the previous days. Plains covered by thick brown shrubs spread to the horizon. The road climbed steeply to the summit of a small rock verge. Once on top there was just sand and desert, and we headed away from the road and across the dunes. It looked like the surroundings at the camp back in Kuwait, and there was something reassuringly familiar about that. Something that made me feel safe.

Dragon 4 had been placed far from any settlements in the hope that the Iraqis would not realise where the forces of the American army were gathering. After crossing the border, 2nd Brigade had engaged with Fedayeen around Najaf before being ordered further north to establish the base. It had been stationed there ever since, the soldiers sent out on operations to continue the sparring with the region's paramilitaries, and its commanders waiting for the reinforcements they had been promised to finally catch up with them. A small airstrip and a field hospital had been built. Vehicle parts, ammunition, food and water were being stockpiled in preparation for the advance on Baghdad. The supplies were certainly needed. At least two of the Black Knights' tanks had broken down, as had the M88. Its engine had blown just east of the new encampment spot, the result of days spent dragging immobilised tanks and Bradleys across southern Iraq. We had been towed the final part of the way, and the mechanics were now busy trying to mend the problem. Sergeant Weaver was distraught. 'I should've looked after you better,' he was saying as he carried out an oil change. 'Come on now, let's get you up and running again. Don't fail me now.'

The soldiers knew that the invasion was behind schedule, yet now they were where they had always been meant to be, and that bolstered their spirits. In the previous days few had managed more than four hours sleep at a stretch. There had been cases of radio operators being discovered asleep at their posts. Now everybody knew they had time to recover. Word spread that hot food was being served that evening. At Bulldog II, Sergeant Whelan was brewing coffee. His crew was planning to put together a makeshift shower hung over the tank barrel. A bucket would have holes punched in it, and a camouflage sleeping sheet would be strung up underneath.

There was still some talk of battle. The Marines had nearly reached their regrouping positions to the east of the Euphrates, as most of the 3rd Infantry Division had to the west. There was concern at intelligence that the Iraqis had Russian-built AT14 Cornets, a modern handheld missile launcher that could hurt an Abrams tank, and which had supposedly been banned under United Nations sanctions on arms sales. President Bush had ordered thirty thousand more troops to the Gulf as reinforcements. But mostly people chatted about where they would go when it was all over. Some planned debauched times in the Philippines. Doc wanted to take a Disney-themed cruise with his wife. Red simply wanted to spend two days in a bathtub, just 'getting all this dirt off me and working my way through a crate of beer'. I began to relax. I poured bottles of water over me to try to clean off some of the sand that had become engrained on my skin. I washed my hair and put on clean clothes under my biochemical suit. I felt a million times better, almost human again and positively cheerful.

In the calm of the camp, the melodic clip of Eminem being pumped out by a portable CD player somewhere in the distance, the fear and franticness of the preceding few days seemed left behind with the previous night's journey through the gusting sand. Sergeant Whelan was shaving by his tank. He turned and, seeing me, grinned his wolfish grin as he shook his razor in the water. 'Don't want any stubble breaking the seal when I have to use that gasmask,' he said. The sun may have been shining, but he knew a new storm still waited ahead.

The following three days of downtime at Dragon 4 were among the most pleasant of the entire campaign. The hot food did appear that first night, and each evening afterwards, and although it was only C-rations – the same ones at which I had turned up my nose in Kuwait – it tasted good after a diet solely of MREs. The company spent their time preparing themselves and their vehicles for the next instruction to move forward. Later, I would be told that there never had been a 'tactical pause' as Major General Blount had outlined while detailing the American plan. However, that time recuperating in the peace of the desert certainly felt like one. Clothes were washed. Tracks were replaced on tanks. The fact that the M88 was immobile at least meant it could not be press-ganged into service. Instead the crew worked on regaining their strength, and with it much of their spirit. Sergeant Weaver was still bumming cigarettes whenever he could, but the anxiety had started to disappear from his eyes, even if the memory of what he had experienced had not gone with it.

At one point I overheard him talking to another sergeant. 'I heard people are saying that I was all set to abandon the M88 when those mortars came in at Samawah,' he said. 'You know that isn't true. I was in control of what was happening. You know I wasn't scared.'

'Don't worry,' he was told. 'Everybody knows you did a good job. Few have done more work in this company than you. It's recognised and appreciated. Relax. No one thinks you panicked.'

Doc and his crew holed up in the back of the new medic van watching DVDs. With the new vehicle had come a new driver, the previous one having requested a transfer after becoming convinced Doc and Frankie were bad luck following the crossfire at Tallil and the hit from the mortar round. The new crewmember, Sergeant Brian Bache, was a true Southern boy from Louisiana, a dip of chewing tobacco permanently pressed in his mouth, an empty water bottle by his side into which he would spit the juices. At six feet five inches he was known simply as Big Sergeant B. He was thirty-six, a bachelor, and as a result had the money to spend on the toys he wanted. A $40,000 Harley-Davidson was being custom-made for him back in the States – he often sported a black T-shirt bearing the slogan of the Outlaws, a motorcycle gang infamous for its scraps with the Hell's Angels – and he had brought with him a far bigger portable DVD player than the pocket-sized one Doc carried. This allowed a little crowd to gather in the back of the new Band Aid and still be able to see the entertainment. The majority were the Disney films Doc loved, but one afternoon I came across him standing outside his vehicle looking slightly strained. 'Just saw *Platoon*,' he said. It had been one of Sergeant B's. 'It was a mistake. All they do is spend their whole time calling for a medic.'

Red was busy trading his pornographic magazines with other crews. The captain was pleased to be back at the front of the American army. Sergeant Pyle, the tank commander I had met on my first full day at the camp in Kuwait, was parked alongside the M88 and occupied himself by itemising the rounds of ammunition his crew needed. Even Sergeant Whelan's temper had cooled. He too had a new driver, and I would pass his crew sunning themselves in deckchairs beside their vehicle.

Only Roman still seemed nervous. Ever since those mortars outside Samawah, he had been shrinking ever further into his shell. Not one of life's great talkers, he was now saying even less, his Russian accent noticeably stronger when he did. I spotted Weaver taking him for walks to try to buoy up his morale. When it became clear the M88 would not be going anywhere for a while, the original plan had been that Red and the sergeant would stay behind and look after it. Roman would join Stazny on the Bradley maintenance vehicle under its commander, Staff Sergeant Gary Harrison. But the positions had been changed. Red would be going forward with the rest of us, while Roman would stay behind. I could only presume that the decision had been made in the hope it would provide Roman with some space in which to regain his confidence. When I talked with him, however, he was uncomfortable about the change of plan. 'I'm not happy with it,' he said. 'It means me and Sergeant Weaver will be alone when we drive the M88 to Baghdad to catch up with the rest of you. Who'll protect us from the Iraqis?'

The days were not entirely without incident. On the Friday there was a gas scare after two Iraqi chemical tankers were discovered nearby and the order was given for them to be destroyed. Too late someone realised they might have been containing biochemical weapons, and with the wind blowing our way we were all instructed to dress at MOPP 4. This was the highest level of protection against gas, in which not only the suits but masks and plastic boots and gloves were worn. The thermometer showed it was 103 degrees outside, and there was considerable cursing at the officer who had ordered the tankers' destruction as everyone hid in the bottom of their vehicles with their kit on and the hatches shut.

The prospect of a chemical attack was still the thing that, above all else, instilled genuine fear. Once gas had been released, no degree of combat skill could enable anyone to avoid it. All you could do was pray there was time to get your protective kit on or antidotes administered. No soldiers doubted that Saddam Hussein had arsenals of weapons of mass destruction. They had been told so by their superiors. It was primarily to remove them that the US military had been ordered to invade his country. The stockpiles of gas had to exist, the soldiers reasoned, otherwise they would not be fighting there.

The only question was when such weapons might be unleashed, and discussing the possible answers to that was one of the most popular ways to kill time. The battalion's intelligence officer told me it had been considered unlikely that they would be used in the far south of the country in the first days of the war, when Saddam was thought still to be hoping French and Russian pressure might enforce a ceasefire. Nor was it felt they would be used near Baghdad, where the majority of people were Sunni, the Muslim community that made up only a third of the country's population but that included Saddam and his most fervent supporters. Instead, it was believed the Iraqi President had drawn a 'red line' somewhere near Karbala, the most northern of the primarily Shia cities, and told the local Republican Guard commanders that once it was breached they were free to use whatever means they had at their disposal to stop the invaders. The suspected location of that line would be crossed in the next advance. It was generally agreed that it would be then that we were most likely to get 'slimed'.

In the M88, dressed at MOPP 4, we had wrapped fresh biochemical detection tape around our limbs and sat looking at its dull brown surface to see if any pink spots started to appear. The all-clear was called, then the wind shifted and everyone was told to completely suit up once more.

At dusk the chow truck arrived. I perched on the digger at the front of the M88 to eat my meal and watched the sun set, its dying rays turning the sand a pale pink as the day drew to a close. Red sat beside me. 'Know any English girls we can call on that phone of yours?' he asked. 'Let's talk to some English girls. Go on, let's call them.'

For some reason I thought of my sister, an English literature student in her second year at university. Once she was over her surprise, I passed the phone to Red. I was amused by how deferential he became. The dirty-mouthed youth I knew was replaced by an imitation of a Southern gentleman. 'Yes, ma'am,' he replied when my sister asked if he was OK. 'Thank you, ma'am. Pleasure talking to you.'

He flashed a saucy smile when he had finished. 'God, she sounds hot,' he said. 'Is she hot? Have you got a hot sister? I bet you do! I think she liked me. I really do. But then again, I am one sexy motherfucker. Let's call some more English girls.'

We watched the sun disappear. 'Can I tell you something?' Red asked. 'But you can't tell anyone else. I don't like any hassle.'

Go on, I said. I wouldn't tell anyone else.

'It's my birthday today. My birthday and I'm stuck here in this fucking desert. Can't even get a drink. Ain't that a son of a bitch?'

He paused to pull on one of his menthol cigarettes. 'Twenty-two. Starting to get old.'

Behind us, MLRS were being fired towards Karbala. They were the most striking to watch of all the American weaponry, the glow of the rocket engines rising at a lazy pace until they reached the edge of the outer atmosphere. Then the secondary thrusters would kick in, sending them faster than the eye could see onward into the far distance.

FIVE

'There Goes Freedom'

Saturday, 29 March–Wednesday, 2 April

Behind the Black Knights' position the colonel had set up his battalion headquarters, a lonely tent marooned at the centre of a sea of armoured vehicles. It was time for me to try to get a grasp on what was actually going on during this invasion. Making my way down the slope of the dune that ran between the two encampments, I came across many of the officers I had met during those first days in the Kuwaiti desert. Major Fredrick – Major Fred, as all referred to him – broke into a grin when he saw me. 'Ahh, roomie,' he said. 'Tough times, tough times, and they're only going to get tougher. Still pleased you came?'

The officers' talk, like that of the men who served under them, focused on the bitterness of the resistance they had experienced. For the officers, the barbarism of the opposition had become a tenet of the war, something unnatural and wrong that required a ratcheting-up of the ruthlessness with which it was met. News was filtering through of a suicide car-bomb attack on an army checkpoint in Najaf, the first such bombing in the campaign. Four American soldiers had been killed when a man drove up in an orange taxi and detonated a device as the troops came forward to search his vehicle. Walking to battalion headquarters was like entering a hornets' nest that had been stirred by a stick; indignation buzzed all around me.

When not rhapsodising to me about obscure 1970s English punk bands, Captain James Montgomery, a twenty-eight-year-old officer with a thin, pointed face who coordinated the battalion's artillery and mortar fire, had talked at length in Kuwait about the importance to Americans of believing they were fighting in a civilised manner and in a justified cause. 'People want to know they're doing what is right,' he had concluded. Now he wanted to discuss the wickedness that he believed his men had witnessed. 'The values of the American soldier are ultimately humanitarian. The American soldier wants to believe that if he's going to kill someone, he's doing the correct thing. But we can't abide by the original rules any more. These people are trying to create a chaotic environment. We were on a recon mission driving through crowds of people, throwing MREs to kids, and then minutes later, when we got under a bridge, we were being fired upon. Women and children were running. They didn't care about civilians. They were happy for their own people to be killed.'

Winning the war on the battlefield was becoming more important than the one for 'hearts and minds'. 'At the start we thought it was going to be a cakewalk,' said Captain Douglas Philippone, the commander of Baker Company. 'The orders were very much to try not to shoot. But this is no parade. We've got to do everything in our power to stop what's happening. In Tallil, we had cars of armed men in civilian clothes driving straight towards us. We fired in front of them and they sped off. We should have toasted them, there and then. These people have been ramming buses into our vehicles. There have been Iraqis attacking tanks in human waves. It's not a normal battlefield situation. These guys have no idea what an Abrams can do. A handgun, even a grenade, isn't going to hurt a tank. They're complete fanatics. They're going to do anything they can to try and kill us, and we've got to do everything we can to protect ourselves.'

The colonel appeared from the tent. He pulled a cigar from a little metal case and clasped it between his lips. We walked to his

Bradley, where he unfurled a map. 'When they came at us in these bullshit vehicles, it was clear these guys were not going to give up easily. Now we're going to get super aggressive and kill them all.'

First, he explained, the plan was for the battalion to engage the paramilitaries fighting around Najaf. 'Like we found out at Samawah, the city proved to be an unexpectedly difficult situation. The 3–7 Cav went in and got attacked, so they withdrew. 2nd Brigade went in and hit hard. They found one of the training camps located on the outskirts of the city and obliterated it. When our forces went in the enemy jumped into bunkers made from dirt and sandbags. Our tanks annihilated them. When they finally surrendered there were just twenty left out of a thousand. These people are not well trained and they're dying in bushels. Those who were interrogated told us they were being terrorised into serving in these Saddam Fedayeen brigades. Their families were being taken to Hillah [a city to the north, on the east bank of the Euphrates] and held as hostages to make sure they fought.'

The next day the battalion was to be involved in an attack on another Fedayeen base amid quarry pits to our north. The area was being used as an observation post to coordinate paramilitary attacks on the American forces. 'We're expecting a far smaller number of enemy soldiers than at the training camp in Najaf, but resistance should still be significant,' I was told. 'These paramilitaries are a problem because they're slowing down our ability to muster forces in this area, so they have to be taken out quickly. They're causing few actual casualties, but they're impeding the drive towards our main objective, which is Baghdad.'

Once the quarry pits had been cleared, the battalion would join other units from 2nd Brigade in assaulting a Republican Guard garrison stationed at a bridge over the Euphrates. As well as dealing with the paramilitaries in the area, the US Army was trying to remove as many elements of Saddam's armoured units as possible ahead of the order to launch the attack towards Baghdad.

'This is Objective Murray,' the colonel said, indicating a small town a short distance to the north-east. 'Not to be reported in the media, but this operation is effectively a feint. We not only want to engage the garrison, we're also trying to give the impression we're sending a considerable force across the river so they decide to send out reinforcements. That should hopefully pull other Republican Guard units stationed further north into the open so we can whack them from the air.'

Through a number of similar manoeuvres to be conducted throughout the surrounding area by thousands of soldiers over the next few days, the United States Army was 'setting the shape of the battlefield', the colonel told me. The strength and morale of the Republican Guard were to be weakened, and the Fedayeen prevented from posing any further significant threat. The American units would then regroup, adopt attack positions just south of Karbala and, in a rapid advance, try to break through Saddam's lines of defence and take the fight into the very outskirts of the Iraqi capital.

'We don't intend to get caught up in street-fighting in Karbala itself,' it was explained to me. 'Instead the main body of the American force will pass through the Karbala Gap, where there are few buildings to slow us down.' He pointed on his map to a thin strip of land between the city and Lake Buhayrat to its west. 'By funnelling our troops through here, it'll enable us to circumvent the main part of the city and catch the enemy by surprise. We'll cross the Euphrates, and then move fast towards the capital. Other units can later concentrate on subduing Karbala and mopping up the Iraqi forces stationed around it.'

His hand skirted a road that led from the city, across the river, and into the south of Baghdad where the two major roads, Highways 8 and 1, crossed. 'This is the route we'll take, and this junction, that's Objective Saints. It's the first target to be taken in Baghdad. If you control it, you control the two main roads to the south of the country. It's this battalion's responsibility to take this objective. We'll be the first in, open up a safe zone for other 2nd

Brigade units, and then we'll hold it as long as required.' He traced a circle around the area underneath the city with his finger. 'While we deal with any counterattacks that may be launched, elements from the rest of the brigade will sweep back down from Saints into this area and attack the Republican Guard units stationed in it from the rear.' These Iraqi units had been arrayed to protect Baghdad as part of the 'ring of steel' Saddam had ordered to be established around his capital, and therefore would be expecting to oppose forces coming at them from the south. 'There's been enough of this bullshit fighting,' the colonel said. 'In the next few days we intend to make clear who controls this war.'

Such was the mindset among the officer class, and it had a warm reception from the men when they grasped what would now be permitted. Maybe it sprang from the conviction held by high command ever since the Vietnam War that people back in the US would not tolerate military operations that resulted in American bodybags; perhaps it was simply the result of a determination by those in charge to do everything possible to protect their soldiers. Whatever the cause, the criteria for the use of deadly force had clearly been loosened. There would be no further instances of soldiers waiting for armed Iraqis in civilian clothes to start shooting before they could be shot at. The experiences of the previous days had been processed, and the definition of what constituted a 'perceived threat' hardened accordingly. Division command had ruled that any vehicle that did not stop at a road-block after a warning shot had been fired was to be treated as hostile. As the colonel explained it, 'If you see a car screaming past with young men in the back then you can be 99 per cent sure it's enemy.'

The problem was that no one had explained these new rules to the Iraqi drivers, many of whom reacted to warning shots by speeding up rather than stopping to see if they were fired at a second time. Across the country there were many deaths at road-blocks in the coming days.

Joe, the *Stars and Stripes* photographer who was now camped near where the Black Knights were based, had noted the new ferocity in the men around us. 'It's basically shoot anything that moves,' was his take on the general mood. 'There's no more trying to distinguish if it's an enemy or not. If it's on the streets, then it's an enemy. People aren't talking any more about what to do with PoWs, as there aren't going to be any.'

He had clearly been shaken by what he had witnessed, and had still not fully recovered from almost being hit at Tallil. The scouts with whom he had been placed were among the most exposed of all the soldiers. Often out in the lead, they drove in Humvees with little armour to protect them, a machine gun and grenade-launcher mounted on the top as their only fixed weapons. It was a role that best suited the confidence of youth, and few scouts were older than twenty-three, most considerably younger. The atmosphere in their encampment was similar to how I pictured a snowboarders' convention. Rap music played over a stereo, and soldiers would high-five each other in greeting then clutch a fist to their chest as a sign of respect. As I walked over to see Joe I could hear one of them, his pockets bulging with grenade shells, his hair cut into a flat-topped Mohican, finishing his account of an engagement. 'It was wild, dude,' he concluded, as if it had just been some particularly exhilarating black run. I doubted whether I could willingly have joined them on such engagements. Joe was beginning to suspect he might not be able to either. 'It's like when I'm out there, I think, "What am I doing?" Then I get back, get it together, and I hear the order to go out again and I'm like, "OK," and it all starts all over again. I don't know how much longer I can cope with this.'

That night I sat on the front of Sergeant Whelan's tank and we took turns peering through his night-vision goggles at the horizon to our north, where waves of American bombers were pulverising the Republican Guard. The United States had complete control of the skies, as the hundred or so fighter planes in the Iraqi fleet had been hidden in the west of the country rather than being sent up against a technologically and numerically superior enemy. With bombing runs unhindered, around 70 per cent were by this point being targeted at the fortified positions occupied by Saddam Hussein's elite forces.

Through the night sights everything was a muddy shade of green, and the thermal shape of anti-aircraft gun tracers appeared as luminous specks rising into the sky. Occasionally there would be a white flash as one of the bombs exploded. Some of the munitions the Americans were dropping onto the area weighed as much as 8500 pounds, causing a ring of destruction that spread for hundreds of yards. 'I don't know why they bother firing back at us,' said Whelan. 'Those jets are at something like twenty thousand feet. They're long gone before the bullets could even reach them.' In the jargon of Major General Blount, this process had been called 'softening up', the operational phase ahead of the ground assault which would break the Iraqi forces' strength and willpower. I remembered the terror those few Iraqi mortar rounds had caused me, and tried to conceive what it must be like for anyone caught at the receiving end of such a bombardment.

Yet my attempt at empathy was mixed with relief at witnessing so much destruction. We were going in that direction, and it was the Iraqi soldiers dying among those bombs who might otherwise have fought the army I was with. It was a contradiction that would struggle within me over the next few days. There was the memory of the bodies of the young men scattered around Nasiriyah and the knowledge that each had his own family, friends, dreams for the future. Then there was the relief that they had died, killed before they had the chance to shoot at me.

It was with the same eyes that I began to look at the men around me. In their guns and tanks I saw the safety provided by the company's efficiency as a killing machine. But then there was the horror at seeing the ease with which they erased lives. Sometimes in the coming days of bloodshed I would view them with something approaching fear as the number of Iraqis the company killed grew, first by ones and twos, then by the dozen, until finally they could only be recorded in the hundreds. I struggled to reconcile this with the banter over breakfast, or the talk of wives and children they loved and missed back home. Of course I had known it was a soldier's profession to kill people, and that these men had been trained to be among the best in the world at doing so. I knew of the cruelties of Saddam Hussein's regime. However, this was not something I was watching on the television, not some graphic of coloured columns illustrating the number of dead. In my time in Iraq, the human cost of the United States's military superiority unfolded in front of my eyes. These men with whom I watched Disney cartoons, argued the merits of 'soccer' over American football, discussed their girlfriends' fine arses – they killed people, lots of people.

I contemplated what it must be like for the Iraqi soldiers as they waited for the Americans to sweep upon them. Whatever the reason they were there – fear of retribution being wreaked on their families, patriotic or religious fervour – few held more than the most basic machine gun or a Soviet-era RPG-launcher with which to defend themselves, a sand berm or foxhole ringed with sandbags their only protection against the approaching army. Their staple food would have been dirty rice and bread. They would know nothing about what was going on around them, radios having been banned to keep them from hearing negative reports about the war's progress.

I imagined the Iraqi conscript standing at his sandbagged post, the cheap polyester of his uniform rubbing against his neck, reaching up one last time to check that his dark green helmet had been pulled down towards his eyes as he heard the sound of the enemy's armour in the distance. He would look to the left and right to see who was still holding the line and who had run. Then he would witness the awesome power of the American tank, its barrel spitting high-explosive shells or armour-cutting rounds, the noise alone so ferocious it had left me flinching, the flash of detonation blinding anyone who stared into it. Then as the Iraqis opened fire they would watch impotently as their bullets and grenades bounced harmlessly off the machines that were passing with barely a pause over their pitifully exposed defences. Max Hastings would write a piece in the *Sunday Telegraph* in which he compared events in the Persian Gulf to the wars of fourteenth-century Europe, when the 'so-called flower of chivalry hacked down the peasantry on the battlefield, secure in the knowledge that they were themselves impregnable in plate armour, unless they were unfortunate enough to be unhorsed, and killed by a dagger beneath their visors'. From my vantage point, it seemed a valid comparison to the events I was witnessing.

I wondered at the bravery of the man lying in a foxhole pretending to be dead, a tactic frequently adopted by the Iraqi forces. His sole aim was to draw a tank closer so he could fire off a few rounds at the American who peered down at his body before he was caught in the blaze of vengeance and lay, dead for real now, in the same foxhole where moments before he had been playacting his demise. It seemed to me almost indecent to be charging at men armed only with small arms in a machine that had sides so thick that barely a tank in the entire Persian Gulf had a round powerful enough to pierce it. 'Dying in bushels', the colonel had said. For the first time I began to dwell on what, if anything, could possibly justify the brutality unleashed by those who had ordered the American troops to invade. And the shooting and the corpses littering the roadside had scarcely yet even begun.

No one in the camp seemed to share any of my misgivings, or if they did, no one gave voice to them. Everyone was focused on the concerns of everyday life: the heat, the dirt, the sand, the occasional possibility of danger. Only once, the day before we again moved north, did I hear a soldier asking the same questions. Everyone else had gone to sleep and I was staring towards Karbala, smoking a cigarette at the front of the M88, when Sergeant Pyle came and joined me, feeding me from his own packet when mine ran out. 'Do you think about them?' he asked. 'About what goes through their minds? How they view us? I think about it a lot. About what it must be like knowing we're coming and there's nothing they can do about it. How they must sit and talk like we do, but they must know they can only face defeat.'

Sergeant Pyle had the most calming of all voices, a gentle mid-western drawl that purred out of his mouth. 'I read history and study the past. I've read about Hitler and Stalin. I know the German people were better off without Hitler. That's why we're here, to stop anyone threatening these people again. Something good will come out of all this fighting.'

It seemed as if he felt he needed to explain something. 'I've never wanted to be anything other than a tanker,' he said. 'When I was a kid I dreamt of it, and then, when I was in my twenties, I got sidetracked, ended up in this job that I didn't really want to do in order to support a wife and my two girls.' I asked him what the job was. He laughed. 'Ah, that's my secret,' he said. 'Only one other person in the company knows what I did. You see, it's not really important what I did before. What's important is that I gave it up and did what I always wanted: became part of a tank crew. It meant I ended up separating from my wife – but I was now a tanker.

'It's my job to fight them. It's what I've been trained to do.' He looked to where we could just make out the fires burning on the horizon. 'And you know, I enjoy commanding that tank. It's given me as much satisfaction as I'd always imagined. It's how I will have spent my life. It's what I believe I was put on this earth to do.'

That morning the chaplain had made his rounds. It was the first time I had talked to him since Kuwait, and he was frustrated that, for safety reasons, his unarmoured Humvee was not being allowed close enough to the fighting for him to support his congre-gation on the battlefield. He took out his little portable altar, set it up in the shadow cast by the M88 and conducted a service for the Black Knights, a service everyone knew would be the last before the resumption of fighting. Around a dozen men attended, among them the captain and Sergeant Swinney. Doc had mentioned to me that, after the events of the previous few days, he was now planning to join the group the chaplain intended to baptise in the Euphrates.

Prayers were said for the injured and for the future safety of us all. The chaplain reassured the soldiers that they were on the side of right. He illustrated this by telling a story that was circulating about some American PoWs who had reportedly been hanged in the centre of Baghdad in an execution shown on national television. The story was untrue – I had checked with the office in London – but it had spread throughout the battalion. As the chaplain flicked through the pages of his hymn book, six MLRS missiles were fired a short distance behind us, their smoke trails clearly visible against the clear sky. He stopped and stared at them, as we all did. Pointing, he shouted: 'There goes freedom!'

And then, surrounded by an army fighting its way through the Middle East, we were led in a rendition of 'Onward Christian Soldiers'.

It was not yet light on Sunday, 30 March when the order was given to move out from Dragon 4 and join the fighting around Najaf. The immobile M88 was to be left behind. My new home would be the 'CP', the company's mobile command post, which travelled with the tanks to act as the focus for radio traffic and to relay orders from the battalion HQ and supply trucks stationed to the rear of the combat vehicles. The vehicle was an M113, an armoured personnel carrier that moved on tank tracks and was based on a design that predated the Vietnam War. On its left wall was a giant radio, and two handsets had been slung on a piece of fraying string tied across its front. Benches covered by thin green cushions had been bolted down on both sides. A black seat was located between them under a hatch, and standing on it provided access to the sole fixed weapon, a .50-calibre machine gun attached to the roof. The area in which the soldiers lived was less than two-thirds the space of the M88. My position was on the left-hand bench, and it was there that I would sit and write my newspaper articles. At the back a section of the ceiling was hinged so it could swing open, and whenever possible I would poke my head through the gap to see what was going on. My main worry was the state of the M113's armour. By the standards of the American army it was flimsy, not strong enough to stop an RPG or even a .50-calibre machine-gun bullet. As my spot on the left-hand side placed me directly beside the fuel tank, I knew that if we were hit things could quickly become very nasty.

The vehicle's crew had consisted of Staff Sergeants Trey Black and Ray Simon. Trey was in command and also manned the gun. After First Sergeant Burt had been hit by the mortar shell he had temporarily taken over the role of most senior NCO in the company, guiding the Black Knights during the days around Samawah. Ray was the driver. A veteran of the previous Gulf War, at thirty-eight his time in the army was drawing to a close. It was only nine months until his second ten-year term of service came to an end, and for the first time since he was a teenager he would be a civilian.

That morning, as I jumped into the back of the vehicle there was also an unfamiliar figure waiting inside. José Rosa had travelled throughout the night from a unit based to the south after being ordered to change battalions and permanently fill the post that had been left vacant due to Burt's injuries. These were my companions, and we would travel all the way to the centre of Saddam's regime together.

The sun had just risen from the horizon by the time the company reached the edge of the quarry pits, its rays struggling to break through the slight mist which had yet to be burnt off by the heat of the day. Tanks were to our right, and in front of us Bradleys stretched forward like fingers on a hand. Behind was the new medic track, Doc in the hatch clutching his M-16 to his shoulder in case anyone did try to shoot at him again. Following them was the remaining company maintenance vehicle, formerly the Bradley repair van, in which Red was now riding. Everyone was moving very slowly. The land was little more than a desert, the occasional low-lying shrub breaking the barren surface, over which were scattered small outcrops of rock. It was near here that the city had once stood where Noah was meant to have built his ark. Looking around, I could see why everyone would have thought him crazy. We passed a rundown farmhouse. Its walls had been made from adobe bricks and the roof from straw under which plastic sheets had been strung. Brittle plastic tubes ran across the plain to provide water siphoned from a well to small patches of green crops, half a dozen of which – none bigger than thirty yards square – spread on either side. A number of the hoses had been crushed by the vehicles advancing in front, leaving a small trickle of water seeping through the broken sides to disappear into the sand.

There were more houses now, five or six of them stretched in a loose line, each as impoverished as the first. Something moved ahead and I peered through my binoculars. Outside one of the buildings stood a girl holding a stick onto which had been tied a tattered piece of white cloth. It was blowing in the slight breeze. She was little more than fifteen years old, her long dark hair also moving in the cool wind, her pale red robe caked in dust. Squatting on the ground was her family. An older woman in a black head-dress clutched a baby to her hip. Four other children were gathered around her. The youngest, who was aged about three, was crying. In the entrance to the house was a man, also squatting, staring silently at the American forces. I began to make out more families. All were huddled close together, their backs pressed against the low walls of their properties. Each held their own makeshift white flag above them for protection. None, except for that first girl, was standing. All their clothes were filthy.

'This is Indian country,' said Major Fred over the radio. 'Watch yourselves.'

One of the infantry units stationed in a Bradley had dismounted, and two soldiers were pushing open the front door of a house while the rest lay on the ground ready to offer covering fire. The infantrymen were soon running between the farms – or rather lumbering, weighed down by the quantities of ammunition and weaponry they were obliged to carry – as they searched the buildings.

A puff of smoke and sand was thrown up in the far distance on our right. A mortar had exploded near an adjacent company. 'That wasn't one of our shells,' Trey said. On the radio a voice reported that two men with AK-47s had been spotted. It was Sergeant Pyle. There was the sound of machine-gun fire. 'They're dead now,' came the same voice through the loudspeaker.

Things were moving faster now. The tanks of the Black Knights were advancing in some sort of attack formation. A white pick-up truck was spotted, its passenger armed with a rocket launcher. It was destroyed with a shell. The captain was barking orders, identifying targets and instructing his men of potential dangers ahead. A small lorry drove up and around thirty paramilitaries jumped out of it, firing machine guns as they ran at the attacking tanks. They too were cut down. There was some American mortar fire. To our rear I saw two shepherds standing with their malnourished flock, a white flag over their heads, seemingly unaffected by the fighting. It struck me how much the impoverished farmhouses in the desert, the shepherds in their flowing robes and headdresses, a barn made from sticks held together with string, reminded me of the nativity scenes I had seen at primary school. However, it was a message of retribution, not forgiveness, which hung over us as the American armoured vehicles climbed over the lip of one of the collapsed quarry pits and the hamlet disappeared from my sight.

It was nearing mid-morning and it was becoming very hot. The CP, Band Aid and the mechanics van pulled into a protective position beside a low-lying berm. José had gone to liaise with the fuel tankers. Trey was standing on the black seat, the top half of his body poking out of the hatch above, the radio helmet on his head, listening to the details of the skirmish.

Ray turned around in his driver's seat. 'Time for lunch,' he said. He was a tall black man from Washington DC, a closely-cut moustache the only hair on his shaved head. Over the radio speaker could still be heard the crackle of combat. 'Good shot,' came the report. 'One kill at four o'clock,' came another. It was hard to work out what was going on, how many of the enemy were out there and how serious the resistance was. All I could hear were targets being identified and then the tanks moving in packs for the kill.

I cut open my MRE and stuck the food packet in the little heater. Ray was talking about his wife. She had recently informed him she would be filing for divorce. 'I knew things weren't good, but why couldn't she have waited until all this was over?' he was saying. 'That's fourteen years she's throwing away. I guess it hadn't been working too well for the last four, but I didn't want a divorce. I should be concentrating on all this shit, and instead I keep thinking about all that.'

He poured a red smear of Tabasco into his food. 'The thing I'm going to miss most is my little ten-year-old daughter and waking up to make her breakfast. I mean, she knew things weren't right, but ... You know how kids can get affected by a divorce. I don't know why I got married in the first place. I was just enjoying life being a player, and then this girl, she just wouldn't go away. My policy had been love 'em and leave 'em. It wasn't right, but I was young, and once I got them I would ignore them. But this one, I began to think she might be special, and then I thought maybe it's time for me to do some growing up, so I married her. And now she wants 50 per cent of my retirement fund. Makes me wonder why I've been bothering doing all this time in the army.'

I knew I should be saying something sympathetic, but I was glued to what was coming over the radio. A group of men, some wearing the black uniform of the Saddam Fedayeen, had been spotted escaping towards a small building, which was then destroyed by an artillery bombardment. A van raced up the road and rammed into one of the Bradleys, causing it to rock but inflicting no serious harm. I could hear mortar and machine-gun fire. The Americans seemed to be killing them all. Christ, I thought, this is a slaughter.

Ray, who became one of the people I cared about most during my time in Iraq, had moved the conversation on. He had a new problem, and he was looking for advice. 'You see, I've been out of the game now for a long time, had hoped I'd never have to be in it again, but there's this girl I like, and maybe she likes me. I think she may well be too good for me. She's university-educated, got a good job, she earns good money. But the thing is, I saw her when I was back in DC over Christmas. She'd heard things weren't going well with my wife, and it seemed that there was something there between us. What do you think I should do to find out if I'm right? What's the best way to get a lady?'

I focused on what he was saying, and gave my best tip to make any woman swoon. 'Well, if you feel something's there between you, it's usually because it is. Why don't you take her out for a meal, buy her a few drinks, then do the lunge and see if she goes for it? It's worked for me.'

Trey stuck his head down. 'Are you listening to what's coming across on the radio?' he asked, his thin mouth pulled back in what looked like a grimace but I realised was an expression of excitement. 'We're fucking killing their army out there!' He popped back up, his leg visibly vibrating with the adrenalin. 'Kill them! Kill them! Show them what we've got!' I heard him shouting into the distance.

Ray raised his eyebrows. 'The thing is, she doesn't drink,' he said.

'That is a problem,' I admitted. 'Well, why don't you at least call her? You can use my satellite phone. She'll love the idea of the brave warrior thinking of her in his hour of need.'

'No, not now,' he replied. 'She might think it too forward, and I don't want to know if it's not going to work out. It's good to have something positive to think about out here.'

We both tucked into our food. 'There's a lot for me to work through at the moment,' Ray said. 'My wife. My family. What to do after the army. My head's busy all the time. I'm thinking of maybe joining the Post Office when I get out. It's good steady work.'

I shook my head. In the US they have an expression, 'going postal', for people who lose it and go on the rampage with a rifle, shooting innocent bystanders. It was coined after it was noted that a disproportionately large number of those who did so seemed to work for the Post Office. It did not seem to me a judicious choice of career for someone who would have been a combatant in two Gulf Wars.

'Well what about Homeland Security?' Ray said. 'I'm from DC, and this terrorism thing seems to be a growth business.'

It was almost dark by the time the battalion regrouped at its new camp, a dusty field somewhere just south of the quarry pits. I stood with Red and the other mechanics talking about the day. Not one American had been injured. No one knew quite how many Iraqis had been killed, but many in the company had noted the one-sidedness of the battle they had just been engaged in. 'It was like shooting fish in a barrel,' was how Sergeant Harrison summed it up. Many of the soldiers were nevertheless very excited, the atmosphere reminiscent of being surrounded by people who were drunk. Two figures emerged from the darkness. They were literally bouncing on the spot, unable to stand still. Their outlines seemed to shimmer in front of me, bright in the fading light from the amount of energy pent up inside them.

'Did you see us? We took those two out. The captain spotted them on a ridge and we turned, I saw them and badabadabada,' one said, mimicking the sound of machine-gun fire, his hands imitating grasping a gun. 'I shot right across the first one, and it caught the grenades strapped to his front and he exploded. This other guy was scrabbling in the ground for an AK-47. Badaba-dabada. His head was shot straight off.'

They were swallowed into the night as they sought out other veterans of the fighting. Red sighed. 'I just went to sleep,' he said. 'It was so dull in the back of the maintenance van, and you couldn't see anything because it was all closed up.' A Disney cartoon was being played in Doc's track, and I made my way over to watch it.

The feint across the Euphrates the following day was a complete success. Three battalions had been sent to secure the area and attack the garrison, where around six hundred Republican Guards were believed to be based. For the men in the Black Knights it was an undemanding mission. The majority of the fighting was the responsibility of the other two battalions, and the company's job was to police the streets that surrounded the main target. Only Sergeant Whelan chalked up a kill. As the company rolled into the town of Alby Muhawish, the settlement that bordered the bridge over the river, a single Iraqi soldier had run out with an AK-47. Whelan shot him three times with the .50-calibre machine gun.

From the spot the M113 had been ordered to guard it was possible to hear the rumble of gunfire, but the main evidence of combat I witnessed was the occasional truck heading east with a few prisoners in the back. There were around fifty PoWs in total, the distinctive red triangle shoulder patches on their dark green uniforms marking them as members of Saddam's best-trained and best-equipped forces. It was the first time American troops had clashed with the Republican Guard in significant numbers since the 1991 war. Two companies of Iraqi tanks had, as hoped, been dispatched from their bases near Karbala to bring help, their movement detected by US aircraft fitted with cameras which relayed pictures of their advance directly to the American high command back in Qatar. They were destroyed dozens of miles to the north of where we were sitting. In a series of bombing runs spread over six hours, the United States Air Force punished the Iraqis' decision to risk sending their equipment into the open countryside.

Trey and Ray were bored by the lack of action. We were stationed at the side of a canal and it was fiendishly hot. José was again busying himself with the fuel tankers. He had spent the morning complaining about his back, which had been wrecked by the requirement for scouts to carry massively overweight packs when they were on reconnaissance. Doc had given him painkillers, but despite the fact that José was eating them as if they were sweets, they appeared to be doing little good. At every bump he would grimace in pain and swear to himself in Spanish.

'I want to get where the fighting is,' Trey was moaning. 'Christ, it seems that if I want to get the chance to shoot things I'm going to have to run off and join the Foreign Legion. At this rate this army's going to take ten weeks to get to Baghdad and we're going to besiege it for three years.'

Trey was twenty-nine, born near Nashville, Tennessee, and in his kitbag he had a Stars and Stripes that he carried with him for good luck but refused to fly until the war was won. He was all skin and bones, so much so that he barely filled his uniform. On his head he wore a dark green bandana that accentuated his hooked nose and pointy chin. When he voiced an opinion that he believed was particularly shocking he had a habit of pushing his head forward, his eyes opened wide, his lower lip pulled up to make his chin jut out in an even more pronounced fashion. And Trey liked to make statements that he hoped would shock those around them. As we waited by the canal he discussed prostitution and Democrats, the former as acceptable, the latter as 'the worst bloodsucking whores in all creation'.

'If I met that Bill Clinton he'd have to watch out, as I might come out with a craziness that means I'd have no choice but to do him harm,' he was saying. 'That man tried to destroy the US military. He bled it to the bone with budget cuts. And that Al Gore. He's an embarrassment to Tennessee. Those two are not real Americans. They should be put on a ship and sent to some country like France where they can feel right at home and we wouldn't have to have anything to do with them. Isn't that right, Sergeant Simon?'

Ray shrugged noncommittally. The two had met while stationed in Germany. Trey told a story from their tour in Europe. A friend of theirs, celebrating on the day his first child was born, insisted they take him to a brothel he knew. 'He was drunk and saying, "I want to fuck a black woman, I want to fuck a black woman," so we took him to where he wanted. His kid had been born, so you had to do what he said, you know the way it is.

'We were sitting outside in the car waiting for him to do his thing. Not that I have anything against prostitution, I want to make that clear right now, everyone has a right to earn a living, but fucking some whore, well, it just ain't me, and it ain't Sergeant Simon either. Anyway, our friend, he was so drunk he couldn't find anyone who was black, so he came out moaning and bitching and we had to go inside to help find him one. As you went higher and higher up the building the whores got more and more ugly.'

'Man, were they ugly!' said Ray. 'When we got to the top I asked her how much it would cost. She said forty marks and I told her, "You'd have to pay me more than that to fuck you."'

'This guy was still crying for a black girl, and finally we found one,' Trey continued. 'She was fat, real fat. He saw her and he shouted out, "I'm having you!" An hour later we came back and he wouldn't come out. We had to go in and drag him away. And all the way home he was saying, "Take me back, I want to fuck her again." She was fat, I tell you. Fat as could be. Alcohol can do strange things to a man's mind.'

Trey revelled in stories about his brushes with the law. There was one policeman in particular who had a personal vendetta against him, he said, and waited outside his local bar in Tennessee to chase him down the highway to try and catch him for drunk driving. 'But he never got me, because I'd just drive faster and crazier than he could cope with. See, people are afraid to die. If you push your willingness to be killed that little bit farther than theirs, then nothing will ever touch you, because nobody can keep up. They'll be too scared. You just have to be determined to go that little bit farther in order to fuck them. That's why appearing mean sets you free.' It didn't really matter if the story was true, it encapsulated his philosophy of living.

The sound of gunfire eased and then stopped. Now that the Republican Guard tanks had been pulled from their defensive positions, the order was given for the American troops to disengage and return to their base camps in the desert. Only a small force would stay to hold the area, and later I heard part of that force did in fact cross the bridge to take on the Fedayeen at Hillah. There had been two American casualties, neither fatal. Large quantities of mortar rounds, ammunition, gasmasks and – most worryingly at the time – anti-nerve-gas atropine kits had been seized from Iraqi installations.

We slowly pulled out from where we had been parked and onto the main road that led back through the town and into the desert. As they passed through Alby Muhawish, the Black Knights witnessed the public mood of the Iraqis tip on some imperceptible fulcrum. In the south the populace had treated them at best with diffidence, at worst with violent hatred. Now, for the first time, people began to emerge from their houses and businesses and wave. A mop-haired child was running along the dusty road beside us, smiling and shouting with excitement. His eyes stared into mine and he cried, 'American. American. Good. Good.'

At first I struggled to interpret what I was seeing. I had become so conditioned to considering every Iraqi potentially hostile that the sight of so many people surrounding us made me nervous. Hundreds, possibly thousands, were lining the streets. Then I realised that they were all shouting encouragement. Whole families stood together outside their homes in the bright sunshine, the children jumping up and down and their parents crying out thanks to the Americans. Groups of young men smiled as we drove past. On the side of many of the buildings had been hung not only white flags to indicate that the occupants were non-combatants, but green ones to show that they were Shia. Beside a small stream, women dressed in black religious robes put down the clothes they had been washing in plastic buckets and waved. I watched as a mother told her children to stop playing in a small walled garden and come out and witness the moment when the United States Army had arrived.

I found myself waving back eagerly. Around me I could see that most of the American soldiers were too, smiling and waving as if they were on floats in a Christmas parade, the delight on their faces mixed with relief that some people, at least, were finally pleased to see them. It was the welcome they had been promised, and the effect on their morale of that twenty-minute drive through the cheering streets was immediate. 'Maybe this is what victory feels like,' Sergeant Harrison said to me later at the encampment. 'They sure seemed happy to see us. Let's hope they're not the only ones.'

Captain Waldron was as affected by the change in mood as his men. 'When I first saw how many of them there were, I told everyone to keep low. But when I saw how enthusiastic they were, I began waving back. I even put a little US flag on my machine gun so they knew who it was who was coming to liberate them.'

Perhaps the power of Saddam and his paramilitaries was beginning to weaken after the numerous casualties inflicted upon the Iraqi resistance in recent days, and people were no longer frightened of them. Maybe the fact that the Americans were now so far north meant the Iraqis were beginning to believe they were here to stay this time. Whatever the reason, in the children running beside the tanks while their parents called out their welcomes, it seemed to me the real attitude of the Iraqi people to the American invasion might finally have begun to be revealed.

I said so to Trey. 'Maybe,' he said. 'Maybe. Or maybe they just realise who's the new top dog in their neighbourhood, and want to make sure they don't get on the wrong side of them. If our ass was getting whipped, they'd probably be cheering as they hung us from the lampposts.'

The time was drawing close for the final thrust past Karbala. The nightly bombardment of the Iraqi positions was continuing unabated, the explosions sometimes so powerful that they made the ground shake underneath us. Supplies were moving up to the front in large quantities now. There were spare parts for the vehicles, ammunition, food and water. The soldiers were ordered to check their anti-biochemical-weapon suits for any rips they may have suffered. An additional medical surgical team arrived. A rumour went round that someone had seen boxes of bodybags being unloaded.

After the welcome in Alby Muhawish, there had been a short period of exuberance. The air force officer placed with the company to direct air strikes, a man known to everyone by the nickname 'Air Force One', had started giving a short recap on the unit's radio each night of the news he had gleaned from the various military frequencies. That evening he said it had been confirmed that Jessica Lynch – the captured nineteen-year-old – had been rescued from a hospital in Nasiriyah in an operation led by navy

SEALs. The British had in custody an Iraqi colonel in Basra who was responsible for suppressing dissent in the city's population. American Special Forces believed they had found weapons of mass destruction in the north of the country, a discovery subsequently found to have been mistaken. 'Maybe things are now going our way,' Air Force One had said at the end of his briefing.

Next morning, however, the captain had come round and individually informed crews that they should check they had all the ammunition necessary for their next mission, which would indeed be the final advance to Saddam's capital. The mood again turned pensive. The Karbala Gap was seen by many as the most likely spot for a chemical strike. The strip of land was thin, only twenty-five miles wide, so American units would be pushed close together and therefore could suffer the maximum number of casualties. The region was Shia, its people held in little affection by Saddam, and was believed to be on the wrong side of the 'red line' beyond which the use of nerve gas could be authorised. The soldiers had been told they would be at MOPP 2 when we moved forward, the next level up in the biochemical protection scale, in which the rubber protective boots would be worn with the suits they had been dressed in since before crossing the border.

Trey unclipped a white metal chair strapped to the side of the M113, a gesture to civilisation that had been carried all the way from Kuwait. Sitting outside the CP, he shaved his head completely, as he did not want anything breaking the seal on his gasmask. Ray passed his time baiting his crewmate that he had missed a patch of hair at the back. Doc decided he didn't want to die without talking to one last woman. He disappeared on a reconnaissance mission, and an hour later returned with a young nurse he had found stationed at battalion headquarters. There they had almost completely run out of MREs – the resupply shipment would arrive later that day – and she tucked into our food while a group of men, myself included, gathered in a semi-circle to stare at her. Everyone seemed a bit unsure how to deal with the situation. Trey decided that the best course was to start talking about his wife. He said his marriage had had its argumentative moments; with Ray receiving his divorce papers, José admitting that he was also in the process of separating from his wife, and Trey's feuds with his, the crew of the CP were evidence in themselves of the harm army life could inflict on people's home lives.

'I love my wife,' Trey told the nurse. 'When I went home at Christmas she got pregnant, and I'm so excited about soon having my own kid that I can't tell you enough about it. My wife, you see, she understands the army, doesn't worry too much when I'm away on operations. She says I'm too nasty to die. Most of the time we get on just fine. But other times, I find I just can't stand her. We're driving somewhere together and she's going on and on, and I just want to put my hands around her neck and squeeze and squeeze and squeeze.' I knew this was just Trey being Trey, but the nurse left soon afterwards.

The battalion was encamped in the middle of an onion farm, and the air was thick with the smell of the crop. Some of the crews had pulled handfuls of the plants out of the ground and were boiling them in water to make a simple soup. Half a dozen children were playing football on a stretch of dusty ground in front of the farmhouse. Their presence was a welcome sight, as it was reckoned that the farmer's family would somehow be warned if there was to be a counterattack. I used the opportunity of the temporary hiatus to walk around the company to try to determine how the troops were coping with the killing with which they were now becoming intimate.

At 'Big Punisher', Sergeant Pyle talked of the quarry pits. 'It wasn't my turn to get shot out there,' he said. 'We had our eyes on the highway and then the CO came on and said he'd seen an Iraqi team behind us. We did an action rear, and I saw them on the treeline and reported on the radio that I'd identified two men with weapons.'

Moe, his gunner, one of the two soldiers I had seen shaking with excitement the night after that skirmish, took up the story. 'I saw them through my gunsight. Both of them had AK-47s. I fired on the first with my coax [the 7.62mm machine gun, manned from inside the turret, which was called the tank's coaxial weapon as it was mounted on the same axis as the main gun]. Then I hit the second one; think I took his head off. I remember thinking that if the CO hadn't identified them, they could have fired first and someone in my crew could have been hurt.'

The driver, Specialist Chris Moore, had popped out of his hole at the front to hear what we were talking about. 'I didn't think about those guys being dead until I saw them lying there,' he said, his boyish face serious under a thatch of dust-covered hair. 'Then I thought, "Fuck, we've killed people."'

'I didn't feel any remorse then,' said Moe. 'I wanted to kill them. But yesterday I was sitting up on the tank thinking, "Damn, I did kill guys." But it was them or us, and if I hadn't acted, my commander, who was exposed out the top, could have been hit.'

'I told my crew before we came up here that it would get ugly,' Sergeant Pyle said. 'I warned them they'd see people being killed. And they have, and it won't be for the last time.'

The captain was going through the intelligence gleaned from the operation at Alby Muhawish. It had been discovered that some of the Republican Guard soldiers were members of the Nebuchadnezzar Division, named after the second and greatest King of the Chaldean dynasty of Babylonia, which was meant to be further east, directly to the south of Baghdad. The Medina Division, the Republican Guard unit stationed around Karbala whose name referred to the site from which Mohammed launched his conquest of Arabia, was apparently being reinforced. A similar conclusion had been drawn from other actions conducted in the preceding days, as well as from the analysis of satellite photographs. As a result, the US generals responsible for conducting the war had decided to bring most of 3rd Brigade forward to join

1st and 2nd Brigades for the upcoming attack. I thought of Major General Blount and his briefing in Kuwait. The plan he had detailed was still broadly in effect: the army and Marines had pushed up both banks of the Euphrates, and the 3rd Infantry Division was now to move past Karbala in a formation similar to the one he had laid out, if one involving a greater number of men. But the journey from the border to the capital had not taken the seven days predicted.

'It really isn't fazing me,' the captain said when I asked him about the recent fighting. 'I'd read a lot in advance on the psychology of war, and was trying to prep myself for what was going to happen, and maybe that's helped me. It meant I had an idea what to expect. But I'll mention one thing: I noticed when my gunner killed someone, another soldier laughed, and the gunner told him, "Shut up, it wasn't funny."'

First Lieutenant John Yaros, a young officer from Pittsburgh, just out of university, was responsible for calling in fire from the mortars and artillery stationed to the company's rear. Because of his unit's title, the Fire Support Team, they were universally known as 'the fisters'. He had called in the bombardment on the uniformed Fedayeen seen heading towards the building at the quarry pits.

'We'd positively ID'd twenty guys, and I could see them running for cover, so I fired mortars and a bit of field artillery,' he said. 'When those shells hit, the scrap metal they release really goes everywhere. When you take hits it takes you apart, and there was a lot of blood. We'd missed three or four of them, and they ran into the building. I called in another strike and the roof collapsed. You don't think about it. You're taught by the army to conceive of them as the faceless enemy, not a real person. In training you spend time shouting "Kill, kill, kill!" to help make it become a normal thing to do. You feel bad that they don't know any better, but they're the enemy, and it's shoot or be shot. In Nasiriyah I had a bullet strike four inches from my head, and I want to make sure I go home.'

I had seen Lieutenant Yaros at all the services the chaplain had held. 'I'm a strong Christian,' he said, 'and there's the question of how you reconcile that. There's St Augustine's theory of a just war, that "War is love's responsibility to a neighbour threatened by force," and I believe that this is such. Saddam Hussein is a threat to his neighbours, his own people and to us. But I was cleaning my M-16 after that fight at the quarry pits, and I did think: "I've killed someone." How does that fit into the scheme of things? Is it fate? Is it all determined by someone else? But when you're out there, your training takes over. You've done it so many times it doesn't feel real until afterwards, you're just on automatic, and that's the way it has to be. Otherwise, if you worry that you're a horrible person, you hesitate, and that means your buddy's going down, and that too is someone's life lost.'

A scout told me that Joe, the *Stars and Stripes* photographer, had left the battalion. I walked to where he had been based, hoping it wasn't true because I urgently needed someone non-military to talk to. He had pulled out the previous day. His satellite phone had been playing up, and his bosses had instructed him to go home, though as he admitted to me when we finally got in contact again months later, 'It was the excuse I'd been looking for.'

I went to look for Ron, the other reporter who had been placed with the battalion back in Kuwait. To my shock he too had gone, apparently moved towards brigade headquarters far to the rear. The captain who had played us Ozzy Osbourne on the CD player strapped to the top of his Humvee told me, 'The thing is, he didn't have the guts to stay.' It seemed a particularly misguided judgement on someone who had no training for combat, and a wife and child relying on him back in Prague. I had always sus-pected that ever since he first arrived dressed in a Palestinian headscarf, the battalion had been suspicious of Ron.

The news that I was the only journalist left, perhaps the only one too dumb to get out of the firing line, gave me pause for thought. I had also learnt from the office in London that the reporter *The Times* had sent as their embed to the US Marines, the only other British daily newspaper journalist with the American ground forces, had requested to be sent home. If others were jumping ship, then clearly I was not being unreasonable in my apprehensiveness about what was awaiting us to the north.

I wondered why, despite everything, I had not thought for even a second about getting out. Part of it was that I felt a sense of duty. I had signed up to do something, and I did not want to let anyone down – whether it was my newspaper, which was relying on me to provide stories, or the soldiers whom I believed, perhaps foolishly, I would be deserting if I bailed out. However, there was another, far more important factor. Despite the discomfort and the moments of intense fear, the guilt and moral navel-gazing, the reason I was going nowhere was that there was a part of me that was enjoying the experience. Every day brought a stream of new challenges to be understood and overcome. There was no time to worry about the normal garbage of life: the broken relationships I picked over, the cigarettes I was never going to give up, the drunken arguments I regretted the morning after. I was living totally in the moment, my thoughts focused on getting through each twenty-four hours and trying to do justice to what I was witnessing in the articles I was producing. I was covering the biggest story in the world, and I was in exactly the right place at the right time. Everything I wrote was flying into the paper. It was the kind of position I had always dreamt of achieving. There was no way I was going to be anywhere but on that highway towards Karbala to see for myself what happened next.

I sought out the colonel for a final briefing. He was sitting at the back of his Bradley. His pistol lay in front of him, stripped to its component parts, and he was cleaning and oiling each mechanism. 'This is when it really begins,' he said. 'You're going to have a lot to write about over the next few days.'

Anything that could be taken out of the battalion's vehicles and left behind was being burnt in pits dug in the sand. As darkness fell the irregular drumbeat of the bombing to our north seemed particularly intense. One explosion was so fierce that our surroundings were lit up as if it was day, and a huge cloud of smoke rose to stretch across the night sky. A lot of people asked to use my phone that evening, their thoughts turned to their families by the inevitable forebodings before battle.

I had been sleeping in Band Aid since leaving the M88, the back of the CP being too crowded for the four of us who travelled in it by day to lie down in any form of comfort. In the medic track four stretchers were laid out, two on either side, the ones at the bottom set up at all times to be ready in case they were needed for casualties. I slept on the one at the top right, my head so close to the metal ceiling that I could feel my breath bounce back off the roof and fall softly over my face.

It was still dark when Doc woke me the next morning. He had barely slept, and was now shaking his crew awake and ordering them to get the vehicle ready. He looked at me, his face intent in the moonlight. 'Be prepared for what may be your last day on earth. It's going to be bloody. It's going to be bloody.' I stumbled across to the CP, where Trey and Ray were already in their bio-chemical protection boots. I told them what Doc had said. They started laughing. Trey had summoned all the NCOs to a meeting the evening before and laid on the line what could happen during the coming advance. 'Man, he scared them to an inch of their lives,' Ray said. 'I thought some of them were going to start to cry. One of them was saying, "I don't want to be here, I want to go home." It was something to see, I can tell you.'

Trey looked pleased with himself. 'I just told it how it was. This is going to be brutal.'

Ahead of us were gathered the surviving units of the Republican Guard, all of whom knew they were the last line of defence before their country's capital. They were encamped in fortifications erected during weeks of preparations. If the regime had chemical weapons, it was predicted they were going to use them now. The next forty-eight hours was expected to be the largest and most bitter battle of the war.

I sat on the ramp at the back of the M113 and struggled to get the plastic boots on. 'So, when are you going to take up a weapon, Oliver?' Trey asked. 'We've got a lot here when you need one, and today may well be the day you do.'

We Were Soldiers, a recent film starring Mel Gibson, tells the story of the 1965 battle between 450 Americans and two thousand Vietnamese in the Ia Drang Valley. It was an early and particularly brutal action in that war, one of the most savage of the entire conflict, that left hundreds of the GIs killed and wounded. Among the fighting men was a reporter, Joe Galloway, who at the time worked for United Press International. In the film, as the Viet Cong break through the American lines, he is depicted picking up a rifle and starting to fight. A large number of the men in 1st Battalion had seen the movie, as the scenes depicting the American soldiers training prior to their deployment in Vietnam had been shot at a 3rd Infantry Division base camp in Georgia. This had partly worked to my advantage. My arrival in the company just days before the invasion had been seen as a confirmation that what they were doing was important, that like the men at Ia Drang, their deeds would not be forgotten. However, it also meant that I was regularly asked when I was going to 'tool up' and join them in taking out some of the Hajji, as Galloway had been shown doing against the VC.

'Go on. When they're swarming over our vehicle, you'll fight back then, won't you?' Trey said.

Beyond any qualms I may have had about being responsible for bloodshed, there is no rule more sacrosanct for reporters than that they never pick up a weapon. I primly told Trey that my plan would be to surrender as quickly as possible. He stared at me. 'Never! No one surrenders in this vehicle. It would be a dishonour to America. Don't worry, I'll make sure no one captures you and takes you to their torture chambers. My last task will be to administer a bullet to your head before those Hajji bastards get to you. Then I'll stick a bullet through my own skull.'

'Ohh, God!' I groaned, to their even greater amusement. I knew he was joking, but I also knew the sentiment was serious. There would never be a moment when Trey Black surrendered. All of us in all likelihood would be dead first from the fighting that marked his last stand.

Trey pulled out an M-16 bullet and pointed it at me. 'I'll keep this one back for you.' He winked and put it in the top pocket of his flak jacket.

Ray was laughing at my distress. Then he sat down on one of the M113's little benches and turned to me, lowering his voice as he confided, 'I've got to admit, though, I'm not looking forward to this. Black may have been laying it on a little thick last night, but this is going to be serious shit. You look after yourself back there. Keep your head down. Don't want you gettin' hurt. Black's really got a bad feeling about this. He thinks he may have to take over one of the tanks when it's over because one of the commanders isn't going to make it.'

I looked at him to see if he was joking, trying to wind me up further. But he wasn't. There was what looked like a trace of fear in his eyes. I asked him if he was afraid.

'Hell, no,' Ray said. 'I trust our leaders. As long as Black doesn't do some stupid shit, I'm sure we're going to be fine.'

The sun was now up and it was a perfect day, not a cloud in the sky. The company had pulled into position in a convoy of two parallel lines, in what was called the herringbone formation, each vehicle pointing slightly outwards at a forty-five-degree angle. Ray was in the driver's seat, Trey had taken his position at the machine gun, José had already dropped a shell into his handheld M203 grenade launcher. We waited, and then the order was given to advance. Ray rose in his seat so his head stuck through the hatch above and called out, 'Come on, you sons of bitches. I'm not scared of you. Bring it to me. I'm not scared.' And we started to move forward towards the road that led to Baghdad.

SIX

England 2, Turkey 0

The shell of a transit van lay on its side in the left lane of the highway, a wisp of smoke still rising from the engine compartment. A lorry had broken in two, its cab thrown across the central partition, what remained of its trailer lying against an earth berm bordering the road. The Black Knights were still more than two hours from the outskirts of Karbala, but already evidence of the fighting that had preceded their order to join the advance was all around them. The line of tanks slowed to weave between two cars, both blackened by scorch marks. In the front seat of the nearest one could be made out a figure slumped over the steering wheel. Further on, a pick-up truck had been reduced to a collage of wheels and metal parts. Buildings burnt in the distance. The smoke drifted up into the still air, dissipating and curling into mutating clusters until it formed a giant Rorschach test hanging in the sky.

The 3500 soldiers in 1st and 3rd Brigade had led the attack, their tanks and Bradleys coming out of the west and the south just before sunrise. Already news was filtering through that they had advanced further than expected. A unit, backed by dozens of Apache helicopters, had secured a dam at the north-east corner of Lake Buhayrat, which it had been feared the Iraqis might detonate to flood the surrounding area and impede the American forces. There had been only limited resistance, and what there was did not appear well organised. Two Iraqi tanks had been destroyed and eighty-two Republican Guards, including two colonels, were reported taken prisoner. A battalion from 3rd Brigade was moving up through the south-east of the city to attack the remains of the Medina Division's 14th Armoured Brigade from the rear. The Iraqi unit had been placed on the western edge of Karbala, with their weapons pointing towards the open land from which they had expected the enemy would come at them. The BBC was reporting that the Marines were also advancing, pushing up through the east of the country past Kut, as the two arms of the Americans' pincer movement accelerated towards Baghdad.

The forces of 2nd Brigade, which now included the battalion I was with, had been held back to push towards the Iraqi capital once the area around Karbala was secured. It was intended that the American attack would gradually shed layers. 3rd Brigade would deal with the resistance around the city. 1st Brigade would focus on securing a bridge over the Euphrates to the north-east of Karbala at Jorf al-Sakhar, thirty-five miles south of the capital. 2nd Brigade would then clear the area that stretched from the river's east bank to Baghdad. As each stage of the road north was taken, units in the front would peel off to secure their targets, bringing other battalions to the centre of the fighting, until they too were ordered to step back and protect a section of the route. The job of 1st Battalion would be to lead the fight into the outskirts of the capital. 'It's like [American] football,' it was explained to me. 'Everyone is blocking, blocking, blocking, and then we carry it into the end zone.'

In his final briefing before the advance, the colonel had detailed to me the state of the Iraqi troops ahead of us. For two weeks they had been under almost perpetual aerial bombardment, which had destroyed a vast number of the tanks the Iraqis had stationed in the area. American intelligence believed that the 2nd Armoured Brigade of the Republican Guard's Medina Division, one of the main units defending the route north, was down to just 13 per cent of its original strength. The other units in the area were estimated to be at a third of their normal numbers, the rest of their contingents killed or deserted. Fewer than forty tanks were thought to be still operating in Karbala itself. Special Forces teams had been directing the air strikes. Sometimes, to encourage desertions, they would climb to just outside Republican Guard positions and leave notes in Arabic detailing how waves of bombers would soon be en route to destroy the Iraqi fortifications.

The most powerful of Saddam's remaining units in the area was thought to be the Hammurabi Division, named after the most renowned ruler of the Amorite dynasty of Babylon, which had previously been stationed to the west of the capital and so had been spared the worst of the aerial attacks. In the previous few days, America's Keyhole and Lacrosse satellite systems had detected it moving south, and it was now encased in defensive positions on the south-west outskirts of Baghdad.

During the 1980s Iraq acquired large quantities of up-to-date equipment, primarily from the Soviet Union but also from France. It was these that had enabled it to survive the 1980–1988 war with the more fanatical and populous Iran. However, the 1991 Gulf War had resulted in Iraq losing vast numbers of tanks, armoured vehicles and artillery pieces. The fall of the Soviet Union and the UN weapons embargo meant it had not been possible for Saddam to replace much of this equipment, nor to update that which had survived intact. Now even the most modern tanks in the Iraqi army were fifteen years old, and its older models were almost museum pieces.

The surviving Republican Guard units that awaited us had been equipped with the most sophisticated of the surviving armoured vehicles, primarily Soviet-designed T-72 and T-80 tanks. Their 125mm guns could disable an Abrams if a shot struck the tracks, but could not pierce its sides unless the shell was fired at less than a thousand yards. The T-80 was the more modern of the two designs, dating from 1984. It had layers of armour at the front which were thick enough to withstand an American tank shell, and it was fitted with a laser range-finder and a ballistic computer system. However, neither of these tanks could compete with the Abrams' range, power and manoeuvrability. The armour of the T-80 at the sides, turret and rear offered little protection against the weaponry available to the United States military. Crews of the T-72 usually had to stop their vehicle to aim their gun before they fired. It was a tank that had first been produced in 1972, and despite subsequent updates it still lacked comprehensive computer technology. In practice, the T-72 and T-80 were hardly more of a threat to the Abrams than the pick-up trucks with machine guns fixed to their backs. I never heard of Iraqi tanks destroying a single American one during the entire war.

As news filtered through that morning of the US advances, it became clear how devastating had been the impact of the continuous air raids. Units surged and spread through the Iraqi positions like a sea on a rising tide. They easily overwhelmed the few Republican Guard units still operating. There was no gas attack. The battalion from 3rd Brigade caught the Iraqi forces from the rear, destroying many of them in a brief burst of combat, or, as it was described on the military radio, 'smoked them'. Even where there was resistance it seemed localised and to involve little coordination. There was no significant counter-offensive. Instead the American troops dealt with isolated defensive positions that they could destroy at their own pace before moving on to unearth the next line of fortifications. By midday the first American units had reached the Euphrates. 'We've got them running,' Trey said excitedly.

We were now pulling into the outskirts of Karbala. Two bombed-out trucks stood by the side of the road, the charred remains of bodies spilling onto the tarmac beside them. A local man dressed in Arab robes came out and watched the American troops, a white flag held in one hand, waving with the other. The buildings were not tall – few stood higher than three storeys, their roofs flat. At each junction a Bradley stood guard. Their crews lazed on the ground beside them, many heating MREs, others simply soaking up the sunshine. One infantryman was contentedly flicking through the pages of a magazine. A few gave the thumbs up as the Black Knights rolled by.

It was hot now, approaching a hundred degrees, and from around the headband of my helmet sweat dripped into my eyes. An Iraqi soldier had fallen by the side of the road, his head split open, brains visible on the ground. A little further on someone had covered a badly burnt corpse with a palm frond. At a corner the convoy slowed to work its way around a crater two feet deep. Beside it was a truck cut in two and a figure lying in the foetal position, unmoving.

Trey received a change of orders. The battalion was going to avoid the Karbala Gap completely because of concern that a chemical attack could still be mounted there. Instead it would pass through the eastern side of the city, along a highway that had been secured by forward units earlier in the day. Rumours began to spread that we might cross the Euphrates that afternoon, twenty-four hours ahead of what had been scheduled that morning.

Even José was quite cheerful: the tarmac road was doing favours to his back, which meant he had less urge to take out his frustration at the pain through his normal practice of complaining about how much food and water the rest of the crew were consuming. As well as griping about the supplies, he would often tell sprawling, incomprehensible stories about him and his buddies watching television or sharing a beer, and then look put out when everyone on board missed the point of the punchline. His face had a certain puffiness that blurred his features, and a small mouth, the teeth crammed on top of each other to fit into the space available, which had a tendency to adopt a pout. However, he had been placed in an almost impossible situation. Now forty, formerly a scout, he had no experience of how tank crews operated, and had been required to take over an extremely well trained and tightly knit unit halfway through a combat operation. Inevitably there had been some tension. At one point he had wanted to take over the gun on the M113, a suggestion Trey had bridled against. He had quarrelled with Doc for letting me, and not him, sleep in Band Aid, and he would mutter that there would be changes when the company returned to its camp in Georgia. Most of the time he perched on one of the benches in the back of the M113 with the BBC tuned in on my radio for company, his Puerto Rican features impassive as he stared at the floor.

José had heard about Trey's promise to make sure I was not captured alive, and thought it hilarious. Concerned that my intended executioner might be incapacitated, he assured me that if the need arose he would be willing to take on the responsibility. 'No bullet though, maybe it not kill you,' he told me. 'This is better. Guaranteed.' He took out one of the shells for his grenade launcher, drew on it a little smiley face with the word 'Oliver' above it, and slipped it into one of the ammo-storing loops on his flak jacket. Every now and then, when he caught my eye, he would tap it and grin at me. This quickly became ever so slightly wearing.

Town turned into desert again. The trees disappeared. Rocks replaced bushes as the only marks on the horizon. Still we drove on. Over the radio could be heard reports of units exploring buildings in the rear, of fuel vehicles getting stuck in the sand, of scouts engaging in sporadic skirmishes against Iraqis still taking the fight against them.

Near a dirt airstrip to the north-east of the city, the battalion adopted its attack formation. Soldiers had been seen nearby. The M113 and the other armoured support vehicles were told to wait at a road junction across which half a dozen concrete blocks had been piled as a makeshift barricade. After the American tanks swept through, gunfire could be heard on the right-hand side. Three Iraqi soldiers were killed.

Trey was growing impatient. 'Everyone's getting things to shoot at but me,' he said. He turned the .50-calibre on a red motorcycle that had been left against a nearby berm. It burst into flames as the bullets hit. 'At least I got myself a motorcycle,' he said triumphantly. 'It may not have had anybody around it, but it was an Iraqi motorcycle and I got it.'

Ray also opened up with his pistol at a box of RPGs that had been abandoned by the road. 'Hell, it's about time,' he shouted. Suddenly everyone was firing at the box and an adjacent wall. 'Cease fire! Cease fire!' shouted José, then muttered to himself, '*Estan comportandose como los niños*' (They are like children).

The unit pushed north once more. We learnt that the bridge over the Euphrates had been secured, but there were concerns of a possible counterattack, so we would not be crossing it that evening. The battalion was in a line driving across a flat stretch of desert, the only marks in the sand the tracks left by the vehicles ahead. A fuel stop was ordered and the M113 drove through the company to see who needed fresh supplies. As we approached an American tank bearing the slogan 'Black Out Fridays' on its barrel, a homage to getting drunk at the start of the weekend, Sergeant Harry Morgan was standing on the turret waving excitedly. He was the soldier Red had sparred with about being homosexual when I first joined the company. In recent days I had found him worrying that he was letting down his unit as he had not killed anyone yet. 'At this rate I'm going to have to shoot a dog so at least I can say I hit something,' he had said.

Now he was smiling triumphantly. 'First kill! First kill! I finally got one!' he shouted. It had been during the skirmish at the airstrip. He raised his fingers in the V for victory sign.

'Good work,' said Trey. 'But I got myself a motorcycle! Everybody's killing people. It's good to get something different.'

The sun hovered above the horizon as the battalion drew to a halt a short distance from the Euphrates. The scouts were dispatched to secure the area. They spotted a line of bunkers and were ordered to investigate. 'There's more stuff in here to light things up than there are lights in Vegas,' the report came back. In the next half hour they found boxes of anti-tank guns, rocket launchers, a battery of four anti-aircraft guns, piles of mortar shells and a number of abandoned AK-47s. Then they reported coming across a 'stack' of Iraqi money.

'How much money?' José asked over the radio.

'There's piles of the stuff,' the answer came back. 'It's filling a whole room. There must be hundreds of thousands of the stuff.'

Doc appeared at our vehicle later that night carrying some of the rolls of cash. He and Air Force One had gone to join the scouts on their exploratory raid. Doc was pleased, as they had let him shoot open one of the doors. 'Don't forget I'm the meanest medic you're ever going to meet,' he told me. He was particularly filthy. A line of dirt was etched around his chin and his greasy hair flopped towards his eyes. There had been fresh wheeltracks and footprints leading away from the bunker complex. Its inhabitants had left so fast that plates of vegetables and rice had been abandoned on a table in a small kitchen. It looked as if Trey was right, and that many of the Iraqis were running from the advancing American army.

We looked at the 250-dinar notes. From one side Saddam's head stared at us. Even if they are essentially worthless, rare is the person who does not enjoy holding large wads of banknotes in his hand. 'How much is this?' Ray asked. 'What's this in dollars?' No one quite knew, though the suspicion was not much. José thought the exchange rate was 2500 dinar to the dollar, others as much five thousand. More than two million dinar had been discovered at the site, and it was loaded onto American vehicles to be handed in once a new base camp had been set up in Baghdad. There were three explosions nearby as the engineers detonated the ammunition and weapon dumps.

I sat next to Trey on the top of the M113. 'Well, we didn't die today,' I said.

'More than time enough for that tomorrow,' he answered.

We moved forward again just after dawn. A light mist still hung over the desert, the tanks resembling ghosts as their pale shapes disappeared into the haze. The company was no longer at full strength. Three tanks, among them Sergeant Whelan's, had broken down during the long advance of the previous day and had been left behind for the maintenance crews to work on. The aerial bombardment had continued throughout the night. At times the detonations had been so close that I could feel their force rattling inside my ribcage.

It took just over an hour to reach the bridge that arched over the deep green waters of the Euphrates. The land grew more fertile as we drew closer. Three-foot-high grass now lined the road and clumps of palm trees flourished along slow-moving streams. Once on the other bank of the river the company would be in ancient Mesopotamia, the area known as the Fertile Crescent that lay between the Euphrates and the Tigris and that had been continuously inhabited for five thousand years. It was the birthplace of civilisation, where mankind first invented the written word and abstract mathematics, built sophisticated cities and extensively utilised the wheel. Already the Black Knights were drawing to its edges, leaving behind the wilderness that had been their home for months, to descend into the lush fields that Biblical scholars argue was the site of the Garden of Eden.

At the bridge, it was clear that those who had been ordered to defend it had paid a heavy cost. Later I would read that eight hundred soldiers in the Medina Division were believed killed or wounded at the spot. Two Toyota trucks stood at its entrance, bulletholes visible in their sides. The mid-section of the bridge was blackened and burnt where the Iraqis had detonated explosives intended to destroy it. The blast had merely ripped away some of the concrete, revealing the metal poles that held the structure together, and a team of engineers, surrounded by armed infantrymen, was now working to plug the gap. At the other end of the bridge an AK-47 rifle was melted to the side of a Mitsubishi truck by the heat of the flames that had burnt within the vehicle.

Crossing the Euphrates was a significant moment for everybody. Ever since leaving Kuwait we had been on its west bank; now – finally! – we were on the east. Only the capital was left to be secured. The units of the 1st Brigade that had taken the bridge were gathered on both sides of the river. Lines of artillery were staged in batteries across the surrounding fields. Tanks and Bradleys were strewn along the main highway. A small group of PoWs behind some barbed wire were being guarded by a soldier sitting in a bright pink picnic chair.

American troops, their faces black from dirt and gunsmoke, watched as we drove through their lines of defence. During the night a unit of Republican Guard soldiers and some paramilitaries had launched a haphazard probe into the area and been fought off. The skirmish meant few of the Americans had slept before morning, and many were still too pumped up to rest. Some of them grasped machine guns, others shotguns, a few brandished grenade launchers. Pistols jutted from black holsters strapped to thighs or hanging under armpits. On the faces of the soldiers was the look of men who had fought a battle and won a victory, and despite their clear exhaustion I found their sense of purpose uplifting. The confusion which had dominated the skirmishing in the southern cities was gone. The American army had massed and pushed forward. The men around me knew they were playing a key role in a decisive battle. Even my blood was running faster through my veins.

There were more Iraqi bodies. I looked down into a line of foxholes and saw the dead lying in them. There was what must have once been a small truck, now just a few twisted metal sheets.

A house to our right had been fortified with sandbags. The brick walls were pockmarked with bulletholes, and through the windows I spotted scouts ambling through the rooms inside. The country-side was still lush and green, and the road was lined by trees which reduced visibility to a minimum. The area was criss-crossed by tributaries forded by narrow bridges. The Iraqis had dug their lines of foxholes at these bottlenecks, most of them not big enough to hold more than one man, who in its isolation had suffered a lonely death. In an orchard there was another dead soldier, lying on his back amid the rotting fruit, his helmet having rolled down the slope to come to a stop at the roadside. An Iraqi tank, one of only a handful I saw that day, had been hit so hard that the debris had been scattered in a circle fifty yards wide. Doc had his video camera out to record the image for posterity.

It was ten to ten in the morning when the shooting started. It began as a salvo in the distance and then spread until it surrounded us on all sides and there was no escape from the constant sound of combat. The Black Knights were out in the front now. Sergeant Pyle's tank led the line. There was no one ahead except the Iraqi army. I had been confused at the dit-dit-dit of those first tentative shots, unsure who was firing. Then the machine gun on a scout Humvee just to our rear opened up, the shock of its roar registered by every nerve in my body. José shot his grenade launcher. Trey started firing bursts with the .50-calibre machine gun.

I tried to make out what they were blazing away at, but couldn't see anything, just a mishmash of trees and buildings. Then there was shooting from behind one of the bushes. The Americans targeted the spot, and it was surrounded by little puffs where their bullets ricocheted off the ground. I hid at the bottom of the vehicle staring up at José as he towered above me, leaning out of the back hatch, calmly pulling the trigger and then reloading as he fired grenade after grenade. His left leg was constantly twitching. The gun casings from Trey's .50-calibre fell through the cockpit in a metal waterfall beside my head before bouncing off the floor around me. I reached down and picked one up. It was burning hot to the touch.

In a moment when there was only silence I forced myself to stand up, and saw two infantrymen outside a house on our left. A dead body lay in front, and a woman in a green headscarf was crying, shaking her fist at the soldiers who had the palms of their hands held out in what seemed to be an apology. Something I had once read by Ernest Hemingway came into my mind: 'War is a crime. Ask the infantry and ask the dead.'

We were slowly inching forward along the road. No one in the M113 spoke, all focused entirely on the task at hand. Occasionally someone would give a hand signal or a shout to indicate where an enemy soldier was hiding. Otherwise there was no noise except for the gunfire. It was only 10.20 a.m. Time was going very slowly. I was not exactly aware of being frightened, just overcome by the compulsion to concentrate very hard on everything that was happening. I tried to distract myself by thinking about a sailing boat I kept by the Solent on which I had spent many great days, but it was impossible to picture anything other than the smoke in the air, the empty rounds rolling beneath me, the blank stares of the soldiers, my hands clenched in my lap. There was no space in my brain for anything but the necessity of picking up every sound that might explain what was happening on the other side of the metal walls in which I was encased.

There was no moment at which one army saw the other, steeled itself, then advanced towards the waiting enemy lines. Instead the situation seemed one of muddled confusion. The American tactics were limited to driving into an area, inviting the Iraqis to open fire so that their location could be identified, and then killing them. Many of the Republican Guard soldiers were hidden in foxholes. Others were perched on the roofs of buildings. Cars and pick-up trucks drove up side roads to get off a round before trying to escape. Banks of missiles were attached to the backs of trucks. The Iraqis' determination to fight terrified me. Men who had been hit half a dozen times still crawled towards their weapons to get off one last shot. Soldiers in the path of tanks stood their ground to fire their machine guns. The air above us was filled with the twisting trails of RPGs and missiles.

There was a pause in the advance. I looked around me once again. An air strike was being called to clear bunkers at a junction ahead. News had just come in of the battalion's first casualty that day, a scout shot in the leg. I was struck by what a lovely morning it was. A slight breeze took the edge off the heat and the sky was a consummate blue. On both sides stretched green fields dotted with groves of palm trees and marsh grass. A cockerel cried. It was so calm, and I smiled at the ridiculous juxtaposition. In a shallow waterlogged ditch that ran beside the road, a frog was swimming from the near bank to a stone on the other. Small white butterflies darted between the blades of grass that broke the water's surface. A slow-moving A10 Thunderbolt support fighter flew overhead, crossing the sky in a perfect arc, so graceful, so lackadaisical, three cluster bombs falling behind it. The explosives were attached to a small net which dropped lethargically through the sky, a flare attached to each to ensure that other planes did not fly into them. I was mesmerised by the beauty of the sight, overcome for a few seconds by a feeling of total serenity.

Then came the explosions and more gunfire. A building just ahead was alight. We passed a burning vehicle, the flames so hot the heat scorched my face. A fire was spreading across the grass on one side of the road. There was a Bradley stationed at the crossroads. The commander was half out of the top hatch. Looking at him I realised it was Mike Golf, the one-time Kentucky dirt-track racer who had taken us to the British firing range. He spotted me and waved in greeting.

Soon afterwards I picked up my notebook. This is what I scribbled down in that place and at that time:

I am watching my crew kill people. I can see them now taking people's lives with barely a flicker of emotion on their faces. No one cares if the Iraqis have wives, children, mothers, fathers, and they are right not to, because everyone wants to make sure that today is not the day that they have to die.

And do I care about what is happening to the Iraqis? Not even for a moment. A few minutes ago a six-foot missile was fired straight towards us. Just before impact the jet burnt out and it fell from the air. It would have cut straight through the fragile armour surrounding me and all of us on board knew it. That malfunction was a stroke of luck that saved our lives.

When that missile was fired, everyone around me suddenly stopped shooting, and that lull frightened me more than the noise previously had. I looked up, and saw those I was trusting to keep me safe staring at something out there. I did not know at that moment what it was. All I knew was something was terribly wrong. And then there was relief on their faces, and they took back up their weapons – became once more machines – and the empty rounds again started falling around me.

All the reasons given for war are bullshit. Only self-preservation justifies the acts it requires soldiers to conduct. I am sitting here and I have no sympathy for the people they are firing at. I feel nothing for them. Not hate, not regret, not compassion, not even that they are human. All I can think is one overwhelming thought: 'Please, please, please kill everyone, as I want to live.'

I would later read that Major General Blount told reporters that the 2nd Brigade encountered resistance from Iraqi forces he estimated numbered 'several thousand' that day. Prisoners would later tell the Americans that they had been issued with vials of liquid PCP, or 'angel dust', into which they dipped their cigarettes before they smoked them. Maybe it was not bravery, but pharmaceutical insanity that fuelled the fervour of their resistance. I almost hoped so. I could not conceive how it could be possible for anyone sane to have engaged the Americans in such an arena.

At one point José reached down and with a knife silently cut free a box of extra ammunition. He stared at me with vacant eyes as he filled his pockets with so many shells that they spilled out and fell onto the floor of the vehicle. News came on the radio that Sergeant Pyle's tank had been disabled and he had been shot in the shoulder. Trey leaned down to light a cigarette. 'You havin' fun yet?' he asked. 'Did you see that missile? It was like the sun was coming at us. Goddamn, this is bloody.'

It took four hours from crossing the Euphrates to fight through the units of the Medina and Hammurabi Divisions and reach the outskirts of Baghdad, but when we did, the shooting that had surrounded us stopped as quickly as it had begun. The M113 parked in a small field beside where the two highways crossed each other on raised bridges, a street sign pointing towards the international airport a few miles to our west. I pulled open the back hatch and stepped out into the dark green grass, its blades wide as table knives, and stared at the men around me. There was a chemical-attack detection vehicle to my right. The Bradley mechanics van was on the other side. The 3–7 Cav were said to be somewhere close. There were a couple of fuel trucks, one of which was stuck in the mud. Soldiers were climbing down from their vehicles, and they too stood staring at each other. Smoke was rising everywhere. A tall black soldier was walking towards me. His name was Sergeant Scott. I had never seen him before, and I never saw him again. 'How do we know when this all ends?' he asked. 'When do we know when it's over? How much longer can this go on? Why didn't they just send in some assassins to do the job of taking out Saddam, rather than killing all those people? There were civilians out there. They have to tend their crops. There's been a whole load of killing.'

Ray was sitting in the driver's seat of the M113 smoking a cigarette, his face shiny with sweat. 'Did you see it?' he asked. 'There were dead people everywhere. I didn't like that at all. It was like the last time [the 1991 Gulf War]. When I see that many dead bodies it's time to go home.'

Doc told me he believed he had fired off more than a thousand rounds in the battle that took us to Objective Saints. 'An RPG hit our side but didn't explode. I saw the soldier who fired it and I put five rounds, perfectly placed, in the centre of his chest,' he said. 'But he wouldn't go down. I could see him still reaching to try and load another RPG and I changed my machine gun to three-round bursts and sent two into his throat and one right through his forehead.

'There was a guy at a big fucking machine gun and I was peppering his bunker with rounds. First sergeant saw him too and fired off his M203. It exploded and I saw this arm fly out and roll through the air. The blast blew up all this dirt. It was so hard it felt like shrapnel and I thought I'd been hit. I reached for my face and found there was no blood so I just got straight back into it.'

Lieutenant Garabato, the XO, pulled alongside in his tank. 'Fuck that. I was scared,' he said.

'You should try being in this thing,' Trey replied as he patted the M113.

Large numbers of American vehicles were pulling in now. Half a dozen medic vans gathered in a corner of the field. Tanks moved in small convoys along the highways. The infantry were going from house to house searching for Iraqi soldiers and weapons. In a nearby mosque, six Iraqi troops and two armed civilians were captured along with a cache of machine guns. Slowly the units spread out and began the work of securing the enclave's perimeter.

After months of waiting and weeks of fighting, days in which they had travelled hundreds of miles, crossed open deserts, withstood mortar and sniper fire, been in constant fear of chemical attack, endured sandstorms, and had now broken through the

Republican Guard, the Black Knights had finally reached their objective. The Americans were on the outskirts of Baghdad.

On the main road I saw Sergeant Pyle and some of his crew. He had been standing out of the turret to fire down into foxholes with his M-16 machine gun when he had been shot in the shoulder. His flak jacket had stopped the bullet, preventing a fractured bone. His tank, 'Big Punisher', had ground to a halt when it had been hit a few moments later by three RPGs. They had struck its rear, the Abrams' weakest spot, disabling it and forcing the crew to climb through a hatch to escape. The tank had been towed by one of the Bradleys and now stood behind them, its back blackened by smoke where the equipment strapped to the top had caught fire.

Sergeant Pyle was still on a massive adrenalin high despite his arm being in a green sling. 'It was my own stupid fault,' he said, a grin fixed to his face. 'I shouldn't have been trying to take on the Iraqi army with a machine gun. Messed up my tank good and proper though. They better give me a new one. There's going to be more fighting to be done.'

A few days later I would talk to Sergeant Pyle about that final stretch of road to Baghdad, a zone that the American military referred to as Objective Cubs. 'It was a bunch of frozen moments,' he said. 'I remember a man getting out of his car burning from his mid-thigh up. He got out as if he was getting a hamburger. He reached down to pick up an AK-47 and I shot him. I remember a man looking up at the tank from his foxhole before I shot him.

'When I was hit, I dropped down inside and said, "I'm hit." I wasn't frightened since I was still so focused on getting down that road. I knew that we were the lead tank and that if we stopped, everyone would stop, so I just wanted to keep going. At the time I felt more shocked that we had to evacuate the tank than about getting shot.

'I was here in Desert Storm,' he continued, 'when they fought us as an army and engaged us in the desert and we defeated them.

It's been guerrilla tactics this time. This has been the heaviest fighting I've ever seen. Guys have found their limit. You can see it in their faces. People have changed. Some don't want to be here and they're scared. They've had as much as they can take. That's something important to learn as a man.'

I was beginning to realise that besides his eloquence and intelligence, this man was above all a warrior. I talked to one of the M113 crew about it. 'Oh yeah,' I was told. 'Sergeant Pyle loves to fight. I've seen him play [American] football. He's a mean motherfucker and doesn't like to lose. That guy's every inch a fighter.'

A crew from Fox News had arrived in their tan Land Cruiser. They set up their camera. The reporter (or 'our front-line hero', as Fox called its embeds), Greg Kelly, had mud all over his face, and like me was sporting a military helmet and flak jacket. Behind him the sun was setting, its final rays turning the sky a fiery red. I walked over to find out if they had any details about casualties in the recent fighting. They were not pleased to see me. 'I thought we were the only reporters here,' the cameraman said. 'We understood we would be the first at this spot.'

I had not thought of it before, but suddenly I realised that I had achieved a professional milestone. I was one of the first reporters, maybe the first, to reach Baghdad with the American troops. 'Who else is here?' I asked.

'Reuters is somewhere nearby. God knows about CNN. Everyone else is trying to catch up,' I was told.

'Any newspaper reporters?'

'No, they're miles behind. No one else is anywhere close. Look around you. There are only a handful of units so far, and there isn't any press with them.'

There was an explosion, closer by this time. 'Come on,' said Greg Kelly, 'let's get this over with.'

*

As a child I would often hear stories about what my grandfathers had accomplished during the Second World War. It was a common thing for many people my age in Britain. We were taught that the old men, when young, had done their duty and come forward to save the world from a great evil. There were photographs curling with age and medals to prove it. In my paternal grandmother's house there was one of my father's father leaning over a stiff-backed chair, dressed in British Army desert uniform, sand goggles hanging around his neck, his face caught in an ambiguous stare. Behind him could be made out a Jeep. To one side was a table with maps on it. A pistol was in a leather holster at his hip. He had been captured as a warrior in a black and white photograph. When I was young, I would look at this picture and fantasise about the adventure of those years fighting across the plains of North Africa. Playing with plastic soldiers, I would cast my grandfather as the hero leading his troops into great battles from which he would emerge triumphant, his rifle barrel hot from the bullets spent and his bayonet dripping with German blood. What virtue, I would think, to be tested, and to find oneself not wanting. What men, to be so strong.

My father's father had been in the Eighth Army, then had volunteered to join Britain's embryonic Special Forces and take the fight to the enemy far to the rear of Rommel's front lines. He had been at El Alamein, promoted to General Montgomery's general staff. When D-Day was being planned he had been part of the team that selected landing zones for parachutists and gliders, units those in command knew would suffer heavy casualties, but which needed to be deployed to ease the pressure on those storming the beaches. Almost immediately after the landings in Normandy, when it had been established that the invasion had been successful, he had a breakdown caused by exhaustion that had required him to be hospitalised.

My mother's father had been a tearaway in his youth, skipping school and drifting through his teenage years. In 1939 he realised that by signing up for the Territorial Army he could get out of having to do the newly introduced national service, so, thinking it might lead to an easier life, had become a part-time soldier. When war broke out this meant he could not join the RAF as he had by then decided he wanted to. After three years of trying to get out of the army he had taken the next best option and signed up for the newly formed Glider Pilot Regiment in the first months of 1942. Shortly before D-Day he caught tuberculosis, and had been invalided out of the battle, unable to pilot one of the gliders sent in to land at those spots identified by the man whose son would marry his daughter.

Standing in that field in Baghdad I thought of them both, and wondered how they had done it. They had spent years at war; the men I was with had changed after only weeks. Those in World War II had seen their friends being slaughtered. These soldiers and I were nervous enough just with a few getting wounded. How had they taken part in a war that lasted so long and not been destroyed by it? My grandfathers' true virtue, I realised, was not, as I had previously thought, the fact that they had signed up to take on the Nazis. It was to have been able to put it all behind them. To get married, bring up children, have fulfilling careers, to manage to appear to escape the traumas of their youth and hide the mental scars that must have come with them.

The day was still not over. The M113, Band Aid and a sole Bradley were sent to guard the fuellers. Their trucks were stationed in the courtyard of a house half a mile from the field where the army was gathering, and had been told to wait for the tanks to come to them to get more fuel. It was completely dark now, and everyone was very nervous. The reality of what had been experienced was beginning to have its impact.

José sat on the bench in front of me in the back of the M113. 'Twenty-one years without having to kill anyone,' he said to me, 'and when it happened you were there to share it. I'd wondered what it would be like. I was surprised by how calm I was. I thought I'd feel more excited, but I was so calm. It's the training as a scout to not feel the emotion. It took over. I felt this great calm in me.'

And then he laughed to himself and, reaching into the straps fixed to his flak jacket, pulled out another shell for the grenade launcher. 'I think I fired your shell,' he said, meaning the one he had written my name on. 'Maybe I was a little bit excited after all.' He took out his pen, drew another smiley face, marked my name, and put my new personalised death sentence back in his pocket.

The fuellers were not happy with waiting around, and nor was I. There had been reports of sniper and mortar fire. One of the fuel-truck drivers came up and asked José for permission for them to get out of there. 'No one's coming,' he said. 'Let's go. They're going to find us and shoot at us if we hang around too long.' Anyone who smoked was told to make sure the flame of the match or the end of their cigarette was not visible, so that we did not give away our position. I began to feel even more uneasy. Ray too was saying to José that it was a mistake to hang around. Trey started to call on the radio to find out where the rest of the company was located, and if anyone was actually intending to be refuelled.

Ray spotted some headlights coming towards us. 'Who's that?' he said. José picked up his M-16. Trey manned the machine gun. There had been no cars passing since nightfall. 'What the fuck is that?' asked Ray. Through his helmet microphone, Trey was talking to the Bradley. They had no idea what it was either, but it was getting closer. Suddenly Ray pointed behind us. 'There's someone with a gun!' José swung around and raised his weapon to his shoulder before he realised it was one of the fuellers who had taken cover, rifle at the ready, behind the wheels of a truck. I was scared. Everyone's nerves were shot. Like the rest, I was only too aware that suicide bombers had been driving up to American checkpoints.

The Bradley commander shouted a warning to stop in English and Arabic. The car kept coming. 'Shoot the fucker,' Ray said. 'What's he waiting for?'

The Bradley opened fire, the shell taking out the front wheels of the vehicle. There was the sound of women screaming. The infantrymen from the back of the tank fanned forward to investigate. 'It's a taxi. It's a fucking taxi,' the report came in. One of the driver's feet was bleeding. In the back were four women, all hysterical with fear.

'That's it. Let's get out of here,' José said, and ordered the fuellers away from the area.

We drove through the dark roads of the outskirts of Baghdad. None of the streetlights seemed to be working, and there was no light from any of the windows in the surrounding buildings. Near the field at which we had first arrived, we pulled into a spot where a wall offered some protection. There were so many air raids being carried out on the city to our north that it resembled a fireworks display. Later I would hear from the local people that there were notably fewer attacks on the capital that night than at any time since the war had begun, but as I watched the flashes of explosions and traces of anti-aircraft fire, it seemed to me that the whole sky was lit up by the bombardment.

I phoned London to check on the copy I had filed. They were pleased with me. My story would be the lead on the next day's front page, under a photo by-line. Beside it would be the strapline: 'By Oliver Poole, the first newspaper reporter to reach Baghdad with US forces.' I had seen the field officer in charge of the 2nd Brigade, Colonel David Perkins, and while he briefed me on events he had also confirmed what Fox News had told me. There were no other newspaper journalists even close. God knows what had happened to all those reporters in their battle fatigues I had come across in Kuwait.

I knew this was the high point of my career up till now. It was certainly a far cry from the film awards and serial killers that had taken up my time in California. Yet amid my satisfaction, excitement and pride, I felt a fraud. I knew that it was just a complete accident – luck had put me with the right unit, luck had meant I had got there first. And then there was the memory of all the dead bodies I had seen on the way, and how I had prayed for others to join them. That night, the bomber jets still flying overhead, the feelings of guilt were particularly strong that I was benefiting as a result of so much suffering.

The foreign desk told me one other piece of news. There had been a football match earlier that evening, a European Championship qualifying match between England and Turkey. A seventeen-year-old striker called Wayne Rooney had made his debut and played a blinder in England's 2–0 victory. The news gave me enormous pleasure. I had been to the World Cup in Japan the year before, and always enjoyed England winning. Then there was the fact that I had once made the mistake of falling in love with a Turkish girl, and two years later had been left with what I can only describe as a broken heart. It had taken almost six months before I started feeling like myself again, but spite meant I was still always happy to hear we had got one over on the Turks. However, above all the news seemed a wonderful reassertion of normalcy in the world. That a teenage footballer from Merseyside would always remember that day for the best of reasons rather than the worst, as all the young men I had been with ultimately would. Across England people would be in pubs celebrating victory in a football match. With those two teams I knew there would have been some crowd trouble – as indeed there was, with ninety-five people being arrested – but it all just seemed so wonderfully civilised after the raw fear and armed violence I had witnessed that day.

I lay on my stretcher pressed against the roof of Band Aid. Air Force One came on the military radio to give his nightly briefing. The 1st Brigade had an hour earlier started its attack on Baghdad's international airport, and had so far faced little opposition. A bar in Russia was refusing to serve British or American customers as a sign of its owner's opposition to the war ('Once a communist, always a communist,' Air Force One commented). Back at Dragon 4 there had been a gas scare that had forced people into MOPP 4. He congratulated everyone on what they had achieved while suffering so few casualties. 'So that's it for Thursday, 3 April. The day we got to Baghdad. Be safe.' A pause, then a final question. 'When do we all get to go home?'

SEVEN

Saints and Sinners

Friday, 4 April–Sunday, 6 April

A bullet fired through his front door told Fawaz Alavan the Americans had arrived in Baghdad. He was reading a newspaper filled with reports of the defeats the United States military was supposedly suffering around the southern cities of Iraq, his wife and sister working in the kitchen, when the lock was shot open and five American soldiers, machine guns held to their shoulders, surrounded him.

'I thought it was Iraqi police, but then I see American men,' he told me the next day as we sat in the calm of his garden sipping sugar-laden tea. 'I could not believe it. They meant to be far away. Not inside my house. It was confusion. Soldiers everywhere. They take us to back room and we hidden there. But my sister needed toilet, so I knock on door and little American answer and he let us out. Then I see damage. Terrible. Terrible. Bulletholes in wall. Bed broken. I will petition for compensation. They damage my property. President W. Bush will hear from me personally. I will inform him that I need new door.'

The American soldiers had conducted the search of Mr Alavan's house because his forecourt had been selected as the spot for the Black Knights to refuel. Before they did so, the site had to be secured. As a result he had been the recipient of what the infantry called 'knocking with authority'. In those first days after the arrival in the capital it was considered prudent to assume that someone inside a building wanted to kill you. Only when it was clear there was no threat would those who lived there be treated as non-combatants.

It was on this forecourt that we had waited the previous evening for the tanks that never arrived, sitting in the dark until we believed we could be the target of a suicide attack. In the bright light of the next morning, when the whole refuelling operation was attempted a second time, it was hard to conceive how we had been so frightened. The area seemed an oasis of tranquillity. A wonderful, clear stream ran through Mr Alavan's garden, the lawn of which was dotted with clay pots filled with flowers. Intrigued to see how the people of Baghdad were taking the sudden arrival of the United States Army, I had wandered over to introduce myself to the nearest resident.

A portly man, his belly pressing against his ankle-length white robes, opened the door a crack as I approached. Behind him I could make out a dozen women and children peering at me. 'I am a reporter for a British newspaper,' I told them.

'That good,' the man answered in halting English, flinging the door fully open. 'You will tell world about petition to President W. Bush.' He pointed at the bullethole in the lock and the smashed glass in the door. In his main living room, the floor was covered in Oriental carpets and the walls were decorated with extracts from the Koran and, incongruously, a striking photograph of the Swiss Alps. He showed me where a side door had been kicked open. The edges of a bed had been pulled off so that the soldiers could check no one was hiding underneath.

Mr Alavan told me he was a chemical engineer, and a Sunni Muslim. He indicated the small room at the back where his family had been marshalled while their house was being searched. As he led me around, the women and children shuffled behind us, staring avidly at my every move. When I touched one of the bulletholes and shook my head in a gesture of appreciative horror, they broke

Myself during a nerve gas scare, after the Americans had destroyed a tanker containing chemicals which it was then realised might be blown towards the camp. Sergeant Weaver is behind me, demonstrating that even at times of stress the soldiers were able to maintain a sense of humour.

Sergeant Ray Simon manning the radio in the back of the vehicle known as the CP, the command point that relayed orders between the various parts of the Black Knights company.

Left: The crew of 'Band Aid', the company's tracked medical emergency vehicle. Left to right: Sergeant James 'Doc' Swinney, the head medic; Sergeant Brian Bache, the driver; and Specialist Terry 'Frankie' Franks, the assistant medic. In the second half of the campaign I slept in Band Aid at night, lying on a stretcher in the back pressed up against the metal ceiling.

Left: Passing over the Euphrates. Since the invasion had started the US army had skirted the west bank; now finally the river was being crossed, and only Baghdad lay before them. It was a moment of exhilaration for everybody, even though the coming hours would bring some of the fiercest fighting of the campaign.

Middle left: Band Aid during the advance to Baghdad. Doc is standing half-out of the front command hatch.

Bottom left: Sergeant Trey Black, the commander of the CP, manning the vehicle's .50-calibre machine gun.

Top right: The final stretch of road to Baghdad. The Black Knights were now at the very front of the advance, under attack from the Republican Guard and Saddam-supporting paramilitaries who shot at them from rooftops, alleyways and foxholes. An air strike had just been called in to this area, destroying an Iraqi gun position and leaving much of the surrounding vegetation on fire.

Right: Sergeants Miguel 'Moe' Marrero and Jerold Pyle and the Abrams, 'Big Punisher', in which they led the Black Knights' advance into Baghdad. The tank had been incapacitated after being struck by RPGs (the scorch marks can be seen on the rear of the turret), and Sergeant Pyle shot in the shoulder.

Left: Sharing tea with the locals on the first full day in Baghdad. Fawaz Alavan (centre, in white robe) discovered the US military had arrived in the city when an infantry unit shot open his front door. The bald man to the right is a taxi driver whose vehicle the Americans had fired at the previous night, fearing he was a suicide bomber.

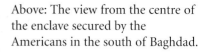

Above: The view from the centre of the enclave secured by the Americans in the south of Baghdad.

An American soldier holds two of the First World War British Enfield rifles that Iraqi troops were still using in 2003.

Above: A destroyed Iraqi tank on the streets of Baghdad. The sky was a reddish colour from the fires burning across the city.

Sergeant Weaver dressed in an Iraqi fireman's uniform found at a Republican Guard barracks.

Above: Myself inside a Republican Guard barracks seized less than an hour earlier by the Americans. The orgy of destruction had already begun: eggs had been thrown at the picture of Saddam Hussein and furniture smashed.

Below: Outside the barracks. A picture of Saddam Hussein had been destroyed by machine-gun fire and a tank shell, and an Iraqi vehicle was on fire.

Above: Trey Black and First Sergeant José Rosa on the day it was announced that Saddam Hussein's regime had fallen.

Below: Trey Black, Ray Simon and me beside the M113 which acted as the CP for the Black Knights tank company.

Above: Residents of Baghdad at one of the roadblocks set up by the Americans in the city. Some came to offer thanks to the invading army, some to ask for food and water, others simply to witness up close the army that was now in their midst.

Below: A Bradley points its gun towards the centre of Baghdad.

into spontaneous applause. Crawling on the ground was a seriously handicapped teenage boy, who pulled himself along the tiled floor by his hands and then started pawing at my leg with his fingers. One of the older children grabbed his foot and dragged him away, the handicapped boy's arm still trying to reach across the widening distance.

'He my son,' Mr Alavan said. 'He not good in head. Now we have tea.'

We sat at a small metal table on the veranda, and one of the boys brought out glasses of hot, sticky liquid on a metal tray. 'These boys my relatives. They live in centre of Baghdad, but not safe with bombing, so they sent to me. Thought be safer. Little know American army come here.'

He leant back in his chair, his belly pushing upwards now, and stroked his black beard. 'The Americans not bad people, despite damage caused. They come in and say "Sorry, sorry" about what they did. Americans good. They good people, they say sorry. That good.'

I asked him about whether Saddam Hussein was good. He leant forward and dropped his voice. 'Still not good to talk about Saddam. Too dangerous. After war over, we talk about him. When he dead, it be safe.'

His handicapped son was approaching again. Mr Alavan saw him, waved a hand, and one of the other boys once again grabbed the hapless youth's leg and dragged him back into the building. 'Yes, America good. They will give me money for new door. Now I give everybody tea to show our hospitality.' He stood up, and at a determined pace headed off towards the American soldiers standing around the fuel tankers on the adjacent forecourt. Behind him, desperately trying to keep a shiny kettle and half a dozen glasses upright on the tray, scuttled the boy responsible for administering the tea.

'My friends,' said Mr Alavan, opening his arms wide. 'Welcome to my home. Have tea.' I could see Trey and Doc staring quizzically at him. 'Tea for my friends,' Mr Alavan tried again, with another flamboyant gesture. They took a glass each and sipped it gingerly.

As well as the American soldiers, there were two Iraqis standing on the driveway. They were the driver and his assistant whose taxi had been hit the previous night. They had abandoned the vehicle after the incident and come back when it was light to try to repair the damage. When I had seen them that morning, I had felt faintly embarrassed at remembering how I had been convinced they meant to kill us, and how close they had been to getting killed. But they seemed remarkably forgiving about the whole episode, smiling and waving as we passed. Perhaps they had simply concluded that it was sensible to keep on the good side of these men who had fired a shell at their taxi. Now they came over to join in the communal festivities.

Asking Mr Alavan to translate, I told them how terribly sorry I was about the previous night. The driver, a tall bald man, smiled, waved his left hand around for a bit, and then said something in Arabic. 'He say no big deal,' our host explained. 'No serious damage done. He hurt his foot, but an American has cleaned it for him. He has no bad feeling.'

This seemed remarkably magnanimous. 'But what was he doing driving around in the middle of a battle?' I asked.

A brief exchange followed. 'He had good fare,' Mr Alavan said. 'Good fare to take women to Babylon. Good money.' Fifty-five miles south-east of Baghdad, the modern town of Babylon still exists where King Nebuchadnezzar's capital flourished 2500 years ago.

'No, I mean why was he risking driving among the American tanks?' I explained.

Mr Alavan stared at me. 'Because nobody knew they here. We told they long way south getting beaten.' He said something in Arabic to the taxi driver who nodded rapidly, his bald head bobbing. 'He thought the tanks Iraqi, and the sound of firing was soldiers excited in celebrating news of some victory. Now, let's all drink more tea.' Mr Alavan clapped his hands and the boy with the kettle rushed around refilling everyone's glasses.

The taxi driver smiled and went into another round of nodding. 'America good,' he said. Pulling out a banknote, he pointed at the picture of Saddam printed on it, then dragged a finger across his own throat.

My day had begun with an infantryman being shot at a checkpoint and Band Aid summoned to provide treatment. A machine gun had been fired from inside a car as it swept past a junction guarded by the Black Knights. An artery was hit in the American soldier's thigh, and there was concern that he could lose his leg. The medics ferried him to a hospital erected beside brigade headquarters in the field where we had first stopped on our arrival in Baghdad. A lot of blood had to be cleaned from the floor of the medic track that morning.

The troops stationed around the medical centre were passing the time exchanging details about the latest dirty tricks the Iraqis were rumoured to have adopted. One told me that dummy cigarette stands had been stocked with cartons filled with explosives primed to detonate when anyone opened them. Dozens of abandoned Republican Guard uniforms had been discovered – some inside buildings, others by the side of the road – prompting speculation that their former owners had changed into civilian clothes to better harass the Americans. There were claims of two more attempted suicide bombings. Sergeant Robert Jones, the driver of an ammunition truck, a position known as an 'ammo dog', was recalling his journey to Baghdad. 'They were surrounding us,' he said, 'but I thought about those Marines who were captured and hanged on Iraqi TV. There was no way they were going to take us.' I had already established that the story was untrue, but it was obviously still having a significant impact. I began to wonder if it had been circulated deliberately.

Gunfire and the occasional explosion could be heard in the distance. The Americans were securing the perimeter of the fifteen-square-mile enclave they had seized at Objective Saints, and this clearly meant more bloodshed. As well as remnants of Republican Guard units and paramilitaries, the fifteen-thousand-strong Special Republican Guard and five-thousand-member Special Security Organisation were stationed in the capital. They were considered the most loyal of Saddam's soldiers.

There were to be no more rest periods until the whole city had been captured, and there was now a constant fear of sniper or mortar attacks. On the company's radio frequency I heard the captain discussing the best way to approach a suspected tank emplacement. 'Damn, I'm just going to blow it up,' he concluded. The infantry were conducting house-to-house searches to ensure there were no enemy soldiers left in the area. 'They can't be too bad,' a GI reported of some Iraqis he had been ordered to guard while their apartment was checked. 'One of them's wearing a Guns 'n' Roses T-shirt.'

I could see that the strain of being at the middle of constant combat was beginning to tell on those around me. At times I struggled to recall the light-heartedness and sense of innocent adventure I had witnessed back in Kuwait. It was as if the days of playful wrestling matches, racing Jeeps across the desert and practical jokes had involved a different group of people. The Black Knights were a company of war veterans now.

Ray was still dwelling on the number of bodies he had witnessed, and the violence unleashed by his comrades. It was an obsession which partly expressed itself through an insistence on photographing corpses. Time after time he would stop the M113, stand up in the driver's seat, and snap a picture of what remained of the latest dead Iraqi. Since leaving Kuwait the log on the M113 recorded that it had covered 824 miles, and it seemed Ray's eyes had sunk deeper into his skull with each passing one. That morning, when he had heard that the company was probing the surrounding streets, he had shaken his head in bewilderment and given a wry chuckle. 'This is getting ridiculous. We wake up, kill people, have lunch, kill some more people, and then go to sleep. It's getting out of control.'

We discussed the changes he had seen in his comrades. 'It's like they were all on Prozac and suddenly stopped getting their medication. They were wild men,' he said. 'Back home we'd be in prison for doing what we've done out here. Did you hear the captain as we went up that road [through Cubs to Baghdad]?' I hadn't. 'He said we should kill as many enemy as we can, and as quickly as possible. I know he just wants to make sure he brings everyone home, but who would have thought he'd be such a killer?'

Later, when others were talking of their surprise at discovering the extent of the captain's ferociousness in battle, I would be amused to hear one soldier attributing it to him playing 'that rugby shit'. Even for soldiers, playing a contact sport without padding was a macho folly that deserved to be respected.

Doc had washed at last, so was looking slightly less primeval. Throughout my time with the Black Knights he had provided me with a safe haven, offering an entertaining distraction from the reality of our situation with his tales of the scrapes he had got into before joining the army. Yet now I would catch him dwelling on the sights he had witnessed here in Iraq, sitting by himself in the semi-darkness inside Band Aid as he went through everything he had experienced. He may still have loved to recount his favourite copulation anecdotes, but now there was an anger in him, fuelled by indignation. After treating the injured scout he had been summoned to examine a PoW who had told his captors the plastic cuffs placed around his wrists were too tight. When Doc came back from inspecting the prisoner he was almost shaking with rage.

'The cuffs were fine, but he wouldn't stop complaining. So I whispered in his ear, "Do you want to be treated like your people treated the Americans taken prisoner?" He looked scared, and told me no. It took everything I had not to pummel the guy.'

Doc was preoccupied by the fact that he may have accidentally killed civilians in the chaos of the battle in the outskirts of Baghdad. There had been Iraqi soldiers shooting at the medic van from all sides, and as Doc returned fire he had hit two people who he now feared might simply have been trying to hide after finding themselves caught up in the fighting. 'I saw the top of their heads behind a berm and I shot them,' I heard him say to Sergeant Black.

'That's why you've got to wait and see them shoot at you,' Trey answered. 'You're here to die, boy.'

'But that's the thing,' said Doc. 'I'm not.'

Of everyone, Trey seemed the least affected by recent events. If anything he appeared strengthened by them, comforted that his pessimistic warnings had for once been proved accurate. Almost uniquely, he had not been surprised by all that had happened, and therefore showed no sign of having been damaged by it. I had begun to realise his distrust of the world was a defence mechanism. In Iraq there was nothing people liked less than surprises. Now life was proving as twisted as Trey had always maintained it was to anyone who would listen. This gave him a certain satisfaction.

For most of that day he held court in the back of the M113 while the rest of the company continued to clear pockets of opposition to our north. Mike Few, the lieutenant who had exchanged some coffee for the use of my telephone back in the field outside Samawah, was with us as his tank had broken down again. He had gained a reputation as a terrible cadger of tobacco, which was becoming increasingly precious as personal stocks started to run low. Soldiers enjoying a smoke now hid their cigarettes when he was spotted approaching. Someone had given him a tin of chewing tobacco in the hope it would satiate his need.

Trey took a break from recollecting good times fighting classmates at high school to conduct a radio check. Of the six Republican Guard divisions believed to be around Baghdad, he learnt, three were now classed as inoperative. Of the remainder, one was to the west and the other in the east of the city.

'Where's the third one?' Trey asked.

'Right here,' came the answer.

'Ahh,' he said. 'I told you all, if it can go wrong, we're always going to be in the middle of it.'

I was typing away at that day's article, and I noticed him sneak a look at what I was writing. 'Do you ever worry that I might be being critical about what's happening here and what people like you are doing?' I asked.

'No,' he replied, 'because I know that you know if you write anything bad about me, I'm going to hunt you down and kill you.'

Yet, despite his bluster and bitterness, there was a kindness in Trey, however much it may have embarrassed him. It was one of the reasons I could not help but like him. When we stopped in Baghdad, it was he who would make sure the men handed out the leaflets to passing civilians explaining that the Americans came to free them, not conquer them. He was one of the few who seemed to be encouraging the confidence-building meetings that were essential if the local people were to trust the foreign army that was now in their city. Trey barely slept, working throughout the nights to make sure every vehicle in the company had all the equipment it needed. He would often take time to talk individually to each crew, to jolly them up and ensure they were coping with the rigours of the campaign.

Unlike many of the men, Trey was not vindictive towards the Iraqi soldiers, but almost pitied them. 'They're just dumb,' he would say. 'I mean, we've got to kill them – this isn't some hippy commune, that's what we're here to do – but they're stupid, and that's why they're dying in such numbers. All they had to do was let us all pass, drawn us into the country, then attacked the supply vehicles, and we would've been stranded up here like Custer at the Little Big Horn. They could've wiped us out at their pleasure.

They've got enough weapons. You can't spit without finding more weapons hidden somewhere. They just don't know how to use them. They've been attacking tanks with machine guns. They ain't been trained about what they're dealing with. That isn't bravery. That's stupidity. They should be listening to their fear and realising it's a dumb idea. Saddam should have hired me to run his campaign. I could have caused a whole heap of misery.'

He had spoken of his wife and the bitter rows that at times erupted between them. I wondered if his pessimism about their marriage was just another attempt to prepare himself in case of the worst. It cannot have been easy to be married to Trey Black. 'I'm not the kind of guy who's good at going to smart events with smart people,' he once said. 'I like bars where I know everyone. You can relax and have some fun, not have to pretend you're something you're not. But she wants us to meet what she thinks are better people: lawyers, doctors, bullshit like that. That causes stress because she wants one thing and I want another, and I feel bad about that.

'I went back this time [over Christmas] and finally she got pregnant. I'd wanted to have a kid for years, but she wouldn't have it. And now it's happening, and I can't stop wondering if I'm going to be a good daddy to that little thing. I've always been an asshole, and sometimes I worry that's never going to change.'

Halfway through the afternoon the M113 was ordered to evacuate when a mortar was fired at the brigade headquarters. Luckily the Iraqi soldiers were now so nervous of giving their position away that they would only let off one or two shells before dispersing. This meant they had no opportunity to work out the correct range. Unless they sent off a freak shot it was very rare, by this point, for their mortars to inflict any significant damage.

The units from 2nd Brigade sent south to destroy the remnants of Saddam's 'ring of steel' had reached their objective. They discovered that it was not only the citizens of Baghdad who were unaware of the United States Army's real location. The Republican Guard tanks had their weapons pointed away from the capital to where they believed the Americans were mustering. The reports of the ensuing fighting all agreed it was a quick, overwhelmingly one-sided affair.

Everywhere the unit's food and water stocks were running low. Throughout the entire advance there had been a struggle to keep supplies up with the soldiers. Now, that part of the battle was temporarily being lost. Bottled water had run out, requiring soldiers to rely on acrid-tasting supplies held in round metal tanks known as water buffaloes. The amount handed out was carefully rationed. The infantry, crammed into the back of their Bradleys, suffered the worst. The first cases of heat exhaustion were being reported at first aid stations. Vehicles that still had supplies of MREs were ordered to share them with those who had none.

The temperature had reached 95 degrees Fahrenheit on the M113's thermometer. I dreaded to think what conditions would have been like if the start of the war had been delayed any longer into the summer. Worse was the humidity that engulfed us now that we were out of the desert, its impact so total it seemed the moisture should have been visible as it hung in the air. Everyone was covered in a sheen of sweat. While I typed on my laptop, drops would roll off the end of my nose onto the keyboard. However, the conditions could have been even more uncomfortable. The order was given that day for the biochemical protection level to be dropped to MOPP 0, as it was considered unlikely that Saddam would launch a biochemical attack on his own capital. For the first time since crossing into Iraq, everyone climbed out of the chemical suits in which they had previously sweltered.

The psychological boost this gave was enormous. There had always been the nagging fear that at any moment we could be 'chemmed'. Ever since the false alarm before crossing the border it had become second nature for me to make sure that my gasmask was always within reach. Before I went to sleep I checked that the strap of its bag dangled next to my head. For weeks we had worn nothing but the same charcoal-lined suits. Mine had become encrusted with dirt and congealed drips of MRE. On a number of occasions I had passively let swarms of flies feed on the stains in the hope that this would remove them. Now the jacket and trousers could be stripped off, and with them went the fear of the grisly death they had grown to represent. For the first time since the war had started I found myself thinking not about what I had to do that day, but what I would do when the whole thing was over. I imagined a beach and the ocean breaking against it. Me lying in the water, staring at the sun as the waves lapped around me. A bar nearby which sold chilled bottles of beer.

In celebration I went for a short walk to take a photograph of a portrait of Saddam Hussein that dominated a nearby road junction. It was only two hundred yards from the central battalion headquarters, but by the time I was halfway there I felt so exposed at being away from the American armour that I turned around and went back, feeling embarrassed at my own timidity.

Back amid the illusion of safety offered by the close proximity of my protectors, I spotted a familiar figure. Standing on top of Sergeant Pyle's tank, which was now being stripped of every useful spare part, was Sergeant Weaver. The battle to resurrect the M88 had finally been abandoned. He had travelled up with Sergeant Harrison's armoured maintenance vehicle that morning after completing the repairs to the three tanks that had broken down on the advance past Karbala.

'Got a cigarette, by any chance?' he asked. I laughed. He shrugged. I asked how he was. 'I don't like not having the M88,' he replied. 'I feel like a passenger now.' Roman had stayed behind with Bill, the sergeant who had been with us during the sandstorm outside Samawah, and would be coming up later when it was deemed safe for the soft-sided vehicles that made up the rest of the supply train to move forward.

Stazny, the Bradley mechanic who along with Red had arrived in the same vehicle as Weaver, came over and asked to use my phone. 'I want to call my girl, if you don't mind,' he said. 'Today's the day we were meant to get married. That is, until I learnt I was getting sent out here.'

Trey grunted. 'The best place to be on your wedding day is somewhere else. You're the only one of us who'd be having a worse time if none of this had ever happened.'

The next morning, the human cost of the recent fighting became clear when the military released an estimate of the number of enemy soldiers killed by 2nd Brigade in the previous forty-eight hours. Around 1600 were believed dead, while 350 vehicles, more than half of them tanks, had been destroyed. 'There's been too much needless loss of life,' Colonel Perkins, the commander of 2nd Brigade, told reporters. 'We have had a number of suicide attackers. These guys are dying in droves.'

The figures shocked me. A whole lot of killing had taken place amid the squat buildings and palm trees that stretched around me. 'It's only half the number who died in the World Trade Center,' Doc remarked when I mentioned the extent of the Iraqi casualties to him. I was not sure the comparison was relevant, and told him so. But later I was not so certain. This wasn't the Tet Offensive, let alone the Battle of the Somme. Maybe 1600 was not a large number of people to be killed during the first stage in the taking of an enemy's capital city. My mind was full of thoughts about how terrible this all was, but what had I expected? What had I thought I was coming to see?

I walked from where 1st Battalion had set up its headquarters and along the road to where the rest of the brigade was encamped. I noticed that a corpse which had lain beside an anti-aircraft gun since the day we had arrived had been disturbed, and part of its leg was missing. I was told that wild dogs had been eating it in the night. One more outrage to add to the burnt bodies, the corpses crushed in destroyed vehicles, brains seeping onto tarmac. I needed to find someone who could give me a perspective on what I was witnessing. Dwelling on the rights and wrongs was no longer making the answers any clearer.

Every hour since our arrival, more and more vehicles had pulled into the American enclave. In tow had come the first journalists I had seen since Kuwait, apart from the Fox News team and those placed with my battalion. There was a fat and grizzled Frenchman, a large Tricolour blowing from the aerial of his car ('An inviting target,' as one of the soldiers put it), along with half a dozen press photographers. Then there was a Spanish reporter and a German journalist who had been travelling with the 2nd Brigade's field hospital. It was to them I turned for advice. I had met the Spaniard, Julio Anguita Parrado, at the Hilton Hotel in Kuwait City during the briefings organised for the 3rd Infantry Division's embeds. He worked for the Spanish newspaper *El Mundo*, and even in Kuwait his huge brown eyes had seemed to be in a perpetual state of surprise at what was happening around him. I had immediately warmed to him, as like me he had realised late in the embed process quite how seriously the Americans were going to take the scheme. 'But I think we could get shot,' he had said after Major General Blount had finished his talk explaining just where we would be located. I could not but agree.

The German, Christian Liebig, was new to me. He worked for a leading weekly current affairs magazine called *Focus*. He was tall and angular, and his welcome was as warm as his companion's. Both were sitting on a stretcher erected outside the hospital tent.

Julio was overcome with indignation at all he had witnessed. He wanted to talk about one subject above all others: how many civilians did I think had been killed? It was a question that was preoccupying every reporter in the region as details had started to trickle out about the extent of this war's 'collateral damage'. The TV camera crews in Baghdad had beamed around the world pictures of fifteen people apparently killed by an American missile that had hit a market. A military investigation was launched after seven women and children were killed near Najaf. Their minivan had been shot after failing to brake when ordered to stop at a checkpoint.

Evan Wright, an American journalist embedded with the Marines, would later say, 'The slaughter of unarmed civilians almost seemed to exceed that of actual combatants.' He had been at a roadblock when a car had not stopped as requested, and American soldiers opened fire. The sergeant sent to investigate the vehicle found a three-year-old girl curled up on the back seat. When he reached forward to see if she needed medical care, the top of her head slid off. As he stepped back in shock, he slipped on the brains that had dropped out and now lay on the ground around him. No weapons were found inside the vehicle. The girl's father kept repeating, 'I'm sorry.' He then asked permission to pick up his daughter's body, and took her away to be buried.

Steve Myers of the *New York Times*, a friend from media boot camp, described how, while with 1st Brigade, he learnt about a family that had been in a car that was caught in the middle of a firefight on a road in Baghdad. They stopped in the central partition of the highway to try to avoid the surrounding tanks and Iraqi paramilitary vehicles. A truck mounted with an anti-aircraft gun drove towards the American column and was caught in a hail of bullets. It careered through the crash barriers and struck the car, causing it to burst into flames. A mother and her three children, the youngest an infant, had been badly injured and burnt. American soldiers had seen the father, barely moving, lying on the roadside.

Across Iraq, reporters were every day witnessing impossible decisions made by people who had been relentlessly trained to ensure only one possible outcome. I had met Alex Perry, a fellow Briton who worked for *Time* magazine, when he was embedded with a battalion of the 3rd Brigade located next to mine in Kuwait.

In Karbala he had witnessed a skirmish with Fedayeen fighters. He was with a platoon of the 101st Airborne, hunkered down on a rooftop in front of a building filled with snipers, when two boys aged seven or eight emerged in the courtyard between them. 'They came spinning out,' he wrote, 'almost as if they had been pushed and began creeping towards an RPG round that had been left lying on the ground. The soldiers were all saying: "Don't pick it up, don't touch that!" Maybe twenty or thirty guys shouting: "Don't do it!"

'A warning shot kicked up dust at the first boy's feet. He stopped and looked up: M-4s, M-16s, heavier automatic weapons, an entire arsenal, was levelled at him. Then, fixing the Americans with his clear, dark eyes, one boy walked forward – slowly, deliberately, defiantly – and picked up the round. "The moment he touched it, you could see a wall of lead slam into those kids," said a soldier who witnessed the scene. "It dropped the first kid immediately. The second one was hit a second later – you could see him tumble as he was running."'

I had not seen anyone kill a civilian. But I thought of the two infantrymen with the crying woman by the side of the road, of the destroyed houses, of Doc's worries, of how easily the passengers in the taxi that first night in Baghdad could have been among the dead. Yet there had also been an incident in which a major had strode into 1st Battalion's HQ and demanded that the soldiers responsible for shooting a pick-up truck still smoking outside be summoned and taken to inspect the vehicle. The people inside were civilians, he said, and the soldiers would have to live with what they had done for the rest of their lives. When they reached the truck they found the remains of two AK-47s and one rocket launcher lying beside the bodies among the scraps of Arab smocks and jeans inside it.

'I really don't know how many civilians have been killed,' I said to Julio.

'I think there are more than we can imagine at this time,' he told me. 'The American soldiers see something and they fire. Then they go to see what it is they have shot. They do not care what clothes their target is wearing. Everyone is considered an enemy until they are found to be unarmed, and that can happen when they walk over to inspect the body.' His eyes seemed even bigger than they had when I had first met him. 'You have seen the burnt-out civilian cars by the side of the road, yes? The buildings destroyed. Just look around us. Things are being destroyed everywhere.'

It was true. Even the highways were scorched by explosions, and their barriers had been crushed by armoured vehicles. Smoke was rising from five spots in the distance, now so familiar a sight that I hardly noticed it. A permanent haze hung in the air. There had not been a glimpse of blue sky since we had drawn into Baghdad.

'Things will be worse now we're in the capital,' the German reporter said. 'There will be fighting beside people's homes. If the American army considers that something is suspicious, it dies, whether they know for a fact that it posed an actual threat or not. Sometimes I worry that they're becoming out of control.'

It was difficult to make a judgement on whether the Americans were being reckless. Iraqi soldiers had been dressing in civilian clothes. It was not easy to tell the bad guy from the innocent. The Americans I had met did not want to kill civilians. Indeed, those who feared they had done so appeared mentally tortured. Maybe it was an inevitability that innocent people would die. Wasn't that just the nature of war, I asked.

'But they promised this war would be different,' Julio said. 'We were told they had the technology to stop civilians from getting killed. America talked of bringing freedom to this country. Of making it better for the people here. But what has happened? They've killed people from one end of it to the other. Women and children are dying. They've used the fact the people of Iraq didn't welcome them with kisses as an excuse to use their weapons even harder. Then they complain that people are still not more welcoming to them.

'It's like America as a whole,' he continued. 'It likes to talk of nice things, but how did the country respond to their fear after 11 September? With violence, just the same as their soldiers did here after they became frightened. Nothing matters as long as Americans are happy. They see any country, any other human beings, as expendable to what they need. It's such shit. I feel sick with what I have seen. Nothing good can come out of this. Not to Iraq, not to these soldiers, not to America, not to us who have witnessed it.'

There was activity in the medic tent beside us. A report had been received that casualties were coming in. Colonel Perkins had ordered a unit of tanks and Bradleys to drive towards the airport through a central area of the city which would take them along the Processional Way, under an arch depicting Saddam's hands holding crossed swords that had been erected as a victory monument to the war in Iran that he had never won. The Americans had realised that many of the inhabitants of Baghdad had no idea that they were so close. As the plan had been to reach the capital and then hope the regime fell as the people rose up against it, Iraqis had to be left in no doubt that US forces were now gathering on the outskirts of their city. The probe into Baghdad, termed Operation Thunder Run, was meant to remove any question as to the Americans' location. Being the furthest military intrusion into the city so far, it was always going to meet fierce resistance. But the risk was seen as justifiable because of the tactical advantages it would bring. A unit of the Special Republican Guard had attacked the convoy. Now the injured were being flown back in three helicopters.

I walked along a grassy path to the M113, and sat in the back hatch as the choppers landed. Half a dozen bodies were carried out on stretchers, the medics running beside them holding drips.

They crossed the road in front of me and went down a bank that led to the brigade hospital. One of the wounded, a tank commander, had been shot in the head. He and another died. I knew that two more Americans had been killed earlier that morning when a supply truck overturned and the crew drowned in a water-filled ditch. Four American soldiers dead in one day was the most I had witnessed since the war had begun. It was nothing compared to the 1600 Iraqis who had died in those forty-eight hours, but it was disturbing enough for the soldiers around me. Many of the Black Knights had known the tank commander who had been killed. He and Trey had been close friends, carousing partners back in Georgia. Now his skull had been caved in by pellets fired from a shotgun.

Those were not the last casualties I saw up close that day. Just before dusk there was the sound of an explosion about a hundred yards from where the M113 and Band Aid were parked. It sounded like a mortar, and the cry of 'Medic!' reverberated across the encampment. I watched Doc and Big Sergeant B hare up a slope to where I could make out the shapes of two bodies. Frankie drove the medic van towards them, with us following in support. The wounded soldiers were screaming until the morphine jabs were stuck in.

On the other side of the ridge was the zone where the American Special Forces were based. Their customised Jeeps, which had machine guns fixed to their backs, resembled Iraqi paramilitary pick-up trucks. These soldiers wore T-shirts and jeans. Pistol belts, rolls of ammunition and grenades hung from them. Their medics also crouched around the pair who had been injured. Another man was present, dressed in non-military clothes. He was older, and had a white goatee and a beer belly. A holster was strapped to his thigh. I heard him congratulating one of the Special Forces medics by name on the job he was doing. The medic looked up and said, 'Thank you, well, whatever your name is.' I later learnt he was CIA, and his identity could not be known by anyone.

One of the wounded had had part of his left foot blown off. I could see a bloodied shoe with some of his toes still in it. The other had lacerations to his leg. The medics cut away their clothes and wrapped their damaged limbs in bandages. The two soldiers had wanted to take a photograph of themselves next to the anti-aircraft gun near where the Iraqi who had been eaten by dogs had lain. The gun had been disabled by MLRS missiles. These work by detonating just above the ground and throwing out dozens of little bombs, none longer than a few inches, which explode around the target. Not all of them had detonated, and the soldier with the injured foot had stepped on one of these unexploded bomblets. He was a casualty of his own country's weapon.

'That's a damn shame,' Trey said as we looked at the boy. His face was sagging from the morphine, but as I stared I realised I knew him. It was Garth Stewart, the twenty-year-old who was in the same mortar crew as Nitai Schwartz. I remembered him saying he didn't want to be in the Gulf, that he didn't believe in the war. His blood had stained the bandages red by the time he was placed in a van to take him to the hospital tent.

When we got back to the nearby field in which the M113 and Band Aid camped each night, we found the scouts had established their base on a stretch of land adjacent to us. Ray had decided that the moment had come to ring his potential lady, the friend who he feared was too well educated for him. He too needed something to provide perspective. When she answered, Ray immediately transformed into some sort of fast-talking pimp. 'Hi, baby. I miss you, baby.' I laughed at his sweet-talking, and he gave me a leery grin and a thumbs up.

I could hear him saying things were pretty bad, but that he was all right. That he had got her letters and that they had meant the world to him. Idly he mentioned that he had just seen someone lose part of his foot. The line clearly went quiet. 'Don't worry,' he said hurriedly. 'I'm looking after myself. It's just the way things are here. Bad things happen to people, but it's not going to happen to me.' Then he reverted to the smooth charmer. 'Look, baby, when I get back, maybe we could meet up and I could take you out and show you a good time?'

I decided to give him some space. The scouts had piles of weapons that they had unearthed in house-to-house searches, and José invited me over to look at them. We didn't see much of the new first sergeant except for when we were travelling in the M113. He spent most of his time with his old comrades in the scouts. It was as if José feared intimacy with his new unit. He was already separated from them by his lack of understanding of how a tank company worked. When he attempted to exert his authority it was accompanied by a seeming inability to back down from confrontation. This just reinforced to his subordinates the arbitrary nature of his position. The previous holder of the post, First Sergeant Burt, had been spoken of with veneration, a respect that he had earned over two years, and his unmistakable strength of character would always have made him a tough act to follow. I heard many in the company cast doubt on José's experience, military worth and personality, and in return he appeared to be ensuring that criticism was literally kept at a distance. I felt sorry for him. He was having a difficult time: getting divorced from his wife, soon to be separated from his two teenage children, seemingly unable to bond with those around him. This was no time or place to feel isolated, although I suspect he would have considered pity from a passenger whom he viewed as a mere inconvenience to be the worst of all insults.

The scouts had found dozens of rocket-propelled grenade launchers and AK-47s, most made in the Soviet Union or former Yugoslavia. José pointed out a pile of about forty dirty wooden rifles. They looked like the Lee Enfields that had been used in shooting practice by the cadet corps at my school. They were freshly greased, and there were frayed cardboard boxes holding dozens of bullets. I picked up one of the guns and found that they were indeed Enfields. I wiped the dried oil from the side of the trigger casing. 'Made in England', it said. Underneath the etching of a crowned lion was the date of its production: 1917. I picked up another. It was from 1918. The most modern of them dated from 1942, the middle of the Second World War.

Britain had invaded Iraq in World War I when it was part of the Ottoman Empire, which had allied with Germany. It proved a bloody fight. In 1916 the British lost ten thousand men at Kut. Their army did not reach Baghdad until March the following year, the same year in which the rifle I had just held was manufactured. I thought of the soldiers who were issued with them, boys from my own country who had marched across the desert through which I had just passed. Now their weapons were being used again, this time to fight the most high-tech force ever sent into battle.

Ray had finished his call. He was pleased with life now. 'Goddamn. Think I might've got myself a date,' he said. 'Now just got to make sure I get home to keep it.'

I was losing my ability to process all that was happening around me, to fit the events I was witnessing into a framework of comprehension. All I had left were emotions, and at that point I didn't even want those any more. Suddenly I believed I knew nothing. Where was the right and where was the wrong? Were the Iraqis welcoming the Americans, or hating them? Were these men I was with bloodthirsty brutes, or just normal people doing what they had to do? Was there a lot of killing, or a little? I felt overwhelmed. There was only one thing I could do: that night we sat in the back of Band Aid and enjoyed the latest episode in the *Star Wars* saga, a simple story of good battling evil a long time ago in a galaxy far, far away.

Beyond the rolls of barbed wire that had been pulled across every road that led out of the American positions stretched a city that no longer functioned. Food was running low. Water and electricity

National Rail Enquiries

2FOR1 offers at attractions when you travel
by train. Go to **daysoutguide.co.uk**
to get your free voucher.

2FOR1 OFFERS
WHEN YOU GO BY TRAIN

Endorsements:

RSP No. 9399   1 BBP 1523 9 8 7 6 5 4 3 2

COLLECTION RECEIPT

Description	Numbers	Value
1 COUPON	38829	£51.50

Issuing office

LONDON WATERLOO

ToD CTR

9794FLR2

NOT VALID FOR TRAVEL

Date of Sale

07-SEP-23

2635890935

CUSTOMER'S COPY

 Selling Office   1749

1333 070923

supplies had been cut off in many districts. Sewerage pipes had been burst in air raids. Phone networks had collapsed and television signals disappeared. For the citizens of Baghdad there was also the fear about what would happen next, about who would join the victims of the violence. No one knew if it would be their homes caught up in the fighting when the battle spread.

At first, the only citizens of the capital I saw were the small groups who timidly made their way out of their homes in the American enclave. White flags were held above their heads or they flourished white handkerchiefs, their hands clearly visible to make clear they had no weapons. It was only on the third day after the company's arrival at Objective Saints that I managed to gain an impression of the situation on the other side of the roadblocks. A patrol was sent out, its orders to gauge the extent of the deprivations being suffered in the district bordering the enclave, and I got a lift in the back of a Bradley. A small convoy pushed along one of the streets leading north, the armoured vehicles accompanied by Humvees fixed with loudspeakers through which propaganda was broadcast. The work of the 'Psyop' psychological warfare units had become a considerable source of amusement to the soldiers in recent days. The sound of the Arabic tapes promising that the Americans came as friends was now a familiar accompaniment to the thud of shells and the rattle of machine-gun fire. As Lieutenant Few had described it: '"We're not here to hurt you, we're here to aid you. Badabadabada." Yeah, I'm sure that message is getting across to people real clear.'

Responsibility for trying to help civilians in the area had been placed with a two-man team of Civil Affairs soldiers. They were reservists, called up for the duration of the war, who coordinated the delivery of medical and water supplies as well as shipments of humanitarian food. Their presence must have looked very reassuring when laid out in a memo in the Pentagon. In reality, when I saw them in action they seemed completely impotent. The humanitarian supplies were stuck somewhere south of Karbala, as it had been deemed not safe to bring the lorries forward into an unsecured area. There was not even enough food and water for the soldiers, let alone to distribute to the local population.

Through the viewing slits in the side of the Bradley I watched the sprawling suburbs of Baghdad roll past. From almost every corner Saddam Hussein's face peered down at us. There were murals depicting him smiling or firing a rifle into the air, photographs of him dressed in army uniform. Some businesses had pictures of him above their entrances. Clearly you could not go far in Baghdad without a reminder of who had held ultimate power.

The streets were lined with rows of identikit square buildings. The majority appeared to be constructed out of concrete that had turned a dull brown from the sand and dust ingrained in the walls. Metal railings topped by fearsome spikes surrounded small gardens. Through them could be seen the occasional homemade bench or small ornate table on a parched lawn. Few of the shops were open; metal grates covered their entrances to deter looters. The most impressive structures were the roads themselves. They were wide and flawless, with a central partition, their sides protected by crash barriers.

The Iraqi vehicles failed to match the splendour of the carriageways over which they passed. Pick-up trucks that could have featured in a *Mad Max* film drove by, one with its windscreen cracked and its front bumper fallen off, another with its entire engine exposed as it chugged forward. There was a donkey pulling a small wooden cart. A boy walked alongside, hitting it with a stick. At the sight of the American tanks it refused to move any further, and the child kicked it in the testicles to spur it forward.

Above all, the street moved with pedestrians. When we were around eight hundred yards from the American checkpoint we were surrounded by men in flowing robes, women concealed by black headdresses, children with their matchstick legs poking out of tattered shorts. They fanned out from the pavement onto the road, and in their hands were containers – empty food jars, old petrol cans – full of water. Many of them were filled so high that the water splattered out and left a trail in the dust that covered the tarmac. In the opposite direction another line of people, their containers still empty, headed towards a canal so heavily polluted that a film of oil floated on its surface and mounds of rubbish cluttered its sides.

On seeing the US troops, the Iraqis began to shout, and some of those with empty containers ran beside the vehicles holding them up to the soldiers. 'Water,' those who spoke a few words of English said. 'Water. Give water.' The Civil Affairs team dismounted, and was swallowed up by a crowd of gesticulating locals. The infantrymen, who were responsible for policing the situation, did not like being so close to people they had learnt to consider the enemy. They stood around their Bradleys trying to keep the crowd back, at the same time attempting to obey their orders to appear courteous. The Iraqis, who were hearing through the Psyop speakers that the United States Army was there to provide assistance, eagerly pressed forward until too many surrounded the soldiers, making them feel uncomfortable. The Americans would push them back a few yards, and the civilians would look confused and slightly hurt at being rebuffed. Then they would start inching forward again, assuming that they had somehow failed to make clear the first time that they just wanted help, and that the order to get back had simply been the result of some foolish miscommunication. Then, inevitably, the process would repeat itself again.

In the middle of the crowd were the two Civil Affairs officers and an Arabic translator, an Egyptian-American dressed in army fatigues and bulbous wraparound shades who clutched a megaphone in one hand. They had been told that the water mains and the electricity supply to the area had been disconnected. People complained that they were also running short of food, as the shops would not open and no one would bring produce to an area near to the fighting.

The person responsible for dealing with the district's water system was sent for, and a dapper little man, dressed in a tight charcoal-coloured sweatshirt and back trousers held up by a gold-coloured belt, hurried forward. He was asked why the water had been turned off. 'Saddam's men came and did it,' the translator said. He was asked why he did not turn it back on. 'Because no one's given him permission,' it was reported. But why didn't he do it anyway? People need water here. 'Apparently that's too dangerous. He's frightened of what Saddam's men might do to him if he does.' One of the Civil Affairs officers, a young man from North Carolina, looked bemused. 'Tell him there's nothing to be afraid of. He can sleep well now, the Americans are here.' And then, turning to the Iraqi, he said directly to him: 'We're here because we've come to help you. America wants to help save Iraq.' The water man smiled and nodded and said in Arabic, 'We trust in God and you.' But still he would not turn on the supply, although he was persuaded to at least tell them where the local substation was located.

The electricity seemed to be a more city-wide phenomenon. It was also not clear if it had been disrupted by Saddam's henchmen or the American bombing. Food was a problem to be dealt with another day.

I found a man, seventy-year-old Abd al-Hamid, who spoke English. Like Mr Alavan, he would not answer any questions about Saddam.

'He is the President of Iraq and he can do what he wants,' he said. 'I cannot say more because I am still afraid. Will the Americans help us?' he then asked.

I said I thought so.

'Will we be hurt?'

'By whom?' I asked.

'By anyone.'

Back at the Bradley in which I was travelling on the patrol, a sergeant – the slogan 'Lord Make Me Swift and Accurate' written in felt-tip on his helmet and a pump-action shotgun in his hands – was trying to keep the crowd in order. He was having particular trouble with two portly men in bright pink shirts, hair descending to their shoulders in little curls, who kept sidling closer to ask for assistance. One of his infantrymen was congratulating him on having attracted the two most obviously homosexual residents of Baghdad. The atmosphere was not hostile, many of the Iraqis were waving and making V for victory signs, but they were lacking basic supplies, and that made it volatile. 'If the shooting starts,' one of the soldiers said to me, 'make sure you get back in the Bradley mighty fast, because we ain't going to be hanging around. We'll be making sure it's raining bullets and getting the hell out of here.'

The Civil Affairs team's work now completed, the order was given to pull out, and the soldiers squeezed into the back of the Bradleys. Through the side slits I could see the crowds of Iraqis still moving to and from the canal with their containers. An old woman, her back so bent that her body was almost horizontal to the road, scuttled forward, a wooden stick in one hand and an empty glass jar in the other.

Captain Waldron, the commander of the Black Knights, was at the checkpoint when the convoy returned. He had been on the patrol and had not liked what he had seen. 'I kept thinking of the film *Black Hawk Down*,' he said. 'It would've taken one person accidentally discharging and it would've been chaos. The whole city could rise up against us here, they know where we are, and there's nothing we could do to stop it.'

In the previous weeks the captain had gained the respect of his men, soldiers who had previously complained that his WASPish manner made him distant and standoffish. He had led them safely through numerous brushes with danger. It was he who determined the company's attack formations, encouraged his unit to be ruthless in dispatching its foes, and had been adept at spotting sites where ambushes could be located. His importance – if there was still any question about it – was confirmed a few days later when, as preparations were finalised for the push into the centre of Baghdad, he was wounded and it looked as if he would not be able to lead the company. The sense of fear that this prospect created, not least in myself, was testament to our belief in his ability to keep us uninjured.

However, the captain held the rigid mindset of the conservative American soldier. It was a mindset that served him well in battle, as it allowed no doubt about the righteousness of the cause for which he fought – protecting the United States and bringing the gift of an American lifestyle to those unfairly denied it – and the importance above all of protecting the lives of his soldiers. The captain would criticise the biased nature of BBC coverage and rhapsodise about the honesty and accuracy of Fox News. He expressed no sympathy after a cameraman for al-Jazeera was killed when two American bombs hit the network's Baghdad offices, because to him the station was a disseminator of anti-US propaganda. The French deserved to be excluded from all international organisations for their treachery, and the Turks were little better for not allowing United States forces to use their territory as a base. Iraqi soldiers were considered barely human as a result of their tactics and their allegedly barbaric treatment of American PoWs.

It was a mindset which, seeing things in clear shades of black and white, made it difficult for the captain to grasp the ambivalence with which the average Iraqi, however much he may have despised Saddam's regime, viewed the army that had invaded his country. That morning he had visited a hospital to ask for spare medicines to bolster the American supplies. He was furious and bewildered to be refused. The staff had told him, 'You have been filling up our hospitals, so how can we have anything to spare?' It was being reported on the BBC that in some areas of Baghdad the number of injured meant supplies were running so low that painkillers had to be used as a substitute for anaesthetics.

'We come here to help them,' Captain Waldron said, 'and they're not willing to help us.' Unprompted, he started to talk about the issue of civilian deaths – because, I suspected, of what he had seen in the hospital. 'On our side, we've made a lot of young guys not so innocent any more,' he said. 'On theirs, well, I think I may have killed some civilians. That knowledge, I tell you, will be something that I will have to deal with once this is all over. But there have been American casualties also. When I hear about them, I don't tell people. I keep them to myself for morale reasons, as do most officers. Americans are dying out here, and I'll do everything I can to make sure none of them are from my unit. My job's to make sure everyone gets home alive.'

I would never know whether the number of Iraqis killed during the second Gulf War was large or small for the securing of a country – how could such a thing be quantified, though I would hear people try to do so – but one thing was clear: the United States Army had embraced the doctrine that placed the security of its forces at the forefront of every thought and action. It was a mantra that I heard espoused not only by the captain but by the other officers in the battalion, both in Kuwait and in the camp outside Karbala. I would later learn that that attitude was taken by leaders and men from units fighting all over Iraq. The American soldiers were not out of control on the battlefield; their actions merely reflected the ethos of the army in which they served. A good war, even a supposedly humanitarian war, was, above all, one in which few Americans died.

I could not blame the individual soldiers – I understood only too well, by then, the fear that comes with combat and the power of the urge for survival, and I could not deny that at times I had been relieved to witness the ruthlessness that came with it. However, training and leadership are meant to encourage the reining in of excess, not reinforce the view that the soldier's life is somehow worth more than that of others. Efforts were made, especially at the start of the campaign, to avoid damaging civilian buildings even if it meant allowing enemy units to escape unengaged. The total number of civilians killed was less than in many previous conflicts; this was an invasion by an army whose political leaders had promised that everything would be done to protect the people of Iraq it was supposedly helping. Yet the reality was that casualty estimates show almost as many civilians as enemy soldiers were killed by the United States military in Iraq. There were shootings at checkpoints, buildings obliterated on only shaky evidence of a military presence, troops firing at ambulances, accusations later of soldiers killing unarmed demonstrators. Everything was justified by those in command with the assertion that the American troops were exercising their inherent right of self-defence.

Once the invasion had been launched, Saddam Hussein's decision to order a section of his military to fight out of uniform contributed more than any other factor to the number of his country's civilians who lost their lives. However, after it was realised that those dressed in civilian clothes could pose a lethal threat, there is no question that the American forces were more willing to kill an innocent person accidentally than to risk the possibility of one of their troops being shot. Even now I can't decide if that is just 'the nature of war', part of its inherent and continual evilness, or if it was a sickening abuse of power by an army whose technology and equipment meant that it should have shown that this time promises could be kept, and that for once it really was possible to be different.

The battalion pulled out of Saints the next day. An order had come down that it was needed to lead part of 3rd Brigade's attack into the centre of the city, so the Black Knights headed west along the ring road that encircled Baghdad. The American forces now had the capital almost completely surrounded. The Marines were taking up positions on the east side. 2nd Brigade had spread across the south, and 1st Brigade covered the south-west around the airport. 3rd Brigade had advanced from the west, reaching as far north as the Tigris. There were reports of Special Forces and units of the 101st Airborne being helicoptered into positions that controlled the city's northern approaches.

As we waited to pull out, the battalion lined up next to the Iraqi gun by which Garth Stewart had had part of his foot blown off, the captain called me forward to his tank. In the cockpit was a computer screen on which was shown, marked by blue squares, the location of every American unit in Iraq. He zoomed in on Baghdad. It was surrounded by a near-constant blue line. 'You're probably not authorised to see this, but you've got to admit it's a pleasing sight,' he said.

The journey west on Sunday, 6 April was notable for how nothing really happened, when even a few days earlier it would have been a terrible flight through combat. There were a lot of military vehicles on the road, so many that they snarled up behind each other as bottlenecks formed at spots where the Iraqis were still engaging the American forces. The distance travelled was little more than twenty miles, but it took over six hours for the battalion to reach its new base.

The longest delay occurred just over a mile from our destination, where determined resistance from remnants of the Republican Guard's Hammurabi Division was encountered. The extent of this opposition had only become clear after about a quarter of the battalion had crossed a bridge at one of the ring road's junctions. Half a dozen fuellers and ammo trucks were left stuck on top, unable to move further forward until the route ahead had been secured. Sitting about 1500 yards behind them in the M113, we listened on the military radio as their crews became increasingly agitated. One driver in particular was not enjoying himself. 'Their mortars are getting closer!' he was squealing. 'We've got to move. They're bracketing us, sir. They're getting very close. We need to move off this bridge!'

The captain's response was unsympathetic. 'Those are our mortars. Now calm down.'

'Those are not our mortars, sir. They're falling only a short distance from where we're located. There are snipers here, sir. I'm going to evacuate the vehicle. It's not safe. I'm going to order my crew to evacuate. We're evacuating.' The emotion in his voice was very raw, but to us, listening in the M113, his predicament seemed tragically amusing. The poor guy's voice had become so high-pitched in his terror that I am ashamed to say we laughed and mimicked his distress. His fear, and the ridiculous situation he had been put in, appeared too comical to be taken seriously. The war had become so repetitive that it had become easiest to view its crises as farce.

'You will not evacuate,' the captain ordered. 'We're trying to clear the vehicles in front. Now wait. It will soon be over.'

From the back half of the convoy, where we were located, we could make out the bridge supposedly being used as target practice. However, no one seemed to care about the possible danger. It was becoming hard to summon the emotional strength to be frightened. I certainly could not. There was just impatience welling inside me, a desire for everyone to get on with it so that it would all be over. I was not alone. Infantrymen were lying against the side of their Bradleys enjoying the sunshine. Tank crews sat out of their hatches, smoking. Many were not even bothering to wear their helmets. The reality of the situation was that we were sitting targets. If anyone had fired at us there was nowhere to go, as the vehicles were so close together few could have turned to escape. But the soldiers knew they had been through worse and were still alive.

Trey, surveying the scene, shook his head. 'No one's even nervous any more,' he said. 'Do you remember at the beginning? Now look at us. It's like people have forgotten how to be scared.'

The attention of the crews of the vehicles around us was instead focused on the central partition of the highway, on the other side of which lay the remains of a bus, gutted and burnt black by the fire that had raged within it. About ten feet behind it lay a body. Like many of the corpses scattered around Baghdad, it was starting to bloat from the heat. One of the problems the Americans were struggling to cope with was that the Iraqis appeared unwilling to risk venturing out to bury the bodies of their dead. As a result they had begun to rot, and it was feared they would soon pose a health hazard. The troops in the area where I was located ended up digging a hole with a bulldozer, which then scooped up the nearby corpses and buried them in a mass grave. Orders issued back in Kuwait about Iraqis being carefully buried pointing towards Mecca had long ago been quietly forgotten.

However, in this instance four Iraqi men had walked up carrying a spade and a large white flag, notable for its size and cleanliness. They proceeded to take turns digging a grave in the earth of the central partition. The American soldiers watched as the men worked. It took them a long while, almost an hour. At one point they turned and made a sign indicating that they wanted some water, their efforts under the midday sun having exhausted them. Ray picked up a bottle – new supplies had finally arrived just before our departure – and had started to climb out the driver's hatch when José told him to sit down. 'If we give one of them food and water they'll all expect us to in future,' he said. Ray looked at him for a moment, and then did what he had been instructed. A private travelling with us commented, 'I wish they'd get on with this, the smell's disgusting.' My sentiments were the same. The odour of the rotting corpse was repulsive, seeming to hang inside the M113 and attach itself to our clothing. At last the four men finished digging, lifted up the body and tossed it in, then filled in the hole. One of them said a quick prayer while another reached for an empty MRE bag that had been thrown away by an American soldier and propped it upright with some rocks to act as a temporary grave marker.

When we did finally pull forward it was impossible to miss the evidence of the fighting that had gone on. There must have been the remains of a dozen Iraqi tanks across the highway and surrounding area. The M113 was ordered to station itself in a field a short distance from the bridge. It was the spot where the battalion's support train, the soft-sided vehicles that had originally been held back around Karbala but had made the journey to Baghdad that afternoon, had also been told to encamp. Everyone gathered around to share their stories from the previous few days as the sun began to set behind us.

There was a report that a sniper had fired into the camp from the west, and conversations were broken off as soldiers huddled behind the armoured vehicles for protection. Those on the western side of the camp opened fire with their machine guns at the spot where the shots were thought to have come from, a small farm-house about two hundred yards away across a ploughed field. There was some dispute about this. A number of soldiers thought the sniper had been in the line of trees, others that there had not been a shot at all; but that did not stop the building being peppered with bullets. One of the cooks picked up an RPG and prepared to fire it. However, he was unable to hold it steady, and the grenade exploded around thirty yards in front of where he crouched, sending up a shower of dirt. José was not amused. He stormed over and proceeded to demonstrate how it should properly be employed.

I was still in a foolish enough state of mind to be indifferent to the possibility of danger, now habituated to the events around me, and started washing with some of the new water supplies. If anything, I was quite enjoying the excitement, though I must admit that I was among the most sceptical that there had ever been a sniper. Nevertheless, there was a morbid pleasure in show-ing that, by casually cleaning myself, I was in my own little way not caring about exposing myself to jeopardy, instead of cringing as usual from any indication of a possible attacker. One of the soldiers had called it 'the secret joy of placing a bet in the game of life and once again winning'.

Just after I had dried off, the order was given for the M113, Band Aid and Sergeant Harrison's mechanics track to change position. The rest of the company was still hunting down the Republican Guard units in the area, and the vehicles were required to move closer to the fighting in case they were needed.

It was dark now. The sight of gunfire was always more striking at night-time. In the day there was only the crash of the explosion and maybe some smoke or a puff of sand or earth. At night there was the sight of the tracers cutting through the sky, and the blinding glare of the detonation. That evening there was a lot of shooting. The crews of the three armoured support vehicles stood in the middle of the defensive circle they had formed and, resembling a family gathered close as protection against the cold on Guy Fawkes Night, huddled together to watch the light show around them. In the sky was the anti-aircraft fire, on the ground the shock of tank shells being fired, a bang that reverberated so loudly that it felt as if the air was being sucked away in a mini version of a sonic boom. At one point a group of infantrymen stumbled on an Iraqi bunker maybe only a hundred yards from where we stood. For twenty seconds the air was filled with glowing tracers and the frantic clicking of machine-gun fire before three Iraqis were left dead and two wounded. No one I was with was in any way put out. It felt like a spectacle provided for our entertainment, the gunfight simply a particularly impressive Catherine wheel.

I was sleeping when the one thing happened that day which would temporarily crack my newfound detachment. Only Big Sergeant B was awake, lying on the roof of the medic van chewing tobacco, when a shell exploded near us. The whole vehicle shook and I woke to find Sergeant B lying face down on the floor, his legs still poking out the driver's hatch through which he had thrown himself head first for protection. We all cowered at the bottom of Band Aid waiting for more rounds to come in, but none did. With no order given to move to the safety of a new position, we climbed back onto our stretchers. A few seconds later I was once again asleep.

EIGHT

City of War

Monday, 7 April–Wednesday, 9 April

One thousand three hundred years ago, the first buildings were erected on the west bank of the Tigris to form the heart of a town that would become the modern city of Baghdad. The settlement's founder, the medieval warlord Abu Ja'far Al-Mansour, named it Madinat Al-Salam, City of Peace, as it was his ambition that its rise would end the tribal conflicts that for centuries had plagued the region. Now, as the Black Knights advanced into the government quarter and to within walking distance of where those first stones had been laid, fighting spread through the streets. Hope may have marked Baghdad's foundation, but this was a city at war.

The blackened shells of destroyed Iraqi gun positions and burnt-out trucks and military vehicles littered the roadside. Buildings lay in ruins, their walls reduced to rubble but many of their flat roofs lying intact on top of them, so that they resembled houses of cards blown over by a breath of wind. Palm trees smouldered from air strikes and artillery shells. Electricity pylons had been bent so that their tips brushed the ground. Few civilians risked leaving their homes as the United States Army moved forward. Only the lines of American armoured vehicles were moving along the city's highways. Lines 'tightening the noose', as the captain called the operation intended to finally break Saddam Hussein's twenty-four-year hold on power.

Two days after the company had moved along the road that ringed Baghdad to its new position in the west, the cordon around the capital was being drawn in to place almost the entire western side of the city under American control. In the operation being conducted on Tuesday, 8 April 1st Battalion led the advance along the Abu Ghraib Expressway. To its north, units of the 3rd Brigade fanned out along the other highways that led to the very centre of the Ba'athist regime. To its south, 1st and 2nd Brigades also pushed forward into the city. Yet even now Iraqis were still fighting back, reflecting either a determination to die for a lost cause or that they were unaware of the hopelessness of their predicament. I would have disappeared long ago, sidled off to some bolthole in the surrounding countryside now that it was clear that the Americans were not only winning, but were apparently invincible. However, at junction after junction, a few ancient tanks emerged from sidestreets, lorries tipped out bands of men, and anti-aircraft guns were lowered to fire not into the sky, but at the enemy advancing ever closer.

'Force protection', regarding the safety of its troops as the number one priority, still defined the US Army's approach. At one point Iraqi snipers holed up in a small apartment complex caused a delay. The solution proposed was simply to destroy the entire building. I wondered what that meant for anybody inside, many of them perhaps too frightened to go out on the streets and find refuge elsewhere. 'Anyone still in that building isn't a civilian,' I was told. The request was sent for a volley of artillery fire to obliterate it.

I stared in awed fascination at the spectacle of MLRS missiles killing a group of armed men who had hidden in the cover provided by a motorway bridge. The missiles flew low as they were released from their launcher three hundred yards behind us, the lines of smoke twisting through the sky, the flash of their fluorescent thrusters making my heart jump with excitement. Peering through a pair of binoculars, I could see the Iraqis disappear as dozens of bomblets exploded around them. The multiple detonations sounded like Chinese firecrackers celebrating the start of a new year. One of the American tank crews reported that they could see one man still standing. Six more missiles were called in. The light-hearted banter that had filled the company's radio communications temporarily abated as the soldiers took in the power of the weapons summoned to remove the obstacle standing in their way.

'Can you imagine being in that rain of shit?' said Trey. 'It's brutal. Makes my .50-cal look kinda weak.' For no reason, all of us in the M113 burst out laughing.

Two A10 Thunderbolt planes circled overhead, their bombing runs bringing them so close to their targets that they disappeared into the smoke still rising from their previous attacks. Even after such a pounding, the Iraqis kept trying to take the battle to the Americans. An RPG hit one of the concrete bridge supports as we pulled through the motorway underpass struck by the MLRS missiles. The American tank crews were ordered to start hunting down these last vestiges of opposition.

The battalion's objective, a series of newly built houses near the Mansour district where weapons and dozens of Republican Guard vehicles were being stored, was only three miles from the city centre. The next day, the Marines would move forward to take control of the east of Baghdad. General Tommy Franks, the head of US Central Command, had said, 'Speed kills the enemy.' Across Saddam's capital, a battle that it had been feared could last weeks was being brought to an end in a matter of days. American units, backed by overwhelming firepower, were securing districts in the heart of the city, taking advantage of the surprise at the rapidity of their final advance to rout an enemy that appeared to have failed to establish defensive fortifications within Baghdad's boundaries.

We were now drawing close to the city's centre. The buildings grew taller, increasing the risk of snipers firing into the vehicles through their top hatches. It was this that was responsible for most of the recent American battle casualties. When the order was given for the M113 to move through the motorway junction cleared by the MLRS missiles, it was accompanied by a command to seal the hatch.

It was a bad moment for such an order to be given, as minutes earlier I had decided to engage in a particularly fetid exercise in personal hygiene. There had been a searing pain in my feet, and with my legs hanging out of the back of the vehicle, I had used the pause that followed the missile bombardment to take off my boots and socks and try to determine its cause. It was the first time I had exposed my feet to the fresh air for at least two weeks. When I went to sleep in Band Aid, I knew that I had to be ready at a moment's notice to evacuate my stretcher if a report came in of casualties. Therefore I would keep my boots on while I slept, to avoid having to rummage around in the dark if an injured soldier needed immediate assistance.

Taking off my socks unveiled my own little biochemical warfare programme. My feet were covered in a green spotty mould, and the flesh had expanded outwards so that my toes had almost disappeared. The skin was mottled from the damp and coloured a pale, greasy white, like a chicken breast fresh from the larder. The smell was so overwhelming that even I gagged on my own odour. The M113's crew stared at me in horror, and tried to suck some last clean air into their lungs before they had to close the hatches as instructed.

'Are they ever meant to look like that?' I asked Trey about my feet.

'Hell, no!' he said.

Ray adopted an expression of exaggerated disgust. 'Looks like we're gonna need those gasmasks,' he commented.

The order came to head forward. Trey kept one hatch open a crack to get some circulating wind. As I squeezed my feet back into my desert boots I found myself laughing. It was all so overwhelming. The shapes obliterated in the smoke. The fact that snipers could be in the surrounding buildings. The reality of moving through gunfire yet again. The condition of my stupid feet. That damn smell. We drove under the motorway junction and the RPG was fired at us, and inside our battered M113 I was almost hysterical, my laughter cracking into high giggles. I tried to control myself. This was no place to stop concentrating on keeping it together.

I was not convinced that everyone else was managing to do so. In the previous forty-eight hours there had been a communal decision by the troops to revel in the delights that victory offered. Military buildings were being looted and their insides smashed up. Graffiti was sprawled on walls, and anything that could be taken as a memento carried away to be stashed in the backs of tanks and armoured vehicles.

Civilian buildings were rarely touched. There was not even a question in the minds of the men I was with of houses being ransacked or their occupants harassed. But with a captured city in their grasp, a version of frat-house rules had quietly been authorised by those in command. A blind eye was turned when American troops acted out their destructive fantasies on the symbols of the Iraqi regime. Anything government or military was considered fair game, and the soldiers grabbed at the opportunities for vandalism this provided. It was time for them to enjoy the spoils of their combat prowess, even if they proved to be merely a pot of plastic flowers or some dead Iraqi soldier's beret.

The day before the advance into the centre, the Black Knights had searched an abandoned hospital and discovered that it was being used as a weapons arsenal. Boxes of shells and bullets were piled high in the wards, and machinery to make ammunition was discovered in the operating theatre. In the adjacent barracks, the lockers were cut open with bolt cutters so that Trey, Doc's assistant Frankie, Stazny and I could rummage through the detritus of the lives of the men who had guarded the site. We found a photograph of a young man, resplendent in his dress uniform, standing beside a pretty girl who stared proudly at him. There were letters, clean socks and a diary, headache pills, half a dozen ornamental holsters. The doors of the lockers had been decorated with stickers. On one Kate Winslet looked buxom and wide-eyed in some fashion photographs. On the one next to it, Sylvester Stallone clutched a roll of ammunition and a submachine gun in a still from *Rambo*. Everything was pulled out, looked through, and then thrown into a pile on the floor. The few items of uniform were the only things worth taking as souvenirs, and even they were tattered and streaked with dirt.

The barracks of a Republican Guard unit was occupied by the battalion at the same time. Sergeant Pyle and his new tank arrived at the site first. The crew obliterated a large mural of Saddam with a shell from the main gun, then threw eggs at the pictures of him that hung in the offices inside. The soldiers who got there next pulled open the drawers of every desk, scattering their contents across the carpet, and smashed up the furniture. Troops were grabbing anything that could make a souvenir. In the back of a Bradley I saw a two-foot-high plastic carriage clock. The uniforms found in a fire engine outside proved particularly popular, their silver helmet with gold visors resembling costumes from a 1950s Flash Gordon film. Sergeant Weaver dressed up in the entire outfit. Another soldier put on a helmet and, quoting Buzz Lightyear in *Toy Story*, ran up and down the parade ground in front of the main building shouting, 'To infinity and beyond.' Around us flakes of black ash fell from the fires burning just outside the compound.

A voluble Red was showing off his haul. 'Now, this is what I like,' he said as he pulled out his collection of cap badges and Arabic documents. 'This is really fun. They're going to let me take sentry duty at one of the checkpoints. I might even be able to do something exciting before all this is over.' He looked at the badges. 'Do you think I might be able to get anything for these on E-Bay?' he asked.

The angry soldier I had seen in the south had been replaced by a youth as excited as a schoolboy who had just finished his final exam. He had previously told me that his best time in the army had been at the end of basic training, when the recruits were allowed to run wild in the garrison in which they had previously been penned. Now he was able to run wild across part of a city. He had come back from a sortie into a school where a sniper had been caught, and proudly showed me some exercise books he had taken, and recounted how he had written abuse on the blackboard. Somewhere he had got his hands on a selection of discarded Arabic business cards and he was passing them out, pretending they were marked with his Baghdad address. 'This is something to tell everyone back home about,' he told me. 'Don't know if there's been a time when someone from Toledo has had this kind of opportunity. They're all going to feel retarded at missing out on this.'

The Republican Guard barracks became the base for the battalion's support vehicles. I returned to them after Saddam's regime had abandoned its capital. The walls had by then been covered in graffiti, most pretty base, such as 'Republican Guard were pussies', or, prematurely, 'Saddam now sucks Hitler's cock in hell'. Every picture had been torn down and most of the furniture destroyed. I have a particularly clear memory of one soldier sitting on a step looking despondent. He had finally found an unharmed picture of Saddam which he wanted to keep as a memento, but Sergeant Whelan had spotted it and ripped it up to demonstrate his contempt for the man who had dispatched soldiers to shoot at him. The senior sergeants were trying to limit some of the worst excesses of the vandalism. An order had gone around to stop their troops defecating in the drawers of the remaining desks. The worst moment came when I walked into one of the conference rooms, climbing over the broken table legs and piles of discarded documents, and saw that the far wall had been smeared with faeces.

On the day the Americans had seized the barracks, I stood watching the soldiers playing American football with a plastic paperweight they had found on an Iraqi officer's desk. One of the sergeants came up to José with a touchingly legalistic question. Even at that point, when the feeling that it was all nearly over was so widespread that the NCOs had to constantly shout at soldiers to put their helmets on and most people were more focused on souvenir-hunting than fighting, it was important to him that this was civilised military conduct. 'It's OK, isn't it?' he asked José. 'This is all military stuff we're taking. Under the Geneva Convention we can loot what we like from military sites. I'm right, aren't I? It's all OK?'

When he had gone off to look for more booty I remembered I was meant to be there to work, so I checked in with the office. They told me a rocket had been fired at the American headquarters back at Objective Saints. It had landed near the field hospital, destroying seventeen vehicles, injuring fifteen people and killing four, among them two reporters. There had been some initial concern in London that one of them might have been me. In fact they were the Spaniard and the German, Julio Anguita Parrado and Christian Liebig, who I had been talking to a few days previously. Both were killed instantly.

The captain was also hit that day. He had been waving to some Iraqis standing by the side of the road when an RPG was fired from behind a ridge. It had exploded on the side of his vehicle, sending shrapnel into his face, right hand and arm. Band Aid had taken him to the battalion medic centre. It was thought that he would require days of treatment, which meant he would not be able to command the attack into the centre of Baghdad. However, the next morning, as the Black Knights waited to commence that advance, he drew up in his tank, the side of his face and his hand still covered in bandages. According to the M113 crew, his hospital bed had been next to that of a wounded Iraqi prisoner. The captain had repeatedly demanded to know why one of the enemy was being given such comfortable accommodation when it was believed the Iraqis were treating American prisoners so badly, and the medics had been forced to move him away from the Iraqi soldier to a bed set up outside the main tent. At dawn he had ignored his doctor's instructions and rejoined his tank, riding through the streets of Baghdad to catch up with the rest of the company. Confidence and relief spread in his wake as he drove through the line of troops to take his position near the front of the column.

There was little finesse now used to clear an area. When the housing estate that was the battalion's objective was reached, some of the buildings storing ammunition were simply blown up with a tank shell. 'Reconnoitre with power', it was called by the soldiers. One house two hundred yards from where the M113 was parked burnt fiercely throughout the night. The air crackled with the sound of detonations when a box of ammunition was caught by the flames. Multicoloured flares soared into the darkness.

'Is this safe?' I asked José.

'There's nothing we can do about it now,' he replied. 'Enjoy the display. Independence Day has come early.'

That night I was woken by Doc, who was on the stretcher underneath me. He was pawing at the cloth above his head and whimpering, caught up in some nightmare about the events by which he was surrounded.

In daylight I came across Nitai Schwartz, the teenager in the mortar team who had been anti-war when I had interviewed him in Kuwait. He was sitting in the front seat of an impounded Iraqi military truck. Its wheels were spinning in the mud. As he saw me coming he turned off the engine and casually smashed the windscreen with the barrel of his machine gun.

'I feel proud of what we've done,' he told me. 'You know that I had doubts before, but I think we've done a good thing. Driving along the street seeing everyone waving, I feel we liberated them. All those women blowing us kisses. I felt like a hero.

'We fought as we were trained. All that training comes to use in the moment when it's needed. Your muscles have their own memory, and you thank them for it. On the final stretch to

Baghdad I saw bodies that were meant to be dead coming back to life. There was a guy and there was a muzzle flash, and I immediately sent three shots and saw him crumble. I really feel bad about it now,' he insisted, 'but I suppose that's something to see the chaplain about.'

The barrages unleashed by the battalion's mortar teams were estimated to have killed more than two hundred people.

'I'm definitely a better man after what we've been through,' continued Nitai. 'I can say I've seen and done it all, and nothing can really shock me now. We went through boundaries that few people go through. I dropped out of high school three times, and used to sit in my room smoking pot. I joined the army because I wanted my parents to be proud that I did what was right, and they'll be proud of me now.'

The night I sat in the M113 watching the ammunition burn in the building opposite, José, Ray and I had talked about our childhoods. Ray was one of eight children, and had grown up surrounded by chaos and compromise. José had been the oldest son of a father with a violent temper. When his dad had been looking for someone to shout at, it had been his responsibility to come forward and make sure it was he, rather than one of his younger brothers or sisters, who was the target.

When the clocks moved past midnight and into Wednesday, 9 April 2003, the day on which Saddam Hussein's regime abandoned Baghdad, the American army on the west side of the Tigris held all but a few square miles of the very centre of the city. Its troops had seized one of the main presidential palaces, and photographs of soldiers lazing on the *faux*-antique chairs inside had appeared on the front pages of newspapers across the world. That night an air raid targeted the Iraqi President himself, four satellite-guided bunker-busting bombs flattening a building where it was believed he was eating dinner. On the other bank of the Tigris, the Marines had been instructed to move forward in the morning to secure the eastern half of the city. The United States high command intended that when midnight next struck, virtually the entire capital would be under American control.

I woke just after 7 a.m., the sky still the same dirty yellow, smoke-created haze that it had been since the storming of the city almost a week earlier. I stood with Doc enjoying the cool air that greeted the new day.

'Hey, Oliver,' he said. 'Are you still coping with all this? You've been less talkative recently.'

What could I answer him? That I suspected I was beginning to lose it, as I couldn't get worked up at the sound of gunfire or the sight of dead bodies any more? That I was emotionally empty? That I was consciously immersing myself in work every minute of every hour of every day so I would not have to dwell on the rights and wrongs of what I was witnessing? That I just wanted to go home?

I told him I was fine. I mentioned his nightmare and asked how he was bearing up.

'Don't worry,' he said. 'I just focus on what's waiting for me back home. The rest is just a job. I think of being in my house with my little baby girl curled up on my stomach, sitting in my easy chair, watching TV.' He asked me if I knew how much extra he got paid for being in combat. 'Three hundred dollars a month,' he said. 'Three hundred dollars a month is what we get for all this. My wife's been saving up mine. She's going to decorate our bedroom in Disney patterns. That's what's waiting for me back in America.'

Frankie and Big Sergeant B joined us. Breakfast was an MRE. It was 7.45 a.m. now, and Big Sergeant B was recalling the mortar that had gone off while he had been chewing tobacco on the top of Band Aid and I had been asleep. He was marvelling at the speed with which he had come down through the hatch. The rest of us were trying to work out which had been more frightening: the blast, or the figure plummeting through the roof in the darkness.

The morning after that fright had begun with another round coming in, this time followed by an order to evacuate the area. We had moved to a position outside the entrance of a hospital, the one that had been discovered to be a weapons arsenal. The M113, Band Aid and the maintenance track established a defensive perimeter and their crews monitored the passing cars.

I had spent most of the time sitting by the roadside sharing cigarettes with Sergeant Weaver, who was still dressed in his bio-chemical suit. He told me he had ignored the order to change into MOPP 0 just in case Saddam did decide to blitz his own capital. Every time we heard a car we would stand so that one of the American armoured vehicles was between us and the road. Weaver had unclipped his pistol and he held it in one hand, kept out of sight, as he peered around the side. With the other hand he would wave a cheerful greeting to the Iraqi driving through the checkpoint.

He had decided he had seen enough of army life. 'There's a programme where you can get out after fifteen years, but you get a cut in your retirement fund. But I now know there are things more important than money. I'm twelve and a half years in. That means I could be out in another two and a half. If I don't get out, how many more of these would I have to go through?' he said.

'What's happened here has made me realise some things about myself. Before, I spent time with my family, but didn't cherish it as much as I could have. Now, every moment I spend with them I'll appreciate. Me and my wife were more or less homebodies before, but I want to take our kids to see Washington DC and all the other sights in the US. I want them to see where my wife was born in New York State. I want to take her out dancing more. I want us to have more fun together, go out and live life as much as possible. I'm thinking of becoming a history teacher. I'd like to teach people about what it was like to be here. Give them an in-depth perspective of what we and the Iraqi people went through. Try to explain what it was really like, not what it looked like on TV, but how it felt to be here and see what happened for real.'

Shortly after 9 a.m. on the day Saddam's regime abandoned Baghdad, a young soldier in the company, Specialist Woodman, wandered over to talk to Frankie, Doc's assistant medic. They speculated about what it would be like once they got back to America. 'When it was my twenty-first birthday on 4 April I spent the whole time dodging bullets,' Woodman said. 'God knows if when all this is over I'll ever be the same again. I might always be looking over my shoulder to check whether someone's trying to shoot me.'

Frankie had his own plans for the future. He had been married on Christmas Eve, and showed me a photograph of his wedding day. He was resplendent in full dress uniform, his elfin blonde wife standing proudly beside him. They had met through a Christian website, and he wanted to do something to thank God for the blessings of his new family. Frankie was another of the many deeply religious soldiers in the US Army. On the walls of the original Band Aid he had stuck not pornographic pictures, but pieces of paper on which he had written phrases from scripture. He joined up because he wanted to help people, and felt that being in the American military was a way of doing so. He had believed that by being a soldier he would be helping to make the world a better place.

It was far from a unique perspective. As I had said to my friend all that time ago in a London nightclub, the majority of people who live in the United States believed they were saving the rest of the world by interfering in its affairs. I had found America still to be a country fuelled by self-belief, whose people really did think they lived in the land of hope and opportunity. In a recent survey, 30 per cent of Americans questioned said they were in the top 10 per cent income bracket in the country. Almost two-thirds said they were either in it already, or expected to be in ten years' time. Statisticians may question the true extent of America's social mobility, but those who live there still largely believe the dream that anyone could become anything they wanted. Whether you were Sergeant Trey Black from Tennessee, Colonel John Charlton, his college-educated commander, or Ray Simon, a black man from Washington DC, there was one thing unquestioned and unquestionable, a presumption so strong that it underpinned everything you did and said. It was the sincere belief that the United States of America was the greatest nation that had ever existed on this earth, and that to serve in its army was to risk your life in the service of something worth dying for.

Before classes every morning American schoolchildren stand, hand on heart, and recite the Pledge of Allegiance, in which they affirm their loyalty to the Stars and Stripes and the Republic. They are taught that the flag is like a sacrament to be respected. Singing the national anthem when it is played in public is something to show off to your friends, not an embarrassment as it is in most of Europe. The President is not only an elected leader but also the symbolic figurehead of the nation, the commander in chief and a focus of patriotic fervour in times of conflict. After 11 September I had friends, people who were not Republicans, who would not allow any criticism of President Bush's response, because to do so would have been anti-American. I know one person who no longer talked to one of his closest college friends because he thought he had betrayed his country by questioning the conduct of the war in Afghanistan.

It is this state of mind that makes the United States an easy country to send to war. Americans feel it is their duty to support their government during a crisis, and ever since 11 September 2001 the United States has felt itself to be a country in crisis. It means that most people will back campaigns abroad because they believe they are aimed at preserving something worthwhile. They will more easily accept the suffering conflict brings both to their servicemen and to the civilians caught up in it because they believe that in its wake is brought the gift of American values. There is an almost universal conviction of their nation's virtue.

That is why Frankie had become a soldier. But after the experiences of recent weeks he was no longer so sure that being in the army was the best way of making the world a better place and giving proper thanks to God for the gift of his new wife. He, more than anyone I met out there, was distressed by the amount of killing that had occurred. Now he wanted to come back to Iraq after the war and preach, to be a missionary. 'These people have so little,' he told me. 'I feel you've got to do something to help. These people have had no choices. By coming back and doing some preaching and charitable work, I hope I'll offer them some choices as to how they can live. It was when we were looking through those lockers at the hospital that it really struck me that the soldiers we've been fighting are people too. I looked at the photographs and realised we've taken someone's husband or brother. I'm pleased this is nearly finished.'

A number of the Black Knights had completed their morning tasks and were relaxing beside their vehicles. Lieutenant Few was scraping around the bottom of a tin of chewing tobacco. Ray was writing the names of the M113's crew on their waterbottles so they would not get mixed up. Trey was shaving. Lieutenant Garabato, the company's second in command, was trying to wash the smell of gunsmoke off his skin. I found the captain at the back of Band Aid having his bandages changed. 'Shame about that finger,' he said about the worst-damaged, the middle one on his left hand. 'That was my wife's favourite.'

The sun was a cold, pale disc in the haze. A palatial mosque, from which the call to prayer had earlier been heard, dominated the horizon to the south-east. In the middle of the housing compound in which we were based stood a manmade lake. I could just make out the sound of ducks quacking as they swam on its surface.

At noon we had to move to a nearby highway to carry out the refuelling rigmarole once again. After the fight the previous day, it did not seem that there could be anyone left who wanted to hurt us. People were starting to wave at the American vehicles instead of walking nervously by with their hands clasped to their heads. There was a report of some of the battalion's soldiers being presented with flowers by local women. I stood on the tarmac beside the M113 and watched the tanks line up and the fuellers scale their sides to put in the gas nozzles. At that moment a sniper opened fire with half a dozen shots. José, who had been guiding the traffic, was very nearly hit, a bullet passing close to his head. I saw another one ricochet off the road ten feet to my left. It was the only time I actually saw a bullet striking near me – which was ironic, as when we had hightailed it out of there to a safe spot I called work, and was told the war was seemingly over.

The news services were reporting that US Marines were being greeted by waving and dancing crowds as they advanced through the predominately Shia Saddam City area of Baghdad. The throng was apparently being bolstered by Sunnis from surrounding areas. International journalists who had been confined by presidential order to the Palestine Hotel – in central Baghdad, but on the east bank of the Tigris – had woken to find their minders, the Ba'ath Party officials who had previously monitored their every move and phone call, had disappeared. There were reports that none of the government's most senior officials had turned up at their offices that morning. Basra had fallen forty-eight hours earlier and a mob had turned on the remaining Fedayeen in the city, killing a number of them. Across Iraq the people who ran the regime had melted away. The international TV networks were saying that the American and British forces had won the military campaign. Now the full-scale victory parade that had long been promised was meant to be kicking off in the streets somewhere near where I was located.

I persuaded Trey to check with the captain, who with the rest of the company had been sent out to intercept a small group of armed paramilitaries that had been spotted approaching a nearby shopping centre.

'Oliver says the war's apparently over. Can you see people dancing in the streets?' Trey asked over the radio.

There was a pause. 'What?' the captain said.

'I said, the international news is reporting that we've won the war, and people are supposedly dancing in the streets,' said Trey.

There was the sound of a whoosh over the radio and someone in the background saying, 'Was that an RPG?' Trey looked at me and grinned.

'No one's dancing here,' the captain said, and hung up.

Indeed, all that day the company was caught up fighting para-militaries in the sidestreets of western Baghdad. Sergeant Whelan's tank ended up taking three or four RPGs, which incapacitated it and set fire to all the supplies strapped to its rear. I would see Whelan a few days later at the battalion's supply centre in the requisitioned Republican Guard barracks. He told me he had been furious when he had realised his stash of Oreo biscuits had been incinerated, and that he was now cold at night because his sleeping bag had been reduced to cinders.

But despite the evidence to the contrary, there was clearly something going on out there, and I knew I had to go and have a look. I took off my flak jacket and helmet and dressed in a blue sweat-shirt and jeans. Opening my bags I grabbed my phone, my note-book, my pile of US dollars (provided by my newspaper before I left England, to be used as bribes to get me out of trouble), my tourist map of Baghdad and my toothbrush. If the Black Knights were moved to a new location after I had started walking into town I would find it very difficult to hook up with them again, so I was preparing for the possibility that my time with the US military could be over. It was not something I had time to dwell on, but my next home – if I could find it – might well be with the press corps at the Palestine Hotel.

'What're you doing?' Trey asked. I told him I was going to walk across the American lines and through the centre of Baghdad, to try to discover what was happening on the other bank of the Tigris.

The M113 had moved again as I was getting ready, pulling up beside the checkpoint that had been erected at the furthest point the US Army had reached into the city. Although the Marines were now at the east bank of the Tigris and the 3rd Infantry Division occupied most of the west, there was still a spot at the centre of Baghdad where no American troops had yet ventured. It was meant to be the next day's objective, the final closing of the vice that had surrounded Saddam. It had always been hoped that the system run by the Ba'ath Party would implode, either soon after the invasion started or when Baghdad was surrounded. However, fear or loyalty meant it took until the United States Army was in spitting distance of the government's main departmental headquarters for the tipping point actually to be reached and the regime finally to fall.

'Say that again?' said Trey. 'You're gonna to get yourself killed. I guess you haven't realised over the last few weeks that there are people out there who kinda enjoy shooting at us.'

I did not really have a choice, as reports were coming in at an ever-increasing rate of widespread Iraqi jubilation. A statue of Saddam within sight of the TV cameras at the Palestine Hotel had been pulled down from its marble plinth by an American M88 after a crowd of sixty or seventy Iraqis had failed to topple it by heaving on ropes. They were now beating it with their shoes, a particularly grave Arab insult. The footage was being interpreted around the world as further evidence of citywide rejoicing at Saddam's defeat. I picked up my collapsible plastic shoulderbag, and hung around my neck the Kuwaiti press pass with its smattering of Arabic writing on it explaining that I was a journalist.

'Be careful,' said Trey. 'We wouldn't want to lose you now. Not after all this.' He smiled his toothless grin, his mouth drawing into an ever thinner line. 'But if you don't come back, can I take your laptop?'

'And I want the GPS,' shouted Ray. 'And the shortwave radio too.'

I stepped through the barbed wire, my army-issue wristwatch telling me it was already almost three o'clock, and out into the city. For a month now I had lived almost every minute of every day with the American soldiers. They had been my protectors, my guides, my entertainment, my comrades. As I walked down that street it was the first time I had been by myself since Kuwait City. This was my opportunity to see what was going on beyond the fighting and manoeuvring of the battalion I had been with – or at least what was going on in the minds of the largely Sunni population of the parts of Baghdad I would be passing through. There had been a few snatched conversations with the PoWs in Nasiriyah, with Mr Alavan, with the crowd calling for water and food, but essentially what had been going on in the minds of the Iraqi people remained a mystery to me. No one really knew if the majority welcomed the Americans' arrival, or hated them for being there. Until now the Iraqis had just been the 'other', the people shooting at me and getting shot. Now I found myself walking among them, with no army to protect me and with no guns to be seen. There was just me and my notebook, trying to interpret what was really going on as TV sets around the world showed crowds cheering in what Donald Rumsfeld, the American Defense Secretary, was describing as scenes reminiscent of those that greeted the breaching of the Berlin Wall.

And so I went for a walk through the streets of Baghdad. I saw a city in which exultation at the taste of freedom mingled with the despair of defeat. My walk took me past looters filling their cars from shops whose windows had been smashed, young men wanting to mob American servicemen with gratitude, and old men who sat on their doorsteps in tears as they contemplated the invaders advancing through the streets. Above all the walk put me in touch with real people – people just like the soldier who had left a photograph of himself with his girlfriend in a military locker at a hospital without any idea that he would never be able to retrieve it – who, even at the end of the world as they had known it, greeted a stranger with only kindness and offers of sweet tea.

The road was broad and clean, broken every quarter of a mile or so by the shaded seating areas which I had already observed were a favourite feature of Iraqi urban planners. Along its left side was a row of small houses shaded by date palms and mulberry trees, on the right the factory chimneys of an industrial estate. I met my first Iraqis less than a hundred yards from the American lines, a group of half a dozen or so men as young as the soldiers I had just left. Word was spreading that something extraordinary had happened, and they had come to see for themselves if it could possibly be true. Many in the group were jumping up and down with excitement. One, Ayass Mohammed, a nineteen-year-old student with jug ears and a thin moustache, spoke English and started pressing me for information.

'Will they beat us if we go close?' he asked, indicating the American soldiers in the distance. 'We hear Saddam is gone. We have heard he has fled and that all that is bad has fallen. We want to say thank you to them for bringing us freedom. I want to thank them, but I am a little bit afraid they will beat us. Will they beat us if we go to thank them for what they have done for us?'

I said that as long as they had their hands clearly visible above their heads the soldiers would be pleased to hear their gratitude. Ayass and his friends were so excited that none of them could stand still for a moment. 'It is a great feeling,' he told me. 'I have never felt this way before. It was only two hours ago when suddenly I feel freedom, when I saw the American tanks and heard that Saddam had run. All my life all I know is Saddam. Now we are free.'

Groups of men stood at street corners. Some were happy and

smiled and waved, the faces of others were grim from the knowledge that the Americans were now in control. 'How would you
feel if there were foreign tanks outside your home?' said Ahmed
Khadra as his two friends nodded their heads in agreement. 'The
young people, they don't know life, they just think it is a revolution
and they can dance and be excited. They do not have a relation
to the land, our country. That is what we die for, that is all that
matters.' He stamped his foot on the pavement. 'This land that is
ours and others are trying to take from us. This is not finished.
There is no balance between the USA and Britain and our country,
no balance, but still your nations will suffer for what they have
done.'

As I walked on towards the city centre a young boy, no more
than ten years old, rode by on a red bicycle. 'Saddam is dead!
Well done America!' he shouted before pedalling into the distance.
Two men walked past, using knurled sticks to guide two sheep
through the urban streets. 'Saddam!' one shouted, pulling a finger
across his neck as his companion smiled and cheered.

'Yesterday I lived in a hell, now we have a future,' said a young
student. 'You don't know how bad it was – the fear, the deaths.
Saddam Hussein was inhuman.' I asked him his name. 'Abdul,'
he answered, but when I asked for his surname he smiled embar-
rassedly. 'I am still frightened. What if Saddam come back and
then he kill me?'

A group of men in Arab robes were standing beside the entrance
to a racetrack. 'Where is Saddam?' I shouted over to them.

'Saddam regime is gone. Everybody know that,' they called back.

I was enjoying myself. Some people would look at me sus-
piciously until they saw the embossed plastic of my Kuwaiti ID,
then they would throw up their hands and grin as they realised I
was a reporter. No one showed any hostility to me personally,
whether they supported the Americans' arrival or were horrified
by it.

Yet there was no sense of ecstatic communal celebration gripping the streets through which I walked that afternoon. I saw no crowds spilling across the tarmac and dancing, just confused people discussing the events of the day and what they meant for their future. Maybe elsewhere there were street parties – it was a big city, and I was only seeing a very small part of it. But although some of the people I met were happy, many were sad at the course events had taken, and those revelling in the moment seemed uncertain whether it was really the right time for them to be doing so.

The Ministry of Trade building loomed over a junction, its windows smashed, whether by an American attack or angry Iraqis it was impossible to determine. I saw a police station, walked in and called out a greeting. No one answered. On the wall was a cardboard sign in Arabic and English that read 'Quality is a Virtue. Aim for Perfection.' The wooden desk at the entrance counter was covered in papers, but it seemed there was no one now willing to man it.

Further on, three men approached me, two of them scowling. 'Tell the world Iraqis are not happy,' one wearing a red Nike T-shirt said. 'Saddam make bad things but he was an Iraqi. And only an Iraqi rule Iraq. The fighting not over. No one accept an American as our ruler.'

In the distance occasional gunfire could still be heard, but I was more preoccupied by the fact that I was utterly lost. All the streets seemed identical, and my tourist map bore little resemblance to the actual street plan. After having found myself at the same block of buildings for the third time, I knew I was in need of assistance. On the step outside his house was Mr al-Ramahi, a veteran of the last Gulf War who professed to despise the US and all its meddling in the Middle East, and who was visibly upset by the events which now surrounded him. Yet he happily walked with me to the nearest junction and showed me the way to the Tigris so that I would not spend any more time aimlessly going in circles. 'Saddam only man brave enough to stand up against America,' he said while we walked. 'Everyone else frightened but he is the only Arab who is not. I lose friends in Iran war, Gulf War, now I will lose my sons as this turns into a new Palestine. There will be years of fighting. It is a tragedy but it is the way it must be.'

A little later, a car drew to a stop beside me. 'No go there,' the driver said, pointing at a warehouse down a sidestreet. 'Thieves. They taking everything.' And then, with a parting 'Welcome to Iraq,' he and his passenger drove off.

At a roundabout, a small crowd had gathered to watch as people ransacked the surrounding shops, piling boxes of pilfered stock into the boots of their cars. I was surprised by how orderly it all was. There was no shouting or firing of guns or fighting: the looters drew up in their cars and patiently waited their turn. A few people were waddling down the street straining under the weight of their pickings. They were laughing and pointing out their booty to their friends. Chairs, particularly desk chairs presumably taken from government offices, seemed to be a particularly popular object of pillage.

Nabil al-Abdil was watching the scene with a look of dejection. 'There have been so many bodies; we had bodies here lying outside on the road that people had to bury in their gardens,' he told me when I asked what was going on. 'Now they have turned us into thieves. We will never forget what has been done by the Americans, or you British.'

I thought it best to say nothing. He turned to peer at me and asked, 'Are you a spy?' I assured him I was a journalist. He looked me up and down. 'You look very tired and very dirty. Come inside and let me offer you a cup of tea.'

It was approaching 5.30 p.m. and I was in fact very tired, so I accepted with gratitude. We walked a few streets to a little two-storey house surrounded by an overgrown garden. We drank tea and smoked cigarettes. He told me he had taught himself English from a book. The women came out to stand on the porch and stare at us. I thanked him for his kindness.

'Our countries may be enemies,' he replied, 'but that does not mean we two cannot be friends. It is not men like us who choose to fight; it is the leaders who tell us to do so. America and Britain may now seek to rule us, but you are still my fellow human being. Hate just leads to more hate. What else is there to hold onto at times like this but common humanity?' Eighteen months earlier in another traumatised city, on the other side of the world, I had been just as moved by the expression of a similar sentiment.

'Do you like football?' Nabil asked. 'David Beckham is a very good player. Many in Iraq like him very much.' And then he looked at me with great earnestness. 'You know, Americans do not even like football. How can we ever live with them? Poor Iraq, always it knows nothing but suffering.'

A married couple who were his neighbours joined us, the husband in a brown jacket with leather patches on the shoulders and a thin dark tie, his wife's hair hidden by a bright orange headdress. Her sister lived in London, and I offered her my satellite phone to call and tell her they were safe. She started crying and ran inside to get the number. I looked at the address written in her notebook, the front of which had been adorned with stickers of the cartoon cat Garfield. Her sister lived in Purley, in suburban south London. It is a district notable primarily for its roundabout, which is one of the gateways to Gatwick airport, a place with rolling streets lined with horse chestnut trees, red pillarboxes, theme pubs filled for England football matches, where police do not need to wear body armour, where at that moment children would be watching Australian soap operas and husbands walking home from commuter stations. That afternoon a phone would have rung as a woman from Iraq received a call from her sister still living in Baghdad, a city where looters had taken to the streets and soldiers guarded every major road junction. I sat on a wicker chair drinking tea as the chatter of a woman talking to her sister filled the air, and around us the shadows spread as the sun drew to the end of its slow descent towards the horizon.

I had no idea where I was by now, and it would soon be getting dark. However, Nabil said he had a friend who spoke English, and who had to walk back to his house which was near where I hoped the Black Knights would still be stationed. Without the unintentional detours I had made, it took us less than thirty minutes to get back to where I had started, the rather humbling reality of the extent of my great trek into the unknown. We talked about the details of our lives, as strangers do when they find themselves walking together.

'You married?' he asked.

'No.'

'Should be. Wife brings great happiness.'

'So, you are?'

'Yes. One year.'

'Children?'

'Not yet. Soon, I hope. Why you not married?'

'I am too busy.'

'Too busy to be happy!'

I laughed. 'Too busy to be happy. That is right.'

'Westerners. Always too busy to be happy! Should have wife, she look after you, make you special. I go to her now. She is making food for me, chicken. She knows I like chicken. That makes me happy.'

I asked him what he thought about the war in his country. He shrugged. 'There is nothing I can do, so why have opinion? There was Saddam and now America. Why worry? All I can do is try and be good person to my family. Everything else will be as it will be. How I can explain? These things are not right or wrong, they just are. I do not want people to die. I do not want soldiers attacking my country. But it is not my position to feel bad about such things. It is the world that is happening, and we just try to live good lives in it. Why take time to be scared or angry or guilty? All that occurs is in the wishes of God.'

Inevitably we started talking about football, that contemporary equivalent of the weather as the stopgap conversation for English-men in any tricky social situation. He was also a great fan, I learnt, of David Beckham. I realised I did not know my companion's name. 'It Mohammed Baghdad,' he told me, adding that he was twenty-two.

'Mohammed Baghdad!' I said. 'You are Mr Baghdad? That is too perfect. Everyone is going to think I made it up as a metaphor.'

He looked confused. 'My name is Mohammed Baghdad.'

The American checkpoint could be made out on the road bridge ahead. There were the barbed wire and the tanks, their barrels silhouetted against the sky that burnt a fearsome red as the rays of the setting sun were refracted through the smoke hanging in the air. I reached in my pocket and pulled out a white handkerchief to hold over my head to make sure I was not shot by accident. Mohammed put his hands up. For a moment he joked, waving his hands in a caricature of someone frightened, but as we got closer he became nervous for real and clutched them firmly to his head.

Just before we arrived at the barricade I met Ayass Mohammed, the young student who had wanted to go and say thank you to the successful invaders. He and his friends were looking confused and angry. 'Reporter, reporter,' he shouted. 'You said it would be safe to go to them. That they would be happy to see us. But they grab us and push us against a wall and check us for weapons. I think they mistake us for officers. Maybe they not friendly. We just want to give them cigarettes. I do not understand what is happening. Why they push us?'

I did not know why the soldiers had pushed them, thought it best to apologise on their behalf, and walked on up the last yards of the incline towards the guards who stood at the bridge's summit. With night now having almost completely fallen it was impossible to make out who they were; all that could be seen was the anony-mous shape of uniforms, the Kevlar helmets imposing and regi-mental against the skyline. I flourished my white handkerchief.

Mohammed and I were told to stop, and a figure came towards us. It was Sergeant Pyle. 'Ahh, Oliver,' he said. 'Good to see you're still alive. There are people out there who want to kill us.'

I walked between the tanks on sentry duty, and saw that the M113 was stationed in the defensive perimeter. Ray was in the driver's seat, and he stood up, waved and grinned when he saw me. Then I noticed a figure making his way back along the line of soldiers. It was Mohammed, my walking companion. He reached out his hand and I shook it. 'Friend,' he said, and disappeared into the night to go and eat chicken with his wife.

NINE

Dog-Faced Soldier

Thursday, 10 April–Friday, 11 July

I flew out of Baghdad less than a week later, the C-130 air force cargo plane banking sharply after it took off and then weaving from left to right to confuse any Stinger anti-aircraft missiles that might be fired at us. The planes would only come in at night, their lights off and their engines left running as they waited on the runway for their cargo to be unloaded. Soldiers combed the treeline to ensure that there were no armed Iraqis in the vicinity. I ran up the ramp that led into the hold, and gripped onto the webbing that covered the inside of the plane to brace myself for the defensive manoeuvres. Once we had reached cruising altitude, an airman handed me a turkey sandwich and a can of Coke from an icebox. He had been looking out of a porthole in the emergency exit door. 'Did you see all those fires?' he asked. 'I'm pleased we didn't have to stay down there too long.'

The intervening days had been a mixture of confusion and boredom. The evening after my walk through Baghdad, I had sat at the back of Sergeant Harrison's mechanics truck and tried to let it sink in that the worst was over. Nearly everyone was too exhausted to talk. A rumour had spread among the unit that they would start being sent back to the US within three weeks. Someone had begun to hum a John Denver tune, and then softly sung the words: 'Country roads, take me home, to the place where

247

I belong, West Virginia, mountain momma, take me home, country roads.'

Doc was emotional, as he had spent a large part of the day caring for some children hurt when they accidentally stepped on one of the unexploded bomblets from an MLRS missile. Similar cases were being reported all over the city, and delegations of Iraqis had started petitioning the Americans for the removal of anti-personnel weapons left behind by the fighting, but there were not enough spare troops to start a clean-up operation. The children Doc had treated had been wounded in the underpass under the road junction through which we had travelled only forty-eight hours earlier. The bomblets were from the missiles I had seen killing the soldiers who had been hiding beneath. I remembered with chagrin how I had casually watched through a pair of binoculars as the weapons threw out their deadly cargo, how I had been excited by the spectacle of such raw power, laughed with the rest at the ridiculousness of such overwhelming destruction.

Doc described how he had heard an explosion, and then some soldiers had reported that a family was running up the street carrying injured children. 'The parents were scared, they thought their sons were going to die,' he said. 'There was a four-year-old, a six-year-old and a seven-year-old, all boys, and they were bleeding badly. The four-year-old had fragmentation wounds to his leg and arm, and a chunk had gone into his pelvis. The seven-year-old was the worst wounded. He had large scalp lacerations, cuts on his head and shoulder, and something had gone straight through his shoulder. The other had small cuts all over his body. The oldest child was angry; you could see that he hated Americans already. The other two were in tears. It was hard not to cry when you saw them. As I looked, all I could see was my own kids in their faces. When I came towards them with scissors to cut off their clothes they were scared of me. I had to hide the weapons we had inside Band Aid – they made them frightened.'

I climbed on top of the medic track where Big Sergeant B was sitting, chewing tobacco as usual. 'Thank God it's all over,' I said. 'Maybe we can all go back to being normal now.'

'We've been part of the longest American ground war since Vietnam,' he replied. 'We're allowed to all be a little bit not normal. Things could've been much worse though. If they'd known what they were doing they could've killed a lot of soldiers. We have this exercise at the National Training Center where we have to go against an enemy equipped with Soviet weapons. They know the territory and they know their weapons, and most of the time they whip the guys with American equipment. If the Iraqis had been sophisticated, a lot of us here could've died. I don't want to think what it would have been like with everyone around me getting killed.'

Before the war, the US Army had run simulated attacks through the Karbala Gap on computers. A captain who had trained on them reported that he had lost every time. 'I died here, like, seven times,' he had said when the real attack was over. It had not been inevitable that American and British casualties would be as light as they had proved to be, even if their troops' vastly superior weaponry meant they almost certainly would have won even if they had not fought cleverly. As it was the coalition fought a tactically sound war, and this had contributed to ensuring its small number of dead. Its troops pushed ahead as fast as they could at the beginning and end of the campaign to catch a bewildered enemy off-guard. Surprise had been achieved by starting the ground war ahead of the full force of the air strikes. Special Forces had been placed in Iraq weeks before the invasion started, with orders to negate any potentially unpleasant surprises. Most crucially, devastating air power was used to flatten Saddam's best soldiers before they could fire a single shot.

However, the success of the invasion had been immeasurably helped by the fact that its opponents appeared to lack a coherent plan of defence. The Iraqi regime could have caused far more damage if its forces had been better marshalled to defend the country's key tactical locations both south of the capital and, most particularly, within the maze of streets of Baghdad itself. Iraq is not an easy country to invade, as it has strong natural defences. There are expanses of desert in the west, mountains to the east, and wide rivers in the centre which block the way to the main area of population. Its rulers had been alerted months ahead of the invasion that war was coming, and should have been able to complete extensive preparations. Dams and dykes could have been destroyed to funnel armoured columns into artillery ambushes. The south of the country could have been heavily mined. Bridges could have been blown to slow attackers, and ports sabotaged. The enormous traffic jams of supply vehicles could have been targeted, instead of resources being focused on the units of heavily armoured tanks. An inferno of burning oilwells could have been lit. The Karbala Gap could have been stoutly defended. But none of these things had happened.

The nature of Saddam's regime was partly to blame for this. Radio reports intercepted by the Americans revealed that senior Iraqi officers were so terrified of Saddam's younger son Qusay, who it is believed was controlling Iraqi resistance in the later part of the campaign, that they repeatedly claimed to have defeated the US forces in battle and to have inflicted heavy casualties. Such disinformation, combined with incompetence and a breakdown in Iraq's communications system – fear of drawing bombs by using electrical signals resulted in many Iraqi commanders resorting to bicycle messengers to contact their troops – meant there was not one large-scale attack on the US military during the entire war. Resistance was primarily marshalled at obvious spots such as road intersections, where it could be easily outflanked. Individual Iraqi units appeared detached from any sort of command structure, required to defend themselves as best they could without hope of significant support, and were mopped up one at a time by American and British forces that were free to move forward at their own pace to deal with each isolated target. After the original surprise at facing widespread units of paramilitaries, the fighting became so one-sided it was, as a Marine lieutenant colonel described it, 'like clubbing baby harp seals'.

That night it was my turn to have a nightmare. I was writhing around on my stretcher so much that I managed to scare Doc and Frankie. When they woke me, I apparently asked, 'Have they surrendered yet?' and then fell back asleep. I have a vague memory that I dreamt I was being crushed by a bridge while sticking out of the top of the hatch on the M88.

By morning, much of the smoke from the nightly bombing raids that had turned the air a bitter yellow had cleared. The unfiltered light seemed harsh and bright after the days of haze. It was sentry duty now for most of the men of the Black Knights. A few tanks were chasing down a pick-up truck in which some men had been seen carrying RPGs, but the rest were in the infantry now, guarding street corners and marshalling the crowds of civilians making their way through the streets.

These soldiers were not the right people to be peacekeepers. For nine months they had trained to be ready to deal with any hostile threat. In the weeks of fighting their senses had become attuned to respond immediately and lethally when anyone fired at them. Now they were expected to be policemen, to calmly keep throngs of people in order despite the wiring in their minds that was geared to treat any sudden movement as a life-threatening danger. 'We did all the fighting, and now they want us kissing babies,' a captain said. 'You can't do that after all we been through, it's just too stressful.'

Some did not want the fighting to be over. Sergeant Pyle talked about how he hoped the company would be sent to Tikrit, the town a hundred miles north-west of Baghdad where Saddam Hussein had been born, which was believed to be the last strong-hold of Ba'athist resistance, and possibly even where the Iraqi President was now hiding. Already the game of 'Where's Saddam?' had begun in earnest. Rumours were flying around, fuelled by civilians who came up to the checkpoints to offer their own suggestions.

It was in the Mansour district near where the battalion was based that Saddam (or, as analysts had speculated, perhaps one of his doubles) had last been seen in public. He was shown on Iraqi TV four days after the international airport had been captured, walking amid a cheering crowd. One local took Sergeant Pyle to a house which he said Uday, Saddam's oldest son, had been using as his military headquarters. Maps were found on the walls with the location of Iraqi units marked on them. Neighbours said Uday had been seen in the district only forty-eight hours previously, but had fled to Tikrit, confirming Sergeant Pyle in his desire to be part of the operation to take that final objective.

News passed down the line that Saddam had been seen in a convoy leaving Baghdad to get medical attention in Syria. Another rumour claimed he was holed up in a suburb to the north-east of the city, surrounded by his paramilitary fighters. A mosque was raided after Saddam was reported to be using it as his last stronghold. At one point a rumour spread that he had been killed, prompting cheering from the American troops who heard it. When it emerged that the news was incorrect, I heard a sergeant confidently comment, 'It's only a matter of time. There's nowhere he can hide from us now.'

When I made my daily call to the office in London, I was informed that my time with the troops really was now to come to an end. The rest of the *Telegraph*'s Gulf team was on its way to Baghdad. One reporter was driving across the border from Oman. Another who had been in Kuwait had secured himself a berth on a boat travelling up the Euphrates. It was time for new hands to take over, and for me to get out of Iraq.

I was driven to the requisitioned Republican Guard barracks, from where I was told I would be taken to brigade and then division headquarters to complete the paperwork that would facilitate my 'dismissal' from the American forces. Trey and Ray dropped me off. I did not know how to express my gratitude for the kindness with which they had accepted me. 'It's been a privilege,' I found myself saying, and then cursed myself for such a terrible line. Horrified, I realised that what had popped into my head was a bit of dialogue from the film *Titanic*. It was the last thing the members of the string quartet said to each other as the ship went down, which made me feel even lamer for having used it.

'Are we ever going to see you again?' asked Doc. 'Or are you going to have come into our lives and then just disappeared?'

I felt I was somehow betraying the men of the Black Knights by leaving them stuck amid the epidemic of looting and the threat of sniper attacks which was the reality of life in Baghdad. 'I'm sorry for going,' I said.

'Don't apologise,' Doc replied. 'We'd all like to get out of this spot and find ourselves sleeping in a hotel. It's not going to be the same without you coming around asking all your stupid questions. You've been through this with us the whole way. You're part of the team.'

'That's why we'll never lose touch. Who else but you guys can understand what it was like to be here?' I said to him.

'Roger,' he answered.

As it was, it took another two days before I could go anywhere. Things were becoming, in one sense, more organised for the US military stationed in Baghdad as camp life was slowly re-established. Areas in the Republican Guard barracks were divided into working zones: one for the mechanics, one for the cooks (it would be hot food again that evening), and even one for the chaplain, who had taken an Iraqi's office as his own and was sitting in it with his driver watching science fiction movies on DVD. He had not been able to conduct his baptisms in the Euphrates, but was now planning to make his own way to the river to collect vials of water in order to perform the ceremony within the safety of the camp.

However, despite the gradual emergence of a fixed daily routine, there was still a severe shortage of working vehicles. American soldiers have a maxim: 'Hurry up and wait.' It means that when an order is given everyone has to jump to it and get in position, and then find themselves sitting around until they are told to actually go ahead and do what they had got ready for. At that Republican Guard barracks it was a case of hurry up and wait. I found one of the few office sofas that had not been destroyed, dragged it outside to the edge of the parade ground, and waited for a vehicle to take me out of there. For almost forty-eight hours I sat on that black leather sofa and watched the soldiers around me finish the job of looting the barracks and reducing its offices to piles of rubbish and debris. At night, lying in the same spot, the mosquitoes feasted upon me.

I saw Roman one last time. He had arrived with the rest of the battalion's supply train. The colour had returned to his cheeks. 'I wasn't good for a while back there,' he admitted, 'but everything's OK now.' Then, remembering the proximity of danger again after his time far at the rear: 'You're lucky to be getting out of here. I'm only eighteen and I already feel I'm too old for all this.' I offered him a last use of my phone, which was gratefully accepted.

On my last night I talked with Captain Robert Ross, a studious red-haired officer in his late twenties, in charge of logistics, who had miraculously kept the battalion supplied throughout the entire campaign except for those first few days on the outskirts of Baghdad. He had been at boarding school in Britain as a child. His parents had been sent abroad by the US State Department and he had gone to Gordonstoun in northern Scotland, the school Prince Charles had once attended, before enrolling at West Point back in the States.

He had seen me on the morning of the final advance into Baghdad, when the MLRS had been raining down on the underpass. 'I looked at you that day and you were laughing and talking with the rest of the crew. Staring at what was going on in front. And I thought, there's someone who's fallen in love with the beauty of destruction,' he said. 'Don't feel bad, it's a common problem. But it's probably a good thing you're getting out now.'

I did not want to dwell on whether he was right. I was only too aware that at that point the unfolding events had left me unwilling to view any of those human shapes getting killed in the distance as real people. I certainly knew I was relieved to be going home.

Captain Ross was worrying about the effect the war would have on the men in the battalion. 'In the next year we'll have a lot of problems,' he said. 'Discipline will be harder to enforce, as people's attitude will be: "Hey, we just fought a war." There'll be soldiers beating their wives because they spent all their money while they were away or were sleeping around. Cases will be reported of people resorting to drugs and alcohol. There'll be fights in the town. These men don't even realise yet what they've done. The simulation of battle training is so realistic that it resembles almost exactly what occurs in the field. They have lifesize tanks that resemble precisely the ones we've been shooting out here. There are dummies of soldiers popping out of doors that resemble the scenario in house-to-house searches. Half these soldiers feel they've been on a field exercise. The problems are going to come when it sinks in that this time it was people they've been shooting at.'

We stood in the dark, me smoking, him spitting out tobacco juices. 'What do you think about this war?' he suddenly asked.

I began the usual spiel about evil dictators and the need for someone to stop weapons of mass destruction spreading through-out the world that it was normally advisable to recite to American soldiers.

'No, what do you really think?' he interrupted. 'Because I'm opposed to it. We had no right to do what we did here. These people had water and an infrastructure before we arrived. Now it feels like they've got neither. We're giving people reasons to hate us.'

I thought about it. There were no certainties in my brain any more, just memories. Those first dead bodies I had seen at Nasiriyah. The night when Doc had dislocated his shoulder and we had sheltered in the M88. The sky that was as orange as Kool-Aid. The truckers driving backwards and forwards along the same road in the desert. The gunfire aimed at us on the road to Baghdad. The emotion of a Spanish reporter. A donkey pulling a cart filled with cartons of water. The men burying a body by the side of the road. Drinking tea in a garden while a telephone call was made to Purley. I did not know if it was my expectation of what was going to happen that had been wrong, or what had happened itself. It was all God's will anyway, I had been told.

The next day, Monday, 14 April, I was still sitting on my sofa, watching the tanks and Bradleys pull in and out of the barracks. A soldier was being treated for a gunshot wound to his cheek, sustained when he had tried to shoot open a metal door and had been struck by the ricochet. Two young soldiers from Sergeant Whelan's tank crew passed by. 'You still on that stupid sofa, Oliver?' one shouted over. I nodded. I had been told their names at the beginning of the campaign, then forgotten them and been too embarrassed ever since to ask what they were.

'You sad to be leaving us?' the taller one asked.

I gave a non-committal shrug and enquired how he was. 'Me?' he said. 'Don't worry about me. It was fun.' That was the last time I saw any members of the Black Knights in Iraq. Less than an hour later a Humvee drew up to take me to brigade headquarters.

In that journey, my last through the Iraqi capital, we passed a few burnt-out cars, a cluster of destroyed AA guns, the remains of a transit van, all reminders of the American advance. There were a handful of civilian vehicles on the highway now, white cloths tied to their wing mirrors. At one point we passed one of Saddam's palaces. It looked like a medieval fort, built of brown

brick on top of a grassy motte, its walls ringed by stylised battle-
ments and topped by a series of ornate towers. There were almost
three hundred Iraqis carrying loot out of it and into their vehicles,
all shouting encouragement and smiling at each other. Some
clutched furniture, a child had a brass lamp, an air-conditioning
unit was being ferried in a wheelbarrow. They resembled a column
of ants swarming over a fallen branch to strip it of its leaves. A
little further on, at a line of abandoned underground military
bunkers, an old woman was pulling a mattress out from an
entranceway while a younger man, presumably her son, clutched
a rug in his arms.

'These people had nothing for so long. It's good they're getting
their hands on stuff now,' the driver said as we drove past. The
BBC was reporting that elsewhere in the city hospitals were being
looted of even their operating equipment. The police had disappeared. Some of the streets were filled with raw sewage. At
night, bandits were robbing homes. With so many weapons in
the city the price of an AK-47 was now little more than a couple
of packs of cigarettes.

When I finally reached the airport after having completed all
the bureaucratic requirements needed to leave my unit, I met
Major Birmingham, the officer who had organised the embed
scheme for the 3rd Infantry Division. He was delighted with how
the experiment had gone. Only one reporter had been removed,
and that was for insisting on using a satellite phone that it was
suspected emitted a signal whose frequency could be detected
by the Iraqi military. Stories about American derring-do had
appeared in newspapers and on news bulletins across the world,
bringing to people's sitting rooms the daily threats the soldiers
had faced and the hardships they had been required to endure.
Above all, they had made clear what battles the manpower and
equipment of the United States military had won. There was no
danger of the world not knowing what the American army had
achieved in the Persian Gulf this time around.

The speed and success of the military campaign meant there had never been a point when the embed system had been put to the test and the army forced to decide whether it wanted the live camera links switched off. Only time will tell whether the Pentagon will repeat the experiment in future wars. The fact that such a gamble was taken in Iraq is a sign of how confident the US high command had been of achieving a rapid victory.

For the media, the problem is to determine what being embedded means for their ability to balance the need to cover an event at close quarters with the requirement to maintain independence and objectivity. On the plus side, the opportunity to see combat at first hand unquestionably added an important element to the campaign's coverage. It also provided the hope that if a war crime was committed or a military mistake made, a reporter would be there to witness it, and thereby hopefully prevent any cover-up.

The controversy surrounding what actually occurred during the rescue of Jessica Lynch has also made it clear that relying on sources in the Pentagon is still not necessarily a method that can be trusted. Despite the military footage of soldiers seemingly risking their lives to show that 'America doesn't leave its heroes behind', it appears that there was no opposition in the hospital they were so dramatically shown storming. Rather than firing her weapon and receiving her injuries in the firefight that marked her capture, as originally reported, it has since been confirmed that Miss Lynch was hurt when her Humvee crashed into the articulated vehicle in front, and that in all likelihood she was unconscious throughout the battle.

On the negative side, by the time I got to Baghdad airport the only objective thought I had left was the siren in my head screaming that I could no longer bear to see any more people on either side being killed or injured. Maybe that is not a bad thing. Detachment is probably the last thing needed from someone trying to explain what it was really like to be there. It is certainly the last thing I could hope to achieve while getting close enough to those caught up in events to understand what they were feeling. The other major problem was that I saw the war from such a limited perspective – my access restricted to one company in one battalion in one part of a country the size of France – and as a journalist for a British daily newspaper I had too little time to adequately investigate the truth behind what I was being told by those around me. This left me unable for far too long to explore the attitude of the Iraqi people, and it also meant I constantly had to resist the temptation to generalise about what was going on across Iraq as a whole from the evidence available from my own isolated viewpoint. Often I would be caught up in gunfire, and later find that things had been totally calm a few miles behind me. I would hear reports from the soldiers of counterattacks or of Iraqi officials being captured that they clearly believed to be true, but which turned out to be utterly bogus when checked with American central command.

The reality is, however, that if the Pentagon does again authorise embedding, such considerations are unlikely to be of primary concern to the people in the news organisations who will be responsible for deciding whether to enlist their reporters once more. As anyone who watched the war on TV already knows, the pictures sent back from the front line were just too entertaining for them not to want to gain similar access next time.

Major Birmingham told me that around 5 per cent of the reporters who had been embedded with the army had died, among them not only the Spanish and German reporters I had met at Objective Saints but also David Bloom, the weekend host of the prestigious American network news programme *Today*, who had suffered an embolism. Indeed, the percentage of journalists who lost their lives during the campaign was ten times higher than among the soldiers serving in the American and British military. Thirteen reporters died and two are still missing, most of them drawn from the brave individuals, like the ITN correspondent Terry Lloyd, who had moved independently around the battlefield to get an unimpeded perspective. They had risked considerable dangers to try to tell the world what was going on across the plains of southern Iraq, going into areas of fighting without the military protection that had been available to the embedded reporters like me. On 8 April a US tank in Baghdad sent a shell into the Palestine Hotel, in which the Iraqis had insisted the foreign press corps be based, after its crew claimed they had come under fire from the building. Two cameramen were killed, one from Reuters and one working for a Spanish TV network. A military investigation was launched into how authorisation could have been given for that shot to be fired. During the entire Second World War the number of reporters killed was sixty-six, in the Korean War seventeen, in Vietnam and Cambodia sixty-five, the Balkans fifty-six and Afghanistan eight. Thirteen journalists confirmed dead in just over four weeks of fighting made the invasion of Iraq one of the most costly wars in history for the media.

Figures have also begun to emerge of the number of military and civilian casualties. No one knows for certain how many Iraqi soldiers were killed. The Pentagon stopped officially releasing details of enemy losses after it became a bureaucratic fetish during the Vietnam War and ludicrous methods – counting five body parts as five 'kills', for example – had undermined US credibility. General Tommy Franks had flatly said, 'We don't do body counts,' and no figures have ever been confirmed by the United States military of the possible number of Iraqi losses in the 1991 war. A Pentagon estimate of ten thousand dead Iraqi troops in the second Gulf War has, however, been widely reported after it was leaked to the American press. It was based on multiplying destroyed vehicles by the average number of personnel on board, and on approximations made after ground engagements in which American forces scanned the area for the number of dead bodies. The true extent of Iraq's military casualties may however be far higher. William Arkin, a former US Army intelligence officer and a senior military adviser for Human Rights Watch, warned that when the full details finally emerge, 'I think we are going to be stunned by the level of carnage caused by this war.'

Figures for civilian deaths are even more difficult to determine, not least because the Iraqi regime ordered a number of hospitals to lie to journalists that all their casualties were civilian even when it was clear soldiers were also being treated. The same Pentagon sources that provided the figure for Iraqi troop losses have estimated that two thousand civilians were killed during the period of combat until the war was officially declared over. Seven reporters for the Associated Press, however, spent five weeks in Iraq reviewing documents from sixty of the country's 124 hospitals and concluded that in those institutions alone 3240 civilians had died from war-related injuries. They believed this total was 'still fragmentary', and that the true figure was 'significantly higher'. An international study that added up all the confirmed Iraqi civilian deaths reported in the world media put losses at between 5500 and seven thousand in the month that marked the official period of combat operations. Other organisations have placed the figure at closer to ten thousand. Nor does the end of the main battles necessarily mean the end of the local population's suffering. A Columbia University public health study of the 1991 war determined that 3500 civilians died in that campaign, but fourteen thousand died from diseases brought on by disruptions to food and water supplies caused by the conflict.

The American military suffered 138 killed and around seven hundred injured either through military actions or as a result of accidents during the period until the war was officially declared over. In the 3rd Infantry Division thirty-five soldiers were killed, twenty-one of them during the fighting around Baghdad. In 1st Battalion, the one I had been with, there were thirty-two casualties, but not one soldier had died. This, the colonel would later tell me, was a testament to the skill of the army's medical teams, as many of the injuries had been life-threatening. The British in Iraq lost thirty-seven men as a result of combat, 'friendly fire' incidents and accidents. Approximately a further 150 were injured. The youngest of those killed, Fusilier Kelan Turrington from Haslingfield, Cambridgeshire, who died in Basra after triggering a booby trap, was eighteen years old.

As I write this, no weapons of mass destruction have been found in Iraq, although the search continues. Tony Blair has shifted the emphasis from locating the weapons themselves to discovering evidence of factories intended to produce them. President Bush has admitted that he made a mistake in the State of the Union address, in which he outlined the justifications for war, by saying that Iraq had been trying to buy uranium from Niger to produce nuclear weapons. Saddam Hussein's sons, Qusay and Uday, were killed in a gunfight with American forces on 22 July. The location of the Iraqi President is still not known, although United States government officials insist that the moment of his capture is drawing near. A series of audio recordings purportedly by Saddam were released, in which he called for the fight against the United States and British forces to continue until the last enemy soldier had left his country. Regular attacks are still being carried out on the coalition troops, resulting in almost a soldier a day being killed or injured. A tape was broadcast by Al-Jazeera which appeared to contain a message from Osama bin Laden calling for the war in Iraq to be used as a justification for more terrorist operations in the West.

Just over a month after I left Iraq, mass graves began to be uncovered in fields outside Baghdad. In them were estimated to be the bodies of fifteen thousand men, women and children believed executed on Saddam's orders during his period in power. Human rights organisations believe that as many as 100,000 people were murdered over the decades by the Ba'athist regime, and perhaps half a million died in their President's pointless wars. Torture chambers whose victims wrote their last words in their own blood on the walls have been uncovered in government buildings. Prisoners freed from jails have talked of being forced to watch their wives being raped by their interrogators, and their children dropped into sacks containing starving cats. Before the war, one Iraqi who had survived Saddam's prisons, a former oil smuggler for the regime accused of being a spy, described to my *Telegraph* colleague Con Coughlin how he was arrested and taken to a presidential compound. He was stripped, given a pair of blood-soaked pyjamas, blindfolded and moved to an interrogation centre. He could hear the screams of people being tortured as he was dragged into the room. The guards tied his feet together, suspended him upside down and whipped him with lengths of wire until he was covered in blood. 'I was more than willing to comply,' he said, 'but I had no idea what I was supposed to confess to. I thought I was going to die there and then, but they were very expert in their trade. Just when I was losing consciousness they stopped and let me down.' Looking beneath his blindfold he saw other prisoners being tortured all around him. One victim was strapped to a table while his fingernails and toenails were removed. A man was receiving electric shocks to his genitals. In a far corner another was being slowly lowered into a vat of boiling water.

When I had arrived at Baghdad International Airport the site was still scarred by the fighting that had gone on to secure it. The tailfin of a destroyed jumbo jet was lying on one of the runways alongside a little two-seater aircraft from which the wings had been sheared off. Around the wreckage were parked lines of Apache helicopters, the stylised sharks' teeth of their insignia painted on each cockpit.

There was one other passenger waiting for the military cargo plane that would take me out of Iraq. It was the translator I had met when the Civil Affairs officers were trying to determine what deprivations civilians were suffering following the US Army's seizure of Objective Saints. He was sitting at the back of a Humvee with his kitbags. 'No one's more pro-army, more pro-US than me,' he told me, 'but I thought I was coming out to help the soldiers. When I got here I realised it was the Iraqi people I'd be helping. There was a lot of killing done. I saw a lot of people die. There were women and children getting hurt. They just wouldn't stay inside. It was a sad thing to see. You were at Cubs, weren't you?'

I said that yes, I had been there on that final stretch of road to the outskirts of Baghdad.

'That was shocking,' he said. 'At one moment there was a white car coming towards us and I was shouting at it in Arabic to stop. I must have shouted four or five times, but it didn't stop. The soldiers wanted to open fire, and even I was beginning to wonder what it really was. Then it came to a halt and a man who had no weapons got out. At least that was one person I was able to save.'

He stared at me, his features indistinguishable in the darkness, all lights having been banned while we waited for the plane to land. 'Did you write what actually happened?' he asked me. 'Did you tell them about the bodies left to rot because the Iraqi people were too frightened to bury them unless someone in authority said they could? About the buildings destroyed with God knows who inside them? About the people killed as they tried to find somewhere to buy food? Tell me you told them what it was really like.'

I didn't know what it had really been like any more.

When I arrived in Qatar I checked into the five-star Hilton Hotel. A pianist was playing beside the reception desk. A Chinese porter in a white jacket wheeled a trolley holding my bags to a room on the fifteenth floor. I stood under the shower and scrubbed myself to get the dirt from my body. I woke in the middle of the night and did not know where I was. The king-sized bed stretched around me as a dark shape falling away into nothingness at its edges. When I had been sleeping in Band Aid and needed to go to the loo, I would climb up through the front hatch and stand on the top to urinate over the side. As I stood there, the vehicle would simply look like a dark shape surrounded by the pale grey of the moonlit desert. I thought in that hotel room that I was still in Iraq, having woken after sleeping alongside soldiers in an armoured tracked personnel carrier. I crawled to the edge of the bed and stood on the side peering into the darkness, trying to dispel my confusion. Then I pissed all over the carpet and climbed back under the sheets, feeling like a small child who knew he had done something terribly wrong but could not quite work out why he would now be in trouble.

The Black Knights did not go home in three weeks, as they had heard they would on the day the Ba'athist regime disappeared from its former capital. It would be three months before they finally flew out of the Persian Gulf and returned to Georgia. On 3 May they were moved to a camp near Baghdad airport, where they were kept in reserve as hopes for a peaceful military occupation during the reconstruction of Iraq came up against the reality of a rising number of guerrilla attacks. Their base was at an installation of Iraqi warehouses. In one were uncovered crates filled with freshly greased machine guns and RPGs. In another were machine parts clearly labelled as exported from France, Germany and Russia. A third held bathroom equipment, mostly toilets and basins. This one had a huge hole in the roof where a bomb had been dropped on it, smashing the porcelain inside so that the floor was covered in white fragments.

The conditions, they later told me, were even tougher than those in the camp in the Kuwaiti desert. There were no showers, barracks or electricity. The mosquitoes were unbearable, and the only wooden building at the site was gradually dismantled, wall by wall, and the planks burnt in the hope that the smoke would deter them. At night, now that there was no action to offer distraction, the nightmares were worse. Trey would describe how when he could not sleep he would entertain himself during the early hours of the morning listening to the screams and trying to work out which vehicle they came from. 'One night Sergeant Pyle was lying on the ground nearby and he was hollering away,' he said. 'It was enough to make even my blood run cold.'

As the combat units of the V Corps moved into the area to take over responsibility for conducting patrols there was little to occupy the company's time. Occasionally there was sentry duty at a nearby university campus. At other times they were sent out to try to limit the looting still occurring across the capital. A member of the unit would describe to me how pointless those efforts seemed. 'The people were like roaches swarming over sugar,' he said. 'When we fired warning shots in the air they disappeared, but as we drove away we could see them emerging from the surrounding buildings and continuing exactly where they'd left off.' One day, as a deterrent, the battalion lined up the cars and trucks seized from Iraqis looting an autoparts warehouse and crushed them with their tanks.

Boredom was the most immediate enemy. Men who had shared the same vehicles for so long could now hardly face talking to each other. Crewmembers billeted down in separate parts of the compound. A few arguments broke out, although there were no actual fist fights, as occurred in other units.

Doc Swinney received confirmation that he had been awarded a medal for his actions near Nasiriyah. He was not the only one. Lieutenant Colonel Charlton was awarded the Silver Star and the Bronze Star. Captain Waldron was given the Silver Star, for gallantry and his leadership of the company, as well as an automatic Purple Heart for his injuries. Sergeant Pyle had also received a Purple Heart, and the Silver Star, primarily for leading the line in the final push to Baghdad and helping protect his crew, despite his shoulder wound, after his tank was immobilised by Iraqi RPGs. Frankie was awarded the Bronze Star with Valor for tending to the injured scout at Tallil. Sergeant Whelan received the Bronze Star with Valor for his part in the evacuation of his crew after his tank had been damaged on the day the Ba'athist regime had abandoned Baghdad. He had stood on the tank trying to extinguish the burning equipment at the back while AK-47 bullets pinged off the armour around him. Among the seventeen members of the company who received Bronze Stars were Sergeant Weaver and José. The Black Knights were one of the most honoured of all the American units engaged in Operation Iraqi Freedom.

Trey received a promotion to sergeant first class. Red got engaged to his girlfriend. Roman occupied his time deciding which motorcycle he would buy when he got back to the United States. The chaplain did conduct his baptisms, though not in the Euphrates. The spot chosen was a tributary of the Tigris, that other particularly Biblical river, which ran through the garden of one of the luxury homes formerly owned by a senior official of Saddam's regime. Located near the airport, there was a lake beside the main building with a little wooden boathouse at the end of a small causeway. The four soldiers who attended the ceremony were immersed to their waists. Among them was Frankie, who was reconfirming his faith, and Doc, who – as he had previously told me – had decided the time had finally come to be baptised.

The company was first told they would be going home on 5 May, then 9 May, then at the start of June. Each time, on the day before their supposed departure, the order came through that it would yet again be delayed. Sergeant Weaver had begun to tell people, 'I now know how to make a soldier crazy: put him in the middle of nowhere with nothing to do.'

It was not until 16 June that they were finally told to drive back to Kuwait, Trey for the first time flying the American flag he had carried in his kitbag since the company's deployment to the Middle East. There they were informed that they had to clean and turn in their vehicles. A programme of reorientation was instigated to prepare them for the real world. As the colonel explained it: 'You take a young kid from the farm who is nineteen years old and his life is in danger and people are dying. It'll have a psychological impact. If you talk to anyone who has gone to war, they'll talk of a great deal of aggression that comes up, and you have to help people come back from that.' Psychiatrists were made available to anyone who needed them. A number of the soldiers were prescribed anti-depressants. Then they just waited for the order, that still did not come, which would tell them they could return to America.

Weeks later, once the company had finally got back to Georgia, I visited Doc Swinney, who filled me in on what they had experienced in the Middle East after I had left. His wife had indeed kitted out their house in Disney designs: a Mickey Mouse sheet dominated the bedroom, and a new plastic shower curtain was covered in cartoon figures. Because of the baby we stood outside, a pale orange baseball cap perched on Doc's head as he leaned against his green Mustang to smoke cigarettes and talk about Iraq. He was bitter by then about what had happened in the Middle East, and that the sacrifices made by the US Army had failed to be recognised by its intended beneficiaries.

'I think it was a waste of time,' he told me. 'Saddam can have those sorry-assed people back. They need to be ruled with an iron fist. They took our good intentions and threw them away. The longer we were there, the more unhappy they seemed to be to see us. By the end, people were saying directly to our faces how much they wanted us out of there right now.

'What happened feels so much more intense now than it even was at the time. While it was going on it was almost normal. But now it seems unbelievable that we all got through it alive. I have a nightmare that keeps coming back about Cubs. There was one moment when I was looking over the edge of my vehicle and there was the body of an Iraqi. I had it covered in case he was playing possum, and he looked up and began to lift his AK-47. I shot him straight through the top of the head, as close as I am to you. It just keeps coming back when I'm sleeping. You know, I'm a medic. I wasn't meant to have to shoot anyone.'

I asked him when he had started to feel safe.

'I don't feel safe yet,' he said.

After I had left, the company had spent almost every day dealing with dead and injured civilians. During the ten weeks since the end of major combat operations had been declared by President Bush, the crew of Band Aid had dealt with sixty-three casualties, all but eleven of them civilians, and the majority children under the age of sixteen. Most had received their injuries as a result of unexploded ordnance left by the MLRS missiles and howitzer shells. Others had become ill because of the lack of water and fresh food supplies in Baghdad.

One day a baby had been brought to them who was having seizures because of a burning fever. Doc called the field hospital, but was told there was no medicine or spare beds. 'I told that lieutenant to kiss my ass,' he said, 'and Sergeant B said to me, "Let's go over there and kill him." We were the ones having to hold that baby in our arms.' In the end there was nothing they could do but provide basic treatment to reduce the fever, pass the baby back to its parents, and hope they had done enough to ensure its survival.

Doc also told me that Private Stewart, the mortar crewmember who stepped on an MLRS bomblet at Objective Saints, had ended up having his whole foot amputated just above the ankle. The wound had become infected in hospital, and there had been no alternative but to operate.

'I got baptised because it was time for a change in my life,' Doc explained. 'There's no way I should've survived what I went through. In Nasiriyah alone I should've been hit. I can remember when I finally headed for cover in the back of a Bradley after our casualty had been evacuated. The sergeant had been shouting at me, "Doc, get your ass over here," and there were bullets coming all around me. I ran straight through them. When I got into the

Bradley, everyone was patting me down and I was saying, "I'm OK, I wasn't hit." They were telling me, "You wouldn't know if you'd been hit." And they were right, because I was that pumped.

'I talked to the chaplain before the ceremony because I didn't feel I deserved to be baptised because of the number of people I'd killed. I said to him, "How can I do this when it says in the Ten Commandments: Thou Shall Not Kill." He said you have to ask for forgiveness, and the Lord will understand that you had to do what you had to do.'

The next day I had lunch in a local steakhouse with another member of the Black Knights. He told me what had really been happening in the Swinney household while Doc had been away in the Gulf, and his wife had been telling him on the phone how much she loved and missed him. She had been having an affair with a member of the National Guard who had been stationed on the base to guard it while the soldiers were in Iraq. It was rumoured that she had gone on holiday with him to Pennsylvania, even given him Doc's mobile phone so he could make calls whenever he wanted. She had spent all the money Doc had earned and more, so that on his return he discovered that he faced thousands of dollars of debt. She had been spotted with her boyfriend by another of the wives, and when the company had returned to Kuwait she had confessed to Doc what had been going on before he could hear it from someone else.

'He was really pissed, but what can he do but try and hold it together? Damn shame though. All Doc ever did out in Iraq was talk about taking his wife and children to Disney World. Now he doesn't even have enough money to take the kids. Still, he won't be the last we hear about, just the first. It's all going to start coming out of the woodwork now that we're back home.'

It had been just after the 4 July Independence Day holiday when I had finally heard that the company was returning to the United

States. 1st Battalion would be one of only a handful of units that returned to America before the end of July. Two-thirds of the 3rd Infantry Division, more than ten thousand soldiers, had been told they would be remaining in the Middle East 'indefinitely' to suppress the escalating number of guerrilla attacks. On Thursday, 1 May President Bush had declared an end to major combat operations in a speech made on the flight deck of the USS *Abraham Lincoln* in front of a banner saying 'Mission Accomplished', but the Iraqis still loyal to Saddam Hussein did not seem to have gathered that the politicians in Washington and London had determined that they should stop fighting. The invasion of Iraq may have been a mostly efficient campaign, but now it seemed those opposed to a US presence were fighting a war on their, rather than the Americans', terms.

A soldier from the 4th Infantry Division was killed near Tikrit when his convoy of Humvees was attacked with rocket-propelled grenades. Two Americans were kidnapped while guarding a rocket demolition site near the town of Balad, twenty-five miles north of Baghdad, and their bodies never found. A soldier from Support Command was fatally injured when men armed with AK-47s attacked a convoy near al-Mahmudiyah, twenty miles south of the capital. Six British Military Policemen were killed when their base at a police post in Majar al-Kabir, near Basra, was stormed by an enraged mob. A women and her child blew themselves up at a checkpoint in Baghdad. An eight-year-old Iraqi boy attacked an American vehicle with an assault rifle. In total, seventy-seven United States soldiers died, as a result either of Iraqi attacks or accidents, between President Bush's declaration on 1 May and the Black Knights' arrival back in America. Five to fifteen clashes were being reported across Iraq each night. The cost of the conflict was running at $4 billion a month. General Tommy Franks warned that the continued harassment meant the American military could be in the country for as much as four years. The soldiers who had been there were predicting it would be far longer.

Despite concerns raised by some commentators – and indeed by some of the American troops themselves – this was not a new Vietnam. The elements still fighting the American and British forces were not a battle-hardened, highly organised guerrilla army like the Viet Cong. Unlike the Ba'ath Party, which in recent times has been associated only with defeat, the VC had beaten the French, secured half the country and brought the anti-Communist government in the south to near collapse. Moreover, it enjoyed the advantage of densely vegetated terrain. In Iraq there is little ground cover, allowing a high level of aerial surveillance and meaning that it is the urban rather than the rural areas that harbour insurgency, and these are relatively small and isolated.

However, in the continued absence of evidence of any weapons of mass destruction, or that Saddam had posed a direct threat to the West, the question was now being asked whether the invasion had simply taken a country that was not a terrorist threat and turned it into one. Foreign fundamentalists were entering Iraq to harass the coalition forces. Not only soldiers but United Nations personnel and oil pipelines were being attacked. The same mis-judgement about the reaction of the Iraqi people to an American invasion, which had led to expectations of widespread and immediate welcome parades, appeared to have meant there was little advance planning of how 'victory' would be policed. However the United States may view itself, it seemed that twelve years of savage sanctions against Iraq and decades of support for Israel against the Palestinians meant that few saw it as their friend, and a significant number as an out-and-out enemy. The capture or killing of Saddam could yet have a decisive effect, but although the war may have been declared over, so far there was little sign of peace. When President Bush was asked about his reaction to the number of militants who were continuing to fight in Iraq, his response had been a brief but defiant demonstration of his commitment to finishing what he had begun. 'Bring 'em on,' he said.

It was not only Doc who was finding some of the Iraqi people's apparent lack of gratitude difficult to accept. The colonel would tell me after his return to the US, 'The Iraqis started to piss me off. They're not showing a whole lot of appreciation for what we did.' The reason for this was something he had dwelled on. 'Some cultures can adapt better to positive change than others,' he said. 'I don't know if those in the Middle East are going to make it.'

I arrived in Hinesville, Georgia, the army town that borders the Black Knights' base camp at Fort Stewart, on Friday, 11 July, the day the company was scheduled to return home. The route from the airport had taken me down Interstate 16, the route along which, in 1864, General William Tecumseh Sherman had led his Union Army on an advance that was one of the most successful modern examples of Total War. It was a march that drove a forty-mile-wide corridor of destruction through the heart of the state, breaking the will of the South and effectively ending the Civil War. Then the people of Georgia used every weapon they could find to try to stop him. Old men and teenage boys were given ageing rifles and dressed in uniforms taken from those who were already dead. The iron gates of houses had been melted down for bullets. The women tore up their best dresses for bandages. However, Sherman had promised his commander in chief Ulysses S. Grant that he would 'cut a swath to the sea', and nothing could stop his men. Singing their marching song to emancipation – 'Hurrah! Hurrah! The flag that makes you free!' – they rolled clean through Georgia. Farms were torched, much of Atlanta reduced to cinders, homesteads looted, until, at the edge of Savannah, there was no enemy left to be killed, and the city pleaded with him to call a halt and show mercy.

Hinesville had been a mere speck on the map before the US Army decided to set up a training camp there during the Second

World War. Now, with the 'war on terror' expanding and the US military budget approaching its Cold War heights, a road sign welcoming visitors declared it 'the fastest-growing town in south-eastern Georgia'. Less than half a mile from Main Street, with its red-brick courthouse and real estate offices, lay the main entrance to the military base. Stars and Stripes and faded yellow ribbons hung from lampposts and mailboxes. Outside shops and res-taurants were messages of thanks to the troops. The hotel I checked into had 'God Bless Our Planet and Our Troops' on a sign outside. The local restaurant: 'Thank You, Our Returning Soldiers, For Protecting Freedom.' An advertisement called for more volunteers to the National Guard 'in these desperate times'. On the radio a song by Avril Lavigne seemed to be on almost permanent request, with its lyrics 'I thought that you'd be here by now' and 'Won't someone please take me home'.

A few weeks earlier, a gathering of eight hundred army wives had descended into chaos as the women had made clear to the military authorities their anger at their husbands' prolonged absence. A colonel who had been sent to soothe their concerns had to be escorted out of the hall under a torrent of abuse and angry questions. As one wife – one of the many in Hinesville who was still waiting for news of when her husband would be leaving the Middle East – put it, 'In the army they say, "If you were meant to have a family you would have been issued one." But the crazy thing is, they mean it.'

Despite many soldiers not having a firm return date, the army had started conducting special classes for the closest relatives of all the troops to prepare them for when they arrived back. The course of instruction had been significantly beefed up after the military had been shocked when a number of Special Forces personnel sent on operations in Afghanistan had killed their wives on coming home. The classes outlined how the women should listen, be undemanding, and not surprised if they witnessed sudden mood changes, or saw the men jump if they dropped a plate on the floor. Above all, they were told, they must accept that their husbands might not at first be the same men they had said goodbye to.

The Black Knights were one of three units scheduled to land at Hunter Army Airfield, in nearby Savannah, at 11 p.m. Families and press were told to assemble at Fort Stewart soon after nine. After the soldiers had been ferried from the airstrip to the base they would line up in formation for a brief final passing-out parade in front of a grandstand from which their relatives would be watching. They would then have four days' leave, and be back at work on Wednesday.

Military Police guided me from the entrance into the carpark. To get to the parade ground we had to pass along a path bordered by thirty-five freshly planted trees, one for each soldier from the division killed in Iraq. Home-made posters had been tied to the metal frame that held up the grandstand. 'Black Knight 1–64 Maintenance Team: Our Heroes!! Welcome Back!!!' read one with the names of Red and Roman, Sergeant Weaver, Sergeant Harrison and Sergeant Bill Jones written on it. Tied to a post was a sign covered with red hearts for Frankie: 'You are my Hero. I Love You Terry. Welcome Back'.

I found the wives and children I had heard so much about. Many were wearing specially printed black T-shirts featuring a picture of a medieval knight holding a yellow banner on which two tank barrels were crossed. Mrs Swinney had come to greet Doc despite withering stares from many of the other women, she and her baby dressed in spangled red, white and blue-striped tops. Mrs Black, a pretty, petite dyed blonde, was there, heavily pregnant – their baby girl Reagan was due only a month later. Sergeant Whelan's wife Christine was present, along with his parents. 'I knew when he went that he'd get through safely,' she said. 'He told all his crew before they left that they would all be making the journey back to the States, and he kept that promise. That makes me very proud.' Lieutenant Few's wife Stephanie, a strikingly beautiful, statuesque blonde, was holding a small Stars and Stripes. 'He's finally coming home,' she said.

I found Kimberly Weaver, Sergeant Weaver's wife. Her children Colin, ten, and Britney, eight, were entertaining the assembled families by performing cartwheels on the grass of the parade ground. 'It will be breathtaking to see him after so long,' she told me. 'I won't believe it till they get here. Only then will I know for certain he's safe.'

We talked about the high school prom to which Sergeant Weaver had taken her and which he had told me about at Tallil. He had given her only a chaste peck on the cheek at the end of the night, and I wondered if she had been expecting a more passionate kiss. 'The thing is, my best friend had a crush on him, so I couldn't let him kiss me because it wouldn't have been fair to her. When he came back from the army and I met him in Wal-Mart, though, he swept me off my feet.

'I love him, I really do, but it has been very difficult with him away so much. When he re-enlisted for a second ten years, I was serious when I said I'd leave him. I didn't marry to raise these children by myself. I married him so we could be together and raise this family, and that hasn't happened yet.' She looked towards where her three children were playing. 'It's been tough these last few months. Before, I had his mother to help, but she died, and now I've been doing it all on my own. I've been bringing up the kids, working, going to school where I'm studying to be a criminal investigator. I have changed. I've become a fully independent person for the first time in my life since I've not been able to depend on anyone but me. I've lost weight. I was over two hundred pounds, and now I'm back to the size I was when I first met him. I've been going out with friends a lot more. I even got a tattoo. I hope he's going to be able to cope with who I am now. It's something we're going to have to deal with day by day. He has got to learn to fit himself back into our life. This is someone we haven't known for the last year.'

There was a tap on my shoulder. It was the captain, dressed in a rugby shirt. He had flown back a few weeks earlier to prepare for a new three-year posting as an instructor at West Point that he would be starting at the end of the month. He enfolded me in a bearhug, to my considerable surprise and appreciation. I said how good it must have felt when he got home. 'It wasn't over then,' he told me. 'My job's only over today, when I know that everyone got back alive.'

I saw First Sergeant Burt, the soldier injured by the mortar on the road outside Samawah. He had undergone six operations, his spleen and gall bladder had been removed, and he still had no feeling in his left hand. He had spent thirty days in hospital before being flown back to the States, and had been told to expect a further eighteen months of medical treatment. 'I knew the risks of the mission and I knew the requirements of my job,' he said when I asked if he felt any resentment.

Another soldier had come back early – Specialist Woodman, the twenty-one-year-old I had heard talking to Frankie of his concern about how he would cope when he got back to the US. He had been flown out of the Middle East after dehydration caused by the heat and humidity caused him to develop a kidney stone. 'It's good to be home,' he said, 'but I'm still not over what happened out there. I used to go out clubbing a lot, but now I don't go to clubs. Before, if there was trouble I knew I'd just walk away. Now . . . Well, I just don't know how I might react if there was trouble.'

A peroxide blonde approached me. She was the stepmother of Private First Class Austin Becker, one of the crew of Lieutenant Garabato's tank, who had been a regular fixture in Band Aid for DVD watching. He was one of the soldiers who had asked to ring home the night before the advance through Karbala. 'Thank you for letting him call us that day. I don't think you can ever understand how much we appreciate you doing that, and what a relief it was to hear he was well and uninjured. It's a phone call that

I'll never forget to the day I die. He sounded very composed, but he told us something big was happening the next day. The impression was that he made the call because he wanted to tell us he loved us in case he couldn't do so again. It was almost like he was saying goodbye. When he hung up I sobbed like I was a wounded animal. I just collapsed. I've never cried like that before.'

Another person I met was Sergeant Pyle's sister, Alison Boyd. She solved a mystery I had been wondering about ever since a conversation with her brother when we were at Dragon 4 watching the bombing around Karbala. He had talked about how he had always dreamed of being a tank commander ('That's true,' Alison said. 'Ever since he was a small boy all he had ever wanted to be was a tanker'), but that he had been sidetracked in his twenties by another career before finally enlisting. However much I had tried to wheedle it out of him over the following weeks, I could never get him to reveal his previous profession.

'Oh, he was a professional dancer,' his sister told me. 'He was very good. He used to win lots of trophies for ballroom dancing, did the waltz, the tango. He travelled all over the world doing displays. He's very graceful, my brother Jerry. It was always so beautiful to watch him dance.' I found this hard to reconcile with the man I had met laughing like a banshee on that first evening at Objective Saints, his arm in a sling, as he described to me how he had been shot in the shoulder.

At a few minutes to midnight the buses carrying the returning soldiers from the airbase pulled in. The gathered families started screaming and shouting, and rushed forward from their seats to stand in a ragged line in front of the grandstand. A sound man from one of the local TV news channels turned to his cameraman. 'There's way too much oestrogen here tonight,' he commented.

Someone was pulling at my T-shirt. It was eight-year-old Britney Weaver. 'Mr Interviewer, someone said you weren't fighting and my daddy protected you,' she said. 'I'm pleased my daddy helped you.'

'He did protect me,' I said to her. 'Your father is a good and humane man. It was very difficult out there and he always did his best. You should be proud of that.'

'I am proud of him,' she answered. 'He's my hero.'

Soldiers began to appear through the line of trees that marked the far edge of the field in front of which we stood. They were coming forward in formation, lined up in the three companies that had arrived back in the States that evening. All of them were dressed in their desert fatigues, their helmets on and webbing clasped at their waists, their kitbags over one shoulder. They marched in time, two unit flags held in front, until they were only a dozen yards from where their families waited. Then they spread out to form one silent block, five men deep, all standing to attention.

There was a lot of screaming now. A black woman behind me was standing on her chair and slapping her behind. 'Here it is, baby,' she was shouting. 'Here's what you been waitin' for. Come and get it, baby. I love you. I love you. I love you.'

The base commander, Colonel John Kidd, stepped up to a podium and gave a short speech. 'Each of you has made great sacrifices and your sacrifices are greatly appreciated. Welcome home, brother soldiers.'

He led them in a rendition of the division's song, and the still night air was filled with the sound of men singing:

> *I am just a dog-faced soldier with a rifle on my shoulder*
> *And I just eat raw meat for breakfast every day.*
> *Just feed me ammunition*
> *And keep me in the 3rd Infantry Division.*

And then everything was over. The formation saluted, broke up, and the families ran forward. I watched familiar faces sweep their sons and daughters into their arms. Trey was being interviewed by the local news. He was not looking at the camera, but staring at his wife, such affection in his eyes that it was humbling that someone could feel so much emotion. I spotted Sergeant Weaver dragging his kitbag along the ground as he looked for his wife and children amongst the jumble of reunions. He walked from one end of the parade ground to the other, where he took off his helmet and wiped his eyes, an expression of utter defeat on his face. Then he saw his family and they ran to each other. They clung together for so long that I could not bear to watch any longer, and made my way towards the parked cars, where I found Ray, who presented me with a beer.